SMALL BUSINESS DIGITAL MARKETING HANDBOOK

THE DEFINITIVE GUIDE TO BEST PRACTICES IN 12 CORE MARKETING CHANNELS

TIM ITO & BONEY PANDYA

— MARKETING NICE GUYS —

Marketing Nice Guys Publishing is a renowned source of insightful and practical information on digital marketing strategies, tactics, and implementation.

Marketing Nice Guys Publishing
2125 N. Troy Street
Arlington, VA 22201 USA

Library of Congress Control Number: 2022919427
Paperback ISBN: 979-8-9869903-0-9
Digital/E-book ISBN: 979-8-9869903-1-6

Marketing Nice Guys Press Editorial Staff
Copy Chief: Tim Ito
Editor: Kenan Pollack
Design: Julien Publishing

_____

This book is dedicated to all the small business owners that work their asses off just running and managing their companies. We hope this no-nonsense book makes marketing easier to understand so that you can do it yourself, not get scammed, and, if you need, hire the right professionals to help you maximize your promotional efforts.

_____

TABLE OF CONTENTS

FOREWORD

You can make 7 figures if you just follow our method!

We'll make it easy to be like us, you just need to take our course!

You've probably seen these headlines, or ones like them, from the many scam artists who know all the tricks to individual entrepreneurs and or individual entrepreneurs. In fact, these ridiculous promotions are everywhere, and one of the (many) reasons we wrote this book.

We saw the need for a reality check when it came to small business marketing. The truth is, what's out there isn't always helpful, or worse, may actually cause a small business more harm in wasting time and money. Indeed, anyone can make a claim about anything when it comes to marketing, especially those opportunists who aggressively push a particular product or service as being the solution to "all your problems."

The truth is there's no such thing. And in many of those cases, those "solutions" are either a scam or require a business to do things it's currently not equipped to do when you actually dig into what it is. After all, who will take the time to fact check anything anymore or even go beyond the bullet points on a page? In such an environment, small businesses often become the victims.

Why do we fall for these things?

Many of us just want to believe whatever it is people tell us, especially if they say things can be easier or better. Who wants to hear something is hard and complicated? But here's the problem: marketing is hard, especially if you're a small business. And the reality is, regardless of who is doing it, marketing is complicated.

That's why in the book we wanted to go more in depth to focus on helping you understand core best practices and approaches not so you can simply mimic them, but you can apply those to your unique situation as a business.

We often say there's no magic bullet to marketing. People that claim upfront they'll drive your revenue or results by a multiplier of 10x are likely lying to you. Why? Because most successful marketing initiatives are a combination of complex factors all at play at the same time, including:

- The strength of the product or service
- The industry (B2B or B2C)
- The length of the buyer journey
- The charisma of the company spokesperson or leader
- The existing brand identity and awareness of the company
- The quality of the messaging/copy and any content
- The use of compelling images and video
- The audience targeting and focus
- The campaign promotion and distribution channels chosen
- The landing page and conversion/e-commerce experience
- The timing of the campaigns
- The quality of your sales team (if you're say, a B2B company)
- The budgets you set
- The goal horizon of your CEO or leadership
- The data you collect and the analysis you do on the data
- The optimizations you chose to make or not make

And of course, the execution of all the little things that matter along the way to encourage people to take the next step toward purchase. As you can see, that takes effort, timing, and probably a whole lot of luck. Marketing can sometimes be a crapshoot in that way. But focusing on best practices and practical tactics in each channel like we do in the book, you can at least start with a better foundation and then use that as the jumping off point to test to see what works for you.

The second reason for us writing the book was that much of what we saw available for small businesses from an educational standpoint focused on narrow topics – what you may or may not want to do in a particular channel. Maybe it was a whole book about content or something on email marketing, which is perfectly fine. But such books don't provide the context of the entire picture of marketing. How what you might do in one channel fits with what you do in another. How does your email marketing work with your content strategy and vice versa?

Finally, the marketing books we've seen also lack the answer to the core question that many businesses have about our field. That is: What are all the things I have to consider when it comes to marketing? In thinking about the answer to this question, we realized that most frameworks out there don't encompass this question, but we think we have an answer. And that answer comes with our PATIO framework, which stands for:

- Planning & Strategy
- Approach
- Tools & Tactics
- Implementation
- Optimization

This should cover everything you need to consider when it comes to doing any marketing in any channel. (More on that as we dive into the various chapters.) Our mission at Marketing Nice Guys, as always, is to help you excel in digital marketing. We hope this book goes at least some way toward that end.

CHAPTER 1

Foundational Principles

Each small business is unique. Some might focus on retail and sell direct to consumers. Others sell products or services directly to other businesses and/or may need a more formal sales team. For each, we can't emphasize enough that the marketing a company chooses to do **should reflect the needs of the business and the audience**, so often there's no single playbook or approach that will work for all. That said, there are core fundamentals when approaching marketing for your business regardless of the industry or type.

Hence, we've developed this guide. Regardless of the stage you're in – whether you have some full-time marketing staff or might still be in startup mode – we will walk you through 12 marketing areas with core considerations and approaches in each area. The tips included are all things you as a small business owner can do yourself (or with some additional help). We know your time is limited so let's get started.

First, let's cover a few basic foundational marketing principles.

The Marketing Funnel: What Part of the Buyer Journey Is Your Audience In?

Many of you may already know or have heard of the marketing funnel. But for those who haven't or need a brush-up here are the basics: In 1898, E. St. Elmo Lewis developed a model that mapped a customer journey from the moment a brand attracted a consumer's attention to the point of purchase. St. Elmo Lewis' idea is often referred to as the AIDA-model, an acronym which stands for Awareness, Interest, Desire, and Action (AIDA). In 1924, William Townsend took what

St. Elmo Lewis developed and turned it into a funnel structure with the book *Bond Salesmanship*.

The funnel structure has held up remarkably well over the years. That's because the structure accurately mirrors customer behavior. To use St. Elmo Lewis' model, there are more people aware of a company/product/service, than express interest in it. There are still fewer people who express a desire or intent to buy, and even fewer that take action. Hence, the funnel shape. Over the years, the funnel structure has evolved to include other terms (not just AIDA), where you might see other terms (brand, engagement, consideration, acquisition, conversion, loyalty/advocacy), but the overall thrust remains the same. At Marketing Nice Guys, we prefer to use terms such as "top of the funnel," middle of the funnel or lower-funnel to refer to different stages. (Graphic right).

Tip No. 1: Pursue a Full-Funnel Strategy

What's important for small- and medium-sized companies to know is that only focusing your efforts on one area of the marketing funnel won't be as effective as pursuing a more full-funnel strategy. For example, you might have a great strategy for pushing your brand out through social media in terms of top-of-the funnel awareness, which is important, but if you don't focus on customer acquisition or conversions in the middle-to-lower funnel you are likely missing out. Similarly, only focusing on those in the lower funnel (those who express the most intent to buy) misses out on an opportunity to brand your company in front of a bigger audience and grow. Think about it this way: The more people you have at the top of the funnel, the more potential you have to make the bottom of your funnel wider. The goal of all marketing is to help you maximize the number of individuals getting to each stage.

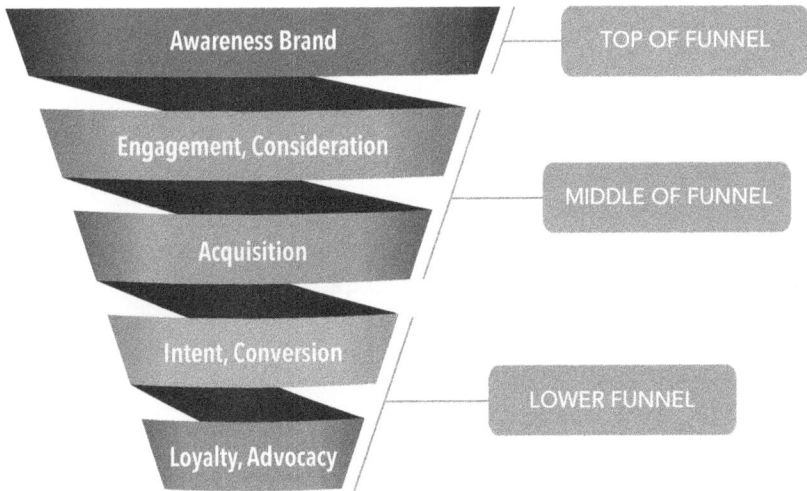

Funnel diagram:
- Awareness Brand — TOP OF FUNNEL
- Engagement, Consideration — MIDDLE OF FUNNEL
- Acquisition
- Intent, Conversion — LOWER FUNNEL
- Loyalty, Advocacy

Tip No. 2: Use a Framework and Create a Plan

One of the cardinal sins of even large organizations is that they decide to take the "Nike approach" when it comes to their marketing – they "just do it." This is bad for several reasons. For small- and medium-sized businesses, lack of a plan often results in marketing that is all over the place with no consistent foundation or lack of coordination on goals. Marketing is one of those specialties where different channels work together (email works with social, which works with paid media and content etc.). So, having an overall plan helps to you think about that big picture and where each channel can help you succeed and feed other channels.

We suggest starting with a framework that helps you understand the steps needed be successful in your marketing operations. We have one called PATIO, which consolidates the major areas you need to focus on in marketing to be successful. Before you do your plan, we suggest walking through the PATIO framework (marketingniceguys.com/patio-a-new-way-to-run-your-marketing/) first.

PATIO stands for:

- **Planning & Strategy**: Typically, this area includes identifying the main goal of your marketing, who you're targeting, budgets and resources, channels you'll use, and how you'll measure success.

- **Approach**: This is really the "how" part in terms of accomplishing your main goals and typically includes identifying the campaigns you'll run, the tone & style and type of content or ads you'll run, the frequency and cadence.

- **Tools & Tactics**: Every digital channel has unique tools that a marketing team needs to use. The volume of the tools can be overwhelming to manage. So, identifying what tools you need upfront is key. Also, given the existing approach and tools identified, there are core best-practice tactics that marketers should know as they look at implementation.

- **Implementation**: From any operations standpoint, this is really the execution piece of what marketers need to do. So based on the plan, the approach, and the identified tools and tactics, teams have to develop content assets, schedule, publish, post, send, and update.

- **Optimization**: These days, no good marketer simply "sets it and forgets it." The departments that are really good at what they do focus on continuous optimization to try to maximize results. They analyze data, make determinations, and optimize for incremental gains in each digital marketing channel. These optimizations and data also feed back into the planning and strategy, approach, and tools and tactics phases so teams can continuously adjust audience targets, budgets, goals, and approaches based on what they're seeing.

The above framework helps you think about all your marketing operations, including the resources needed, and the considerations and decisions you'll have to make as a small business. For the marketing plan itself, we suggest a modified version of our best-practice template (https://marketingniceguys. com/how-to-develop-a-modern-day-marketing-plan-free-download/) for small- or medium- sized business who don't have a large staff of marketing already on hand. There are six core areas we'd cover in a plan:

1. Goals

Defining the overall goal of your marketing is critical. What does that mean? In most cases, a marketing department's primary goal is to drive revenue of some kind for the year, either through its own efforts or through sales, depending on the industry. So, if your goal is to drive $25m in revenue for the year, say that upfront. If you have other goals, you can include those as well, but it's important to define the primary overall goal first. An example might be:

Primary goal: Drive $25M in revenue for 2022

Secondary goals:

Drive 10 percent improvement in sales-qualified leads for 2022 over 2021.

Drive a 10 percent increase in website traffic from the previous year.

Etc.

When crafting your goals, it's always a good idea to use SMART goals, which stand for:

- **Specific**: What exactly are you trying to improve? This is something you could state to any CEO and he or she would understand immediately.
- **Measurable**: Goals that are amorphous and aren't trackable with any data aren't useful for a marketing plan. Make sure you can measure the success of what you put in place.
- **Attainable**: It probably goes without saying but putting in goals that set wild expectations won't do anyone much good. It's important to use a past benchmarks here as a guide.
- **Relevant**: Ask yourself why you're setting this particular goal and how it helps the company. Why is it significant to mention?
- **Time-Bound**: State when you plan on achieving this goal. For the period we're recommending that the plan cover (1 year), it's important to note that upfront. If you have a different timeframe, it's important to list that as well.

2. Executive Summary/Current Market Environment

Most marketing plans include an analysis of the current marketplace. This doesn't have to be long but it should cover:

1. The key competitors, including:
    a. The companies' names
    b. What particular strengths they have in certain marketing channels and what the specific threats they pose to your business
    c. Company sizes, revenue, market share (if available)

2. Your strength/weaknesses in the market, including
   a. What digital channels you're strong in
   b. Which channels need improvement
3. Trends that you've seen in the last several years (of the company's business or the marketplace in general).
4. Your opportunities based on competitors, your own strengths and weaknesses, and trends

Another option might be to do a quick SWOT (Strengths, Weaknesses, Opportunities, and Threats) analysis. While it doesn't list out specific companies, it does cover most of the areas above – and it comes as an easy-to-read chart at a glance. Also, specific company threats can be listed within the Threats section. The SWOT is a great option if you're attempting to provide a quick visual glance at the marketplace and your company's role in it.

STRENGTHS	WEAKNESSES
OPPORTUNITIES	THREATS

3. Budget and Resources

In the ideal world, your marketing plan should be done in coordination with your company's budgeting processes for the year, to align revenue and cost expectations for the company as a whole. According to a recent study, most companies spend about **11 percent of revenue on marketing costs** (https://deloitte.wsj.com/cmo/2017/01/24/who-has-the biggest-marketing-budgets/) (it varies by industry and some include staff in that calculation while other companies don't.) For newer companies, it's suggested that marketing might encompass up to 20 percent of expected revenue given the need to build the brand. That's why setting a realistic revenue goal and secondary goals come first. Here are some questions to answer as you set your budget and staffing/resources, as well as some other suggestions:

Budget Total: First, state the overall marketing budget (we suggest including fully-loaded staffing costs if you can get them).

Additional Staffing Considerations: To hit the primary goals that you have outlined (revenue or secondary goals), what can you do with existing staff? If you've set goals that require additional staffing, what types of positions do you need? How much do those positions cost fully loaded for quality staff?

Staff Allocation: How will you allocate those staffing resources and other marketing costs in the budget to best allow yourself to hit the goal? Make sure you've covered all the digital channels you'll use, as well as understand the time it takes for staff to do what you need them to do to be successful.

Detailed Budget Inclusion: We are big believers in marketing transparency. We suggest including a line-by-line budget, splitting out where you'll spend the non-staffing costs. Where you allocate money (particularly paid media) will depend on the industry and your goals. In this case, it's also important to know the benchmarks. For example, paid search takes up roughly 45 to 60 percent of the total marketing ad spend. How you spend that money will depend on the channels you aim to use to hit the goal.

4. Target Audience

Part of the prework to any marketing has to be updated research on your target audience(s) and/or segments and personas. If you haven't done a lot of persona work before, we detail out a few tips here in our post on **Audience Research and Personas** (https://marketingniceguys.com/what-are-personas-why-audience-research-matters/) as well as what we'll cover below. This section doesn't need to be long but is a great reminder of your focus on the key audiences that will drive your business. If you have several different persona types, it's good to list those, along with a statement or bullet points about how you intend to help them.

5. Distribution Plan (Marketing Channels & Funnel Target)

After you've detailed the goals, studied the competitive landscape, finalized the marketing budget and the resources you need, and included the persona research, it's time to provide some detail as to how you're going to drive toward those overall goals. This is where you can detail the core marketing channels you're going to employ in the coming year, and the strategy you have for targeting your audiences in different parts of the funnel. (We also list a lot of the core channels below.)

Depending on the industry, a great majority of the marketing resources might be dedicated to driving brand awareness at the top of the funnel. (Think of a Coca-Cola for example, which focuses heavily on brand marketing.) For others, it may be the opposite, where your industry (or your CEO) dictates that you focus on lower-funnel activities.

For most companies, however, you'll need a full-funnel marketing approach. That doesn't mean spending a ton on brand awareness for a Super Bowl commercial but it may mean being more deliberate about planning for the investment in, say, quality content that makes you and your company a thought leader or the go-to resource for helpful information. A couple of tips here:

It's useful to list out all the digital channels you currently use, and any ones you plan on adding in the coming year. For the latter, be sure to emphasize new upcoming initiatives, such as if you're going to undertake a SEO (search engine optimization) initiative, launch a website redesign, or build a new app.

Think about the role that each channel plays in driving your success and at what part of the funnel you're wanting that channel to play. Remember, in best practice, not all channels have to be immediate-term revenue drivers but serve more as a touch point that helps the customers get more comfortable with the brand. With any channel, we suggest thinking about the three to five core areas that align with the funnel:

    a. Will this channel potentially make more customers aware of your brand?

    b. Will it help you acquire more potential customers?

    c. Will it help you engage those you've acquired?

    d. Will it help you convert those you've acquired and engaged?

    e. How will it encourage loyalty and referrals?

Alternatively, you can look at the above questions in more of a macro view and list the channels you'll use to achieve those particular aims. Either way, it's a good exercise to help you reflect on your practice and make sure you emphasize a more full-funnel approach.

6. Measurement

Once you've laid out the goals or the critical success factors, it's important to state upfront how you'll measure the progress toward those goals and lay out the KPIs (key performance indicators) that you'll use to see if you're on track. Why put measurement in the overall marketing plan? Because it gives you markers along the path toward a goal and benchmarks that allow you to transparently communicate how you're doing against what you said you would do. And no, that doesn't set you up for failure. What it does do is set you up so that can make adjustments as you go, so that if you're falling behind in a particular KPI, which is causing you to not be on track for the overall goal, you can switch gears. For example, if your overall goal is hitting $25M in revenue, a set of KPIs might look something like this at each quarterly check in point:

- 1,500,000 website visits per month
  - » 15 percent traffic driven from advertising
  - » 40 percent from organic search
  - » 15 percent from email
  - » 20 percent direct
  - » 10 percent from social media
- 45 new marketing qualified leads per month from website forms
- 15 sales qualified leads from email per month

Final Thoughts on a Marketing Plan

We know what you're thinking right now: "I don't have time to plan!" But trust us, doing even a short one-page plan using this information will help you set the foundation for your activities later on. And it will actually help you save time and likely money, as it will improve your focus and targeting. By setting those goals, you'll be able to work backward to figure out what you need to do to be successful to hit those as well. It may be that you make adjustments along the way. That's OK. Just keep documenting them as you go. For small- and medium-sized businesses, you can also include short areas to cover your intended brand voice/tone/and content approach (to help reinforce how you want to speak to the customer). Or, you can also include campaigns you intend to run, particularly if there is a season or timeframe which is a large revenue-driver for the business. The important thing: Keep the plan iterative and relevant, and it will continue to guide your activities in marketing

With that, let's go next to the 12 core marketing areas and channels that small businesses should consider and continuously focus on to improve.

CHAPTER 2

Audience Research/ Personas/Your Narrative

Don't I already know my audience? On the surface, it seems like you should if you've started a business and developed the products or services. But to do marketing really well, it's important to build a fuller picture of who those audience members are – as you have to speak to them consistently and come to understand their core challenges and pain points. If you don't do the work to find that out or you don't have a narrative that matches what those issues are, your messaging will inevitably fall flat. In this section, we'll start with audience research and developing customer personas and then we'll transition into your narrative as a business.

1. **Interview current or prospective customers**
    - Before marketing agencies do any work on a website, they will interview people – typically current or prospective customers. This is probably the number one thing you can do in terms of audience research. We suggest seeking out five buckets of information:

    A. **Current Professional Background:** Typically, title, company, and other professional history

    B. **Demographics:** Gender, age, income, location, race

    C. **Psychographics:** Ambition, goals, values, opinions/beliefs

    D. **Behavior:** What sites do they visit, where do they go to look for information, how do they find out about your industry's products and services?

E. **Challenges and Pain Points:** What issues do they face? And then, figure out how your company can help solve them

2. Create a focus group

Similar to the above, you can gather a group of current customers and potential customers for a focus group session at a particular time. You can solicit the same information you do with the individual interviews. But typically, the goal is to walk them through a user experience (website, app, landing page, checkout process) and have them provide feedback on it. Do they know where to go? Do they know the next step in the process? Do the people understand the experience? Do they know what you stand for as a brand? What's their response to what they see? During the pandemic, it's a good idea to do any session virtually and most will participate if you provide a small fee, say a $25 Amazon or Starbucks gift card.

3. Collect other quantitative and qualitative data

When thinking about quantitative data, the first place to look is your website – in particular your data analytics. Most companies use Google Analytics as it's free and connects to other critical Google platforms. if you haven't yet, you can easily install it yourself on most websites, particularly those that use WordPress. We like the Google Analytics plugin from MonsterInsights, usually one of the top-rated ones. Here are some quick steps (if you have WordPress) (https://www.monsterinsights.com/how-to-properly-setup-google-analytics-in-word-press/). Once you get it downloaded and configure your Google account, you're off and running. From there, we suggest setting up goals, conversion tracking, and other data that you can capture (see our Analytics chapter at the end of the book). Most small businesses don't have access to specialists who can do this well but it's worth it to hire a contractor to help you configure this easily. Google Analytics contains a treasure trove of information about your current website visitors. Here are some areas you should collect information on:

- What are the popular areas of the site?
- What are people searching for?
- What are the most purchased products/services?

- What content are audiences consuming?
- Are there seasonal trends?
- What's the mobile percentage? Demographic breakdown?
- What site goals are getting completed?

For qualitative and quantitative data, we like to collect information through surveys. This is where you gather information on not just user preferences specific to your product, but also on attitudes, outlook, challenges, pain points, and other key psychographic or interest data. While it's relatively inexpensive to run a survey through a company such as SurveyMonkey, a few critical areas are important:

- Have a research professional look through the survey so there's no inherent answer bias
- In order to get decent results, try to get at least a few hundred replies to the survey for it to be statistically significant (That means you have to send it out to probably a lot more individuals.)
- Offer some sort of benefit to taking the survey. Perhaps a discount on your products or services or some other inexpensive way to reward people who participate.
- Use your existing email list. (Hiring a separate company to survey its customized list for your industry or consumer area can be expensive but if you can afford it, it's an effective way to go beyond your existing customer base

Tip No. 1: A few things about psychographic data

In 2016, some might recall the rise of Cambridge Analytica, which illegally pulled user data from Facebook and targeted individuals (voters) based on a psychographic model known as OCEAN. While the firm itself was discredited, the model was not. What the company did was analyze audiences based on five core areas: openness, conscientiousness, extroversion, agreeableness, and neuroticism with individual criteria in each area helping to determine where those individuals fell on a scale from high-to-low. Based on that criteria, the company successfully targeted individuals that would be more likely to be sympathetic to certain campaign messages. Evidence suggests that it worked in 2016[1] and you can imagine how powerful this is for companies to understand as well. A graphic at right illustrates the core concept. *(Thanks to CB Insights).*

Psychographic Model 'OCEAN'

Quality	Low Scorers	Range	High Scorers
Openness	Down-to-earth Uncreative Conventional Uncurious	←——→	Imaginative Creative Original Curious
Conscientiousness	Negligent Lazy Disorganized Late	←——→	Conscientious Hard-working Well-organized Punctual
Extroversion	Loner Quiet Passive Reserved	←——→	Joiner Talkative Active Affectionate
Agreeableness	Suspicious Critical Ruthless Irritable	←——→	Trusting Lenient Soft-hearted Good-natured
Neuroticism	Calm Even-tempered Comfortable Unemotional	←——→	Worried Temperamental Self-conscious Emotional

mng) marketing nice guys

As a small company, you may not be able to get the volume of data points that Cambridge Analytica pulled (nor should you attempt to do so the way they did), however, the fact that psychographic data works is not in question. Whenever you can better understand an individual's ambitions, challenges, issues, opinions or beliefs, you'll be better equipped to market to them because you're better able to tailor a message to what they're feeling at that particular moment.

4. Putting it together: Creating a persona.

In the ideal world, you take all that research you've done and create a customer persona or a few different personas based on your audience. What are personas? It's essentially a picture of a hypothetical customer that is a composite of different qualities. Companies use "personas" to more accurately identify segments with common needs and pain points, so they can:

    A. Better tailor content to existing audiences, improving market reach;

    B. More accurately identify potential new markets

---

[1] Cambridge Analytica analyzed audiences on behalf of the then-Trump candidacy.

C. Better align marketing, product, sales and other business groups within the organization around the offering to these core groups.

Our personas consist of 6 core elements, many of which we detailed earlier:
- Professional background
- Demographic/geographic
- Psychographics
- Behavior
- Challenges/pain points
- How do we help

Hopefully, at this point, you've gathered a significant amount of data on your audience – enough to put together a composite picture of common elements of your customer base. A few tips here:

- **Name your persona:** Give your persona a name that will remind you of the challenges or behaviors that composite individual exhibits. For example, "Time-strapped Tina."
- **Keep the number of personas manageable:** For small businesses, we'd suggest in the range of one to three (maximum). The tendency is to want to do a lot but you'll find with resources thin, segmenting different messages to those different audiences takes time.
- **Keep those personas in mind when you market to audiences:** One of the benefits of doing persona work is that it forces you to keep the audience in mind when you're speaking to them and it can provide rigor in terms of your messaging. For example, if you know your audience needs practical help, your messaging should reflect that. If they care about the environment or other causes, point out the environmentally friendly packaging etc.
- **Measure success and update personas so they evolve with what you're seeing in the data.** Let's say you try messaging to a particular persona segment and it falls flat. But then you test something else and the audience responds to it. It's inevitable that some of the characteristics or issues you described upfront with a certain persona

might not be 100 percent accurate. So, make an adjustment to that persona and the subsequent messaging. You might even realize you need a new persona based on the feedback you get from your initial and ongoing marketing efforts. Discovering that is key to opening new potential opportunities for your business as well.

Your audience research and resulting personas should focus your marketing efforts and help to make your messaging more relevant. Consumers want to see themselves reflected in the products and services they buy so the more focused you can be on their needs and behaviors, the better.

Your Narrative as a Brand

The next thing to do is figure out how you project your own brand in a way that matches up who you are with those audiences you identified. We recommend taking a step back and giving the following questions some additional thought:

1. Purpose: What's my mission as a business? (e.g., I want to help individuals do ____) _____
   _____

2. Uniqueness/Strengths: What makes me or the services I provide unique? What are my businesses' emotional, practical strengths or what knowledge do I have that can help prospective audiences?
   _____
   _____

3. Cultural: How does my background affect my perspective? What does it mean about how I view the world in a way that others can relate to?
   _____
   _____

4. Values & Beliefs: What are those core tenets that I believe about life? Business? About how I deal with customers? Or, how I show up for my customers? _____
   _____

The reason for the four questions is that these in particular can help you think about what your narrative really is. Because as you project your "brand," you'll want to make sure it's consistent (that you reinforce the same narrative arc) every time you and your business show up in, say, social media, or any marketing collateral. Let's take a look at how one business does this: Alex Goldstein, a realtor in Florida. (Realtors are basically small businesses that have to do a lot of their own marketing so we'll use them as an example.) If you follow his account, he always photographs himself in front of expensive homes with pools etc. His narrative is always about a seller getting the maximum price on a home. And he's consistent with how he treats his brand, using the same hashtags, for example with #goals #dream #paradise – after all, that's what he's selling: high-end real estate. Here's what he does effectively: Because he's consistent in how he shows up, Goldstein has made a connection between luxury homes and himself in the minds of home sellers in Florida. That's a big hurdle but one you can do in your business as well, whatever you want to try to be equated with.

mralexgoldstein
Golden Beach, Florida

...

929 likes
mralexgoldstein Green Estate of Mind 🌴 🏖 #Scary #Massive #Goals #GoldenBeach #water #ocean #beach #sky #sun
View all 35 comments

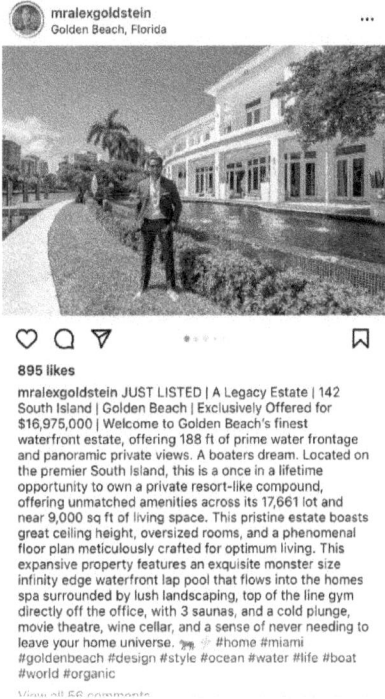

mralexgoldstein
Golden Beach, Florida

...

895 likes
mralexgoldstein JUST LISTED | A Legacy Estate | 142 South Island | Golden Beach | Exclusively Offered for $16,975,000 | Welcome to Golden Beach's finest waterfront estate, offering 188 ft of prime water frontage and panoramic private views. A boaters dream. Located on the premier South Island, this is a once in a lifetime opportunity to own a private resort-like compound, offering unmatched amenities across its 17,661 lot and near 9,000 sq ft of living space. This pristine estate boasts great ceiling height, oversized rooms, and a phenomenal floor plan meticulously crafted for optimum living. This expansive property features an exquisite monster size infinity edge waterfront lap pool that flows into the homes spa surrounded by lush landscaping, top of the line gym directly off the office, with 3 saunas, and a cold plunge, movie theatre, wine cellar, and a sense of never needing to leave your home universe. 🐾 ✨ #home #miami #goldenbeach #design #style #ocean #water #life #boat #world #organic
View all 56 comments

You can establish that narrative consistency based on any of the 4 questions or a combination of those. Just make sure to reinforce that theme constantly, whether that's you as a trustworthy business, a knowledgeable authority on some topic, or whether you understand the needs of certain groups or types of people. A few tips as you develop your personal narrative:

- **Be Authentic to Who You Are:** In other words, if you're all about money, that's fine. Help those clients who also want to maximize their money as well. If you're about truly helping people, that's great too. But don't try to be something you're not, just because you think it sells.
- **Be Consistent Everywhere:** After you've established your narrative, be consistent in reinforcing that in everything you do, including the copy you use, the images you select, and the approach you take (which we'll cover in a later chapter on Content.) This will allow you to project a brand identity in the marketplace that people come to recognize you for.

If you want to delve into your narrative more, we're happy to suggest our partners at The Narrative Playbook. (https://thenarrativeplaybook.com).

CHAPTER 3

Website Design & UX

Of all the marketing channels available to most small businesses, the website is perhaps the most foundational and important. In many ways, it's the center-piece of any small businesses' digital marketing efforts and has to serve as both a source of information and conversion. Because the user experience is so poor on many websites, small businesses lose potential customers constantly – those who might otherwise convert if the site improved even just a little.

So, let's talk about some core practical areas upfront.

1. **Selecting a hosting provider and a website CMS.**
   - Most small businesses can't afford to pay an agency to design and build their website. So, they have to look at options that are both affordable and can be built by a layperson. If you have money to hire an agency, then you should definitely move forward. If not, we suggest first following these steps:

   a. **Choose your domain and the right hosting provider.** There are many options available for you to build a website. Hosting providers such as GoDaddy, Bluehost, or HostGator offer various options to easily find an available domain and begin hosting services for a relatively small amount of money.

   » *Tip No. 1 (Dedicated Hosting):* If you aim to build a greater volume of traffic to your website, you'll want to think about dedicated hosting services. Shared hosting can mean slower page loads, leading to customers not being able to open your website pages in an efficient manner. It can also hurt your SEO rankings. You'll pay a little bit more, but it will be worth it.

» *Tip No. 2 (Domain Names):* In choosing a domain name, there are no hard and fast rules. You want it to be memorable and creative. If your business already has a name but the first choice you want isn't available because it's already being used, think about shortening or abbreviating it to get closer to what you want. It also never hurts to have the domain reflect what people are looking for. So, if an audience is looking for, say, plumbing services, having plumbing as part of your title will help as well.

» *Tip No. 3 (SSL Certificate):* Before you take any site live, make sure to get a secure socket layer certificate for your website! It's the 's' in the http(s), which indicates a secure website. The reason you need this is many browsers will now flash warnings – some won't even let customers navigate to sites that aren't secure due to information that they submit can be stolen. Most hosting providers offer SSL certificates for free too. So, it's just a matter of turning on the setting.

b. **Selecting a content management system (CMS).** Most hosting providers allow for an easy connection to a content management system. WordPress, a free, open-source CMS is the most popular for businesses and the one we'd recommend. WordPress allows for a layperson to be able to develop great-looking website pages without knowing coding or other more technical development. There are a number of other content management systems options out there for smaller businesses – Wix, Squarespace, Shopify (for e-commerce) etc. – and it doesn't really matter which one you use. You can also find industry-specific platforms that allow you to get your website up and running and also bundle other services too. One thing to avoid: Having a single developer build your site and being the only individual who can update it. We've seen too many small businesses make that mistake, where the business owners can't update the site themselves. Oftentimes, the developer holds the business hostage – no one can get in and make any changes that might be needed for SEO reasons or otherwise. That's not to say that you won't have any need for development resources. But your developers may not know or understand some of the basic marketing best practices in SEO or content development. Let's face it they're coders. That's why we recommend a content management system such as WordPress (especially for non e-commerce type websites), where most of the on-page updates can be made by business owners. Given it's the most widely used platform, we have a few tips for using WordPress specifically:[2]

» **Tip No. 1** *(Themes)*: The out-of-the-box WordPress templates might be a bit limiting for your business. We do recommend choosing a paid "theme" – really just shorthand for a set of templates/look-and-feel that use consistent styling and fonts. Paid themes are inexpensive – usually less than $100 per year – but offer more advanced templates. If you foresee needing an e-commerce function, WordPress has plugins available such as Woo Commerce, which can be added easily to certain themes.

» **Tip No. 2** *(Plugins)*: One of the great aspects of WordPress is that it has third-party plugins that help with everything from SEO and analytics to chat and community functions. Downloading new plugins (some are free, some are paid) is easy and you shouldn't be afraid to use them. But one thing to note: There are some plugins that can cause issues with elements of your theme and/or pages. So, only use the ones that you absolutely need and deactivate the rest.

» **Tip No. 3** *(Logos and Favicon)*: If you have access to some basic design resources, it's helpful to get a couple things: various sizes for your logos, and a favicon. The logo sizes are generally determined by the theme you pick and most WordPress themes now set the various logo sizes for mobile and other areas where you'll show on bookmarks etc. The favicon is the small 32x32 pixel icon that appears in the browser tab. Make sure to either cut one for that size too (or make sure your theme can reduce the existing square logo you have and use that)

---

[2] If you have questions about other platforms feel free to email us at contact@marketingniceguys.com and we'll be happy to provide our opinion based on what your business circumstances are.

as it general distinguishes a professional vs. non-professional website. One other tip with logos is to create versions that are also "transparent" – they can be used on a dark background or a light background and don't have an existing white or black background built in. One more thing: It's good to set these up first so you can see pages that come in with your logo already in place.

2. **Setting up the site with marketing in mind.**

- One of the big mistakes we see small companies make is that they don't realize the importance of systems integration and data sharing when they set up a website. In the ideal world, your website will be able to track user behavior and translate that into more personalized messaging based on that behavior. The key word here is: data! Because the website is typically the centerpiece for activity, monitoring user behavior and sharing that with other systems is critical. And thinking about your marketing holistically is also important. For example, if you know that a logged-in customer left something in a cart, do you have the capability to send an automated abandoned cart email reminder? Or send an alert for it? These little integrations will help make it easier to convert potential customers. Obviously, there are lots of website integrations you'll want to develop but here are a few core ones.

a. **Connecting your website to your marketing automation/email platform.** For those sites which focus on lead generation and forms, you'll definitely want those leads and the data you collect pushed into your email/marketing automation platform. In some cases, the marketing automation platform itself will have a form you can embed on a page of your website or the platform will allow you to develop great looking landing pages with forms on them so you can track traffic and leads to that page in one place.

b. **Connecting any e-commerce platform to your CRM.** At some point down the road, you'll want to be able to know which of your customers bought which products. Because you can then automate the e-commerce experience for those customers, having them see related products based on what they already purchased. From there, you'll also want to **connect your e-commerce platform to your marketing automation platform.** As noted above, you'll want a way to send any logged-in customers an automated email reminding them to purchase anything they have left abandoned in a cart. Also, when you get more sophisticated and can store customer site behavior in your CRM, you can then start marketing to people based on what they are browsing! But our recommendation is to start with the other two integrations first. If you have trouble, you can let your site developer know what you want to do.

c. **Connect your website to Google Analytics.** Not only is Google Analytics free and easy to connect to your website, but it also comes with a number of benefits. First and foremost, it's a great tool for you to be able to analyze your website traffic, including popular pages, total unique visitors, and even the devices and geographic areas your audience comes from. If set up correctly with goal and conversion tracking, it can also tell you information about which products are selling, where people are coming from (organic search, paid search, email, etc.), and who buys your products. Lastly, it's a critical component of data if you're going to do any paid search or paid display campaigns in the Google Ads network. Connecting your paid ads to analytics helps you understand which ads are most effective and producing the best ROI.

3. **The seven website UX areas to focus on.**

   - When agencies design and relaunch new websites on behalf of large customers, it can often cost millions of dollars. But as a small business owner, you can still get great results doing it on your own through WordPress or another CMS of your choosing. We'd definitely recommend this route rather than trying to build and manage your own site from scratch. For one, WordPress has more built-in elements that will allow for more consistency across websites, including a cascading style sheet (CSS) to establish your brand fonts and colors), as well as modules you can transfer from page to page.

Many business owners ask us about what to focus on when it comes to the website experience. We look to boil it down to seven elements. (Note, if you have an additional e-commerce platform, we'll cover that separately later in the book.)

Element No. 1: Speed

Think about it: How many websites have you tried to visit but if it didn't open within two seconds or so, you decided it probably wasn't worth it? You abandoned that site. It's a really common practice. So, having a fast site is critical to your success. Typically, there are several reasons small business sites don't load quickly: shared hosting (as mentioned earlier), large image sizes, lack of page caching, unnecessary JavaScript and/or other coding on the page that inhibits browsers from displaying your content. One place you can do a quick check on various pages of your website is with Google PageSpeed Insights: https://developers.google.com/speed/pagespeed/insights/

Just enter in your URL and Google will giving a speed ranking for mobile (default) and for desktop. Google will also give you suggestions for areas that are causing the slowness, and typically you can hand this off to your developers to have them try to fix most of the issues. If you don't want to use Google, other tools developers use include GTMetrix: https://gtmetrix.com/ and Yahoo's YSlow browser extension: http://yslow.org/

Element No. 2: Navigation & Headers

Two big mistakes we see small businesses make with navigation:

    a. Labels that don't mean much to their customers

    b. Navigation and a header that take up way too much space.

Let's take each separately.

First, navigation should be customer-focused. What we mean by that is that it should have user-friendly labels that resonate with how the customer wants to drill down into the site to find information. The mistake many businesses still make with navigation is that it can reflect the company's focus (perhaps the name of the division or company jargon) but not always helpful to the way a customer looks at finding his or her way around the site. Many great websites will now purposely employ more action-oriented labels for this reason. "I Want to: Take a Course | Make a Payment | Explore Content" rather than having more traditional labels such "Education Courses | Finance | Content & Tools," etc. There's no right way or wrong way, but it's again important to put yourself in the customer's shoes – **make sure the focus of the action/label is about what they want to look for, not about what you simply want to call it.**

Second, we often see websites take up way too much real estate for the navigation and the header. Remember, the point of navigation is to help people move through the site quickly. And on any page, the quicker you can help people get to content, the better. So, choose a template (theme in WordPress) that keeps the website navigation "thin" taking up no more than 15 percent of the viewable window on a standard desktop browser. (Note: Most WordPress themes are responsively designed, which means typically your navigation will resolve to a "hamburger menu" – the three horizontal lines usually in the top part of the page on a mobile device.)

Lastly, make sure not to overload the main navigation either. Having too many choices in the nav can overwhelm a customer. Keep it focused on the core areas. Many themes will now allow you to fly out submenus or even do a megamenu (a drop-down menu on hover) that will help you further expose secondary navigation or areas for customers to visit. If so, definitely take advantage of those rather than crowding the main navigation. In general, put less important items such as your privacy policy or links to your social media in the footer of the site.

Element No. 3: Mobile Experience

One of the reasons we recommend WordPress is that most of its theme templates come responsively designed. That is, the pages will respond to the device that's being used. So, if someone comes from a desktop, it will provide a desktop layout. If someone comes from a tablet, it will show a tablet layout. And, if someone comes from a mobile phone, it will display a mobile layout. Templates can do this because they have built-in break points at which content is programmed at to appear as individuals scroll down a page. Be warned, however, some website templates aren't actually responsive. So, make sure to choose one that is.

The other thing to watch out for as you're building out your website or building new pages is to make sure to ALWAYS check your published pages in mobile. With some sites, more than half the traffic comes from mobile devices. That means, regardless of whether your business is B2B or B2C, your mobile experience is just as important (if not more) than your desktop experience. Many people also use mobile to do research and it's now become standard for purchases. A few areas to consider:

a. **Take a look at how headers and text on "hero" (top of page) images appear in mobile**. Make sure both are legible and clearly visible.

b. **Test any entry forms in mobile**. Make sure the forms have the same fields and a consistent labeling that is clear and not overwriting the entry field itself.

c. **Go through a mobile purchase (if you have an e-commerce site)**. Similar to the above, it's important to test forms and checkouts in the process of using a mobile device.

d. **Thoroughly review landing pages**. Oftentimes, landing pages (such as your home pages or section pages) don't always translate well into mobile. Make sure the core elements appear the way you want and in an order that makes sense to the customer.

Element No. 4: Use Personalization

For many small businesses, integrating more personalized experiences into a website can be challenging, particularly those that don't have development resources at their disposal.

That said, if you can muster some resources for the effort, it's worth it. Here are a few ways you can approach a more personalized experience for your website visitors:

- Personalization Based on Geography: Let's say you have a few brick-and-mortar retail stores in a local area and you sell goods both online and in the store. One easy thing you can do is provide the nearest store to that individual based on the geographic location of that visitor's IP address or phone geolocation. It's an easy reminder of a place they can shop. Most all web developers can easily help you execute this function.

Knowing that IP address will also give you the ability to personalize deals to particular geographies. So, if in the winter time, you want to provide winter boots to the northeast but sun tan lotion to Arizona, you can do that pretty easily by building a module that changes based on various states and ZIP codes.

- **Personalization Based on User Choice on Input:** Let's say you sell a particular set of products or services, each with a distinct set of audiences (in other words, not much crossover in terms of audiences who might be interested in one solution and another). One thing you can do for those website visitors is have them take a quick upfront survey or have them select particular preferences when they visit the site for the first time. Those selections and interests then determine the experience they receive. One example might be a wine shop that asks website visitors what their taste profile is like: Do they like California fruit-forward wine? More European style? And then, based on the outcome, personalize the offering to show the customer those choices that fit their preferences on a home page. Make sure to encourage the visitor to create an account profile and sign in so they receive the personalized experience and save their settings to the site. It will take some development effort to customize this but, in the end, you'll find it's worth it.

- **Personalization Based on User Behavior:** As stated earlier, if you have given thought about the systems that you can connect to together (especially your CRM and the website, or the e-commerce platform and the website), you can begin executing this aspect of personalization. For example, if you can store data within your CRM or e-commerce platform for signed-in visitors such as pages they visited or items they've put in a cart, you can easily carve out a space in the home page or header to show them the pages they've viewed (so they can easily navigate back) or the abandoned cart items. Also, if you have a shopping cart function, it's pretty easy for a developer to display a return visitor a site alert saying they should "check out now" with the products they were intending to buy.

Element No. 5: Search

There are really only two ways that website visitors find the content and products/services they are looking for on a website. They navigate to it or they search for it. And the latter plays a huge role in the overall website user experience. If you're using a WordPress theme, your site will simply come pre-loaded with a basic search that will primarily find only exact word matches as part of it. If you don't have a lot of pages, that's OK. But if you have lots of products and services, a store, or other pages where your visitors might need to drill down a little deeper, you'll definitely want to think about a few options.

First and foremost, you can work with a developer to replace the search on your website with another search appliance. Pre-2019, many sites turned to the Google Search Appliance, given its notable capabilities in its own search realm. However, Google phased out the platform in 2019, leaving many companies to scramble for an equivalent search engine. For small companies, it was likely a bit on the expensive side regardless. Other options for smaller companies include:

- Solr
- Amazon Cloud Search
- Sharepoint Search
- Sinequa
- Oracle Endeca

If you have a WordPress site, you can also enhance your search with plugins. Among those that are quite highly rated include:

- Search & Filter: If you have a site that requires "facets" – drilldown filters to help narrow the search for a website visitor, this plugin is generally pretty feature rich. It includes a combination of categories, tags, taxonomies, post-types, and can be displayed with checkboxes, radio buttons, range sliders and other functions.
- FacetWP: Another cool plugin that can do "facets," this add-on uses shortcodes to determine the placement of search control features and results. It includes custom fields, tags, and categories.
- Advanced Search: This isn't a plugin but a PHP framework that can be used by developers to create an advanced faceted search experience.

Not a great option if you don't have WordPress developers but it's pretty straight-forward for them if you do.

- Solr Search for WordPress: With features similar to the Solr search appliance, this is a good option in that it's also used by Netflix, Ticketmaster, and Instagram on their respective websites. The plugin features the ability to do facets by category, page type, author, and custom fields.

Every search engine appliance or plugin is slightly different and allows for different experiences. We would suggest investigating a few key areas of functionality:

- Autocomplete. When a visitor types in a search, it's important to help them by giving suggestions for what others have looked for as they type in their query. Google has clearly set the standard for this.

- Non-Exact Jargon. Let's say you're a toy store and the customer types in "action toys" when the known exact name/jargon is actually "action figures." Does the search still turn up a useful result with action figures being displayed? Great search engines will understand and help the user out. They might even suggest more accurate terms.

- Faceted Search. As mentioned above, it's the ability to drilldown by category, or other tags, page types, or fields so the website user can find exactly what they're looking for.

- Contextual Snippets. Does the website return a small description (typically the meta description) on what the page is about? That short description helps website visitors decide if this is indeed a relevant page. If it's a product search, does it bring up a product image or other details?

Element No. 6: Visual Design

One of the most critical areas of the website involves visual design and user experience. We see a lot mistakes that small businesses tend to make here. Mostly, this is because they don't use a good WordPress theme or template. We'll walk through several key areas below:

- Simple, 'airy' design: One mistake that we see websites make too often is that they pack information into a small viewing window and cram call-to-action buttons everywhere. Best practice would dictate that landing pages only have 4 to 5 separate items in each viewing window on a desktop browser. That means more "air" and fewer choices to make the viewing experience less chaotic.

- Using visually compelling images: Images need to be both fast-loading and high resolution to meet the SEO criteria, which we detail later on. They also need to be contextually relevant. If you don't have access to good stock photos or in-house photography, you can get high-quality, copyright-free images at sites such as Unsplash.com or Pexels.com. Just credit the photographer and you'll be ready to go.

- Clear hierarchy of promotion. The key element here is don't bury the lead. For landing pages or article pages, make sure to highlight the most important information at the top of the page, starting from left to right. The top left is the most important real estate followed by the top right on a desktop. Obviously, on a mobile device, make sure your responsive website focuses on the most important content at the top.

6 Elements of a Strong Small Business Brand

When you're just starting out running a small business, the hardest part is often simply gaining visibility beyond your initial network. Indeed, for many small companies the first buyers are people you know or people you know who have referred you to someone else. Steadily – we hope that's the case! – you gain more customers from that network over time who get to know your business and what it stands for. That's great as you continue to spread word-of-mouth, which hopefully comes from the great products or services you provide. But at a certain point, your business ends up running through your network connections and their friends. And then, many companies get stuck. How do I attract more customers? How do I make them aware of my company and what I do?

Marketing and Your Brand Identity

In those early stages, many companies don't think about their brand. They may have done a little marketing, for example – perhaps some digital advertising or social media – but they may not necessarily consider the brand in those activities, as much as sales or other immediate rewards. And it makes sense in many ways. There are so many things a startup or new company has to do around other core areas – the products and services offering, dealing with finances, trying to get those immediate term sales, and even all the administrative stuff – that oftentimes the owners or leadership might de-prioritize what they might view as some esoteric, intellectual marketing exercise.

After all, it's not exactly a common refrain at small companies to ask: "What's our brand stand for?" as you attempt to navigate those first crazy years as a business. That said, as any marketing professor will tell you, it's a question that businesses need to ask themselves.

And also answer.

Indeed, your company's brand identity is perhaps the single most important reason why others buy from you. And that's true whether you're just starting out or at that point where you've reached your network saturation. (In those early stages, with network word-of-mouth going, much of your brand identity may be wrapped up with personal identity, as it may be friends recommending you to other friends based on who you are and what they know about you and your reputation.)

The Six Core Areas of Small Business Brand Development

With a brand, much like your own personal identity, you have to start establishing that same (hopefully strong) reputation and narrative, if you will. Larger businesses clearly have an advantage here. Many can spend on brand advertising on TV, radio, digital, mobile, and other formats to get the word out about what they stand for. Because they have a longer-term horizon, they can invest in awareness and developing their unique brand equity among potential customers. But small businesses don't often have that luxury or the dollars needed to more broadly spread the word about their products or services, even in a local community.

So, how does a small business do it? This is where it gets a bit tricky and pays to take a step back and think through several things, including:

- Your Mission as a Business
- Your 'Ideal' Audience and Your Brand's Relationship to Them
- Your Uniqueness
- Your Visual Identity
- Your Content & Other Promotions
- Your Narrative

Your Mission as a Business

As a company, what do you believe in? Many small businesses don't actually state that upfront. And because they haven't figured out their values, or what they stand for, they end up sounding like one big sales pitch when it comes to talking to their customers. Your mission – or what you believe about how you're serving customers and/or your role as a company itself – needs to be front and center when you communicate with audiences. And it needs to be repeated. Often. This is especially true as you think about how your brand identity comes across. The key word here is trust. Your mission helps establish that in the minds of customers, getting them to know about bit more about you. The reason: People buy from companies that they trust and come to know, especially today when it pertains to values.

Your 'Ideal' Audience and Your Brand's Relationship to Them

The reason we say "ideal" here is that you may be currently serving and attracting an audience that isn't ideal, one that isn't going to help you grow in the future. And, in that case, maybe you have to transition or re-imagine your brand for a different audience. An example might be the company Old Spice, which in the last several years has made significant moves to attract a younger male audience, as it faced competition from Axe.

As you start thinking about that ideal audience, how do you see projecting your brand to meet their needs? Do you need to make adjustments in the way you...

- Talk about things (voice, tone)
- Visually represent things (design, colors, images, video)
- Interact with customers

When companies talk about "audience-focus," this is what it truly means.

Your Uniqueness

What's that one thing (or few things) that makes your company unique as far as the industry you're in? Some in marketing call it that "special sauce" that's something only you do. Maybe it's a process you have that's more efficient, maybe it's a special touch when you execute on something, a unique product or service, maybe it's the way your treat customers, or even a mission. For example, the company Tom's was known for giving away a pair of shoes to under-served communities whenever someone bought a pair of theirs. They've continued to evolve that mission of giving back – and it's what makes them unique in the marketplace. As you think about the way your company's brand projects itself to others, are you repeating that uniqueness or message about what makes you different often enough?

Your Visual Identity

Does your "look" represent and project both who you are and who your ideal target audience is? Is your look outdated? As mentioned earlier, does your use of images, video, graphics and color scheme speak to audiences? Is it consistent across various different mediums – website, email, social, sales or marketing collateral, for example. How about the fonts you use? Do you present a consistent font, similar to what Apple does in all its promotions? (They use different sizes of SF Pro everywhere.) Visual is typically the area that most small businesses will want to address first because it's the most obvious. Sometimes that translates into small adjustments – establishing more consistency and rigor around colors or fonts. But typically, if something is off with the brand "look," it often means that it's time for a complete rebranding.

Your Content and Other Promotions

As mentioned above, many small businesses won't have the kind of capital it takes to conduct a broader advertising campaign focused on awareness. (Sure, traditionally lower-funnel ads will provide some aspect of brand awareness as well, but it's probably not equivalent to broader awareness advertising in many industries.) So, many companies will look to more cost-effective ways. One of those ways is developing content.

We have often stated that content is the guerilla marketing of today. That is, content is both cost-effective (it only takes time and effort to produce) and a great way to spread the word about what you represent as a brand. Content also allows you to highlight your expertise, which is a key aspect of bolstering your brand story and narrative, which we'll talk more about below.

Your Narrative

How are you telling the story of your brand value? We think of a narrative as being both strategic and operational. Your company narrative – in this case we're defining it as the "story" about your brand – has to encompass all of the elements we discussed above in a strategic, considered approach. But it also has to be implemented in a consistent way. In other words, your brand only has real value to customers if you've been relentless in communicating and operationalizing that story about who you are and what you stand for all the time.

We often see companies that have the core aspects of a good brand but when it comes to telling the story, they lurch from being one thing to another. That's an issue with the narrative they're telling. An example might be a company that wants to be a high-end retailer but then, every month, offers discounts on the products they sell. The brand strategy they've created – about a high-end retailer doesn't match the story in the market, which is that they're a discounter.

Element No. 7: Colors and Fonts

Too often we see small business websites use a barrage of colors and varying fonts, which do nothing but add to a chaotic visitor experience. If you think about a company such as Apple, which is known for its stalwart brand consistency, it uses a single font (SF Pro) with varying sizes. It also defines a more limited number of colors in its CSS (cascading style sheet) and all within a single-color palette. Sites that use too many colors will create an un-focused experience, where the eye may be drawn to different colors on the page but not actual content. Two tools you can download to your Chrome browser as the extension: WhatFont?, which provides information about any site's fonts, and ColorZilla, which has a webpage color analyzer. There's no hard and fast rule, but you should generally only use one type of font on your site. And you should generally try to limit your color usage to under 20 defined in your CSS.

CHAPTER 4

Search Engine Optimization (SEO)

SEO stands for search engine optimization. These are the activities a website owner does to increase organic referral traffic from search engines. In particular, those activities that make a page more relevant and useful for a search engine's users. For most websites, organic search accounts for anywhere from one-half to two-thirds of traffic. And despite the obvious evidence that it's the single best method for sites to acquire new, interested audiences, many small businesses don't have a plan to focus on this. For the purposes of this book, we'll break down the basics of search engine optimization into a few core areas.

How It Works

With a search engine such as Google, no one outside the company really knows "exactly" how its algorithm works. Many attempts have been made to gather evidence, particularly through the years as Google has evolved the factors that play a role in website rankings, but none absolutely conclusive. That said, there are clearly fundamentals that will help you and your small business as you go forward.

Google's 7 Core 'Systems'

Google has a number of 'systems' that play a role into what a searcher sees. These come from our friend Myron Rosmarin, one of the top SEO experts in the United States. They are:

- **Authority**: Authority is a system for search engines like Google to determine the credibility/trust of the information source. It is based on a few things: Strength of brand, and who points to who. So, if an authoritative site links to a second site, that second site receives a boost in the eyes of a search engine such as Google.

- **Discoverability**: This is the system used by search engines that discovers (crawls) content on the web and determines what to index. In order for a search engine to rank your website, it has to be "discoverable" by its crawlers. The first goal of any website is to ensure its pages are discoverable by Google. Most sites do this by pushing pages live and then promoting them, in say, Twitter (which Google indexes first) or other social media.

- **Context and Setting**: Google will look at other signals such as geography, ratings/reviews, past search behaviors to determine what to show a particular user.

- **Content Quality**: This system evaluates whether the content is robust and well written.

- **Presentation of results**: Determines how results should be displayed to the searcher.

- **Relevance**: Determines if content on a page is considered a match for a user's query, considering word similarities, geography, and past behaviors. Typically, search engines look for a "preponderance of evidence" that something is a match, usually based on a number of on-page and off-page factors.

- **Site quality/UX**: Evaluates whether searchers will get a good user experience with content that loads fast and is easy to consume.

Individual businesses don't have much control over systems such as Context and Setting or Presentation of Results. But the others are areas where the businesses do have influence: Relevance, site quality, content quality and, to a certain extent, authority. Let's cover more about those areas that are within an organization's control and will impact ranking.

Relevance

Google determines relevance by several on-page and off-page factors that match for a particular query. This "aboutness" test is done when a search engine looks at the following:

On-Page Factors

- **Title Tag:** The title of the page. Make sure the title tag follows the recommended structure: <article title 60 characters or less if possible> | <site name>. Title tag should include the keywords people are searching for.
- **URLs:** The URLs should include the page title (which should have keywords people are searching for).
- **H Tags** (aka Heading Tags, esp. H1 but H2 and H3): Every one of these should be keyword-driven or use correlated keywords based on the main set of keywords the page is about. (Example: If the page is about George Washington, a correlated keyword headline might be "Revolutionary War" or "First President").
- **Related Keyword Usage (topic models):** Ensure the text has correlated keywords. If the page is focused on leadership, for example, it's important to include keywords related to that – emotional intelligence, change management, vision, ethics, responsiveness, etc.
- **Link Text (on-page pointing out, especially in article body):** Linked text on the page should include keywords that the page is about. (Example: If this is a page about motivational speakers, the link text pointing to other pages should also be about motivation or motivational speakers or correlated keywords.)
- **Meta Description:** The meta description does not influence page rank but it is useful as this is the description Google will often use when describing the page. (It may also just choose its own snippet on the

page as well.) It's important to make sure the meta description has the keywords embedded into it as you want to give anyone searching in Google the reason to click to your site.

- **Image Alt Tag (describes images, equates to link text)**: Make sure the image alt text includes all the keyword or keywords that the page is about.
- **Image URL**: Similar to the page URL, name the image so that the URL for the image location (all images are published to an imager server with a unique URL) has the keywords in it. Use hyphens to separate keywords.
- **Typography**: Bold or italicize the core keywords and correlated keywords on the page. You can also put those high-value keywords in bullets to highlight points on the page, or change font sizes, which will draw the attention of the search engine.

Off-Page Factors

- Inbound links and link text: Certainly, Google looks at the "authority" of sites linking to your site. But it also looks at the relevance of the text on the links from external sites, as well as links from the rest of your website. The more those inbound links have text that resembles the user's query or keyword, the more relevant Google determines the site to be. So, if your website is about knee replacement surgery, and the inbound link says: "knee surgery" that's better than an inbound link that just says: "more" or "click here." (One tip: With any page of your website, make sure you have at least 5 other pages linking to it. After all, if you don't link to the page yourself, Google may think the page isn't important enough to rank highly.)
- A note about social media: Not all inbound text links are treated as providing authority or relevance. Indeed, the ones from social media have no direct bearing on your SEO ranking in that links from such sites are generally discounted by Google. That said, it's still important to link to your content and pages from your social media platforms because it aids in the discoverability of your site by Google (previously

mentioned), it improves your brand awareness, and it increases the likelihood of those who see it, will link to the pages directly from their own websites or from company websites.

Authority

A number of factors influence your website's authority. First and foremost, it's your brand penetration and awareness. The more recognizable your business and brand, the more people engage with it. The more people engage with it, the more they search for it and link to it from other places. Recognized brands have natural authority that automatically helps their SEO. That's one case where doing brand-awareness-type marketing helps in ways you might not immediately be able to measure.

As you might guess, for this cross-linking reason, authority is also passed between sites. So, if one site is an authority in a particular space and it links to another site, it will help pass that website authority onto that receiving site. Receiving inbound links from particularly authoritative websites is critical to helping improve the ranking of your pages. That's why some marketing departments focus on link-building campaigns (generally email reach-out campaigns asking other sites to link back to your company website.) How do you start the link-building process? Here are a few things you can do:

- Reach out to websites that already mention you but perhaps don't currently have a link to your site
- Exchange a link out to an external site for an inbound link in to yours
- Put your content in front of publishers in your industry or area and have them link to you for additional content for a story
- Do the occasional press release through, say, a Cision/PRNewsire. These don't create inbound authority but they do allow for more opportunities for those to discover you.

How about link-building services? There are a number of different services out there that provide link-building. Some services do guest posting on websites and provide links back to yours. Others get your site listed in directories or particular listing services. If you do decide to move forward with one of them, make sure the links they provide are from high-domain-authority websites in the same industry or focusing on the same thing that you do as a business. A link from a medical website to a construction website has very little value, for example. Some businesses also sell bulk links from "100s of websites." Those are scams. Don't fall for them as this will not help your site rank higher.

7 Ways to Tell a Scam from a Really Good Service

As a small business ourselves, one of the things that dismay us more than anything else is that we're inundated on daily basis with lies – all of which come from those selling us the promise of something. We're all familiar with the guru who will transform us "if you just take his course" or the snake-oil salesmen who will relay to you that secret to making 7-figures if you just sign up. But it's also those who overpromise on everyday services they provide. Some might call this "good marketing." But there's nothing good about it if the service was set up to be a scam or doesn't deliver on a consistent basis. You work too hard as a business owner to deserve the con artists we all seem to encounter.

And we're not just talking about Theranos here either. We're talking about everyday scams, especially the ones that involve marketing. We've seen some of our own small business clients get suckered in by promises that other firms have made such as:

- "Getting in front of an audience of 1 million investors"
- "You just sit back and get all the leads"
- "Buy these 100+ backlinks to your website at the push of a button!"
- "I want to see you 10x your income. Just follow the link."

If you just take a step back and consider those statements in isolation, you probably would be immediately skeptical. After all, 1 million investors? Who exactly are those people? And why would all of them be interested in investing in my product? Second, anything that suggests we can sit back and enjoy life while someone else does the work for us (at especially a low cost) is, sorry to say, fraudulent. Third, if everyone could just buy 100 backlinks (to boost SEO) they would, if it actually worked. (It doesn't.) Lastly, 10x your own income? One of the recommendations here was literally learning to start with the right car (to impress people.) If that isn't a joke, we don't know what is.

But the truth is, we often get suckered in. Because that's what opportunists do – they prey on our desire to make things better or easier for ourselves.

The tough part is that it can be hard to tell the difference between a valuable service and a scam. For that reason, we wanted to tackle here the 7 ways we've found to uncover a scam, something we hope you can apply to evaluate any product or service you buy.

No. 1: Ask the Company About How the Product/Service Works in Detail

Any good product marketing team will work to put a product or service in the best light. They'll make sure the landing pages, brochures or anything marketing-related addresses the core audience challenges and pain points. But as a business owner, we always recommend taking the next step. When you talk to a representative from the company, ask them detailed questions about how the process works. How do they justify the price? If it's low, ask yourself what the value really is or what automation is there that allows them to cut the cost? Does that automation make sense for your business? Ask them basic questions about jargon you don't know. Can the representative explain it things in layman's terms? If they can't explain it well, it's likely been made up. What really happens if you do this or that with a particular service? Finally, not every product or service will do this but see if you can take it for a test drive. As you dig in, if you're not comfortable with the answers or what you find, it might start to smell more like a scam.

No. 2: Ask Your Friends, Not Theirs

Testimonials from the company are fine, and the assumption we all make is that such individuals aren't just made up, so hopefully real people have been impacted by the product or service. But it also pays to ask your own friends in the same industry or area if they have used that that particular product or service. What did they think about it? Was it worth it? You can often get a lot more insight this way than you would on your own.

No. 3: With Leads, If They Promise That You Can Sit Back and Just Watch the Leads Come In, Be Afraid. Very Afraid.

We often see a lot of turnkey products and services, especially when it comes to website development, SEO, lead generation and marketing automation. And there's nothing wrong with such services on the surface. If you can get a low-cost website built (even if it's more templated), one that understands the needs of your business with tools that allow you to customize it and connect to a marketing automation platform, that's great. So far, so good. The problem, in our view, comes when you hear promises of automated ads that will allow you to "watch the leads roll in" or SEO optimizations that will increase your page ranking for that same low cost. If you start to hear that, be afraid. Very afraid.

Why?

Because lead generation and SEO, in particular, are complex and in most cases, still require a lot of manual effort (or human touch). Let's take advertising as an example. Having a built-in, design template is great, but that's just one part of the process. There's copy, targeting, budgeting, dayparting, tracking, the image quality, the call to action, and your own narrative as a business – each of which can mean the difference between something that works well and something that doesn't. A machine or a low-cost offering won't be able to do those things well for you or be able to provide you that personal touch.

Similarly, SEO is all about attention to detail. And we mean little details that require hands-on adjustments to on-page factors and off-page tactics. If you do come across a low-cost SEO service bundled into an offering, ask them what you really get for the money. Does it makes sense? And why can't they do an optimization once, then check in less frequently (assuming you have a smaller website).

No. 4: Watch Out for Subscriptions That Lock You In

Subscriptions to ongoing services can be a great thing. We love, for example, Canva, which is worth every penny of the $12 a month we pay for it. But we'd be wary when it comes to paying for ongoing subscriptions for something such as a website (which really should be a one-time cost even with more complex integrations) or, as mentioned above, SEO. That's because if SEO is done right for a small business in particular, there are probably limited ongoing things that need to be done. If it's link-building, OK, as long as it's legitimate but there are many illegitimate offers out there. This is where even a low monthly cost can add up over time. One thing you can do here is step back and think about what you're paying over the entire year or if you do it for two years or three years. Will it be worth it rather than spending to do it once?

No. 5: Know Yourself and What You Have to Do Within Their System

It's probably true that the same product or service that can seem fraudulent to one individual, might be transformational for another. A lot of that has to do with the individual doing the buying. A few questions to ask yourself here:

- Are you willing to do what the product or service requires?
- Does the product or service really fit into what you do every day? Or will you have to make a big transition in terms of how you operate? Are you willing to do that?
- Does it just make life easier for you (which we all would love) or are there harder things involved?

- Are there things that you're annoyed by? Does the product or service have anything that would suggest it could trigger you in a negative way?

Remember, products or services can only be transformational or helpful for you if you're willing to change yourself in some way. If you're not, you might consider another alternative.

No. 6: Does the Company Produce Its Own Content? Is It Any Good?

When we say content, we don't mean they do a fancy video on Instagram that promotes their services. We mean real thought-leadership content – a book, a regular blog, a series of videos or podcasts that you can look at to know the company truly is a leader in the space and have thought about those issues that are pertinent to you. In other words, is there any meat behind what they do or are they simply a shell of a company that hasn't really considered the customer in any deep way? If they haven't and don't produce a lot of content, it might be there is also nothing behind the actual product that is worth paying for.

No. 7: If It Sounds Too Good to Be True, It Probably Is

It's an old adage but it's appropriate in cases such as these as well. Few companies are out there underselling the value of what they provide. True, it might be the company is new and/or trying to bring on new customers so you might be getting advantageous pricing or great value for your money. But make sure again to ask the right questions. If your first instinct is to believe something is too good to be true, it probably is.

Site Quality & Content Quality

What determines site quality? A number of factors, including:

- **Robust content that is grammatically correct**. What is considered "robust"? Google uses a topic model to determine robustness and depth. For example, if an article is referring to the Kentucky Derby, Google would normally expect that article body to include "Triple Crown," "first Saturday in May," "Louisville," or even "hats" and "fashion" as those elements are all connected to the event. The more you can create content that is robust here the better. That doesn't mean you simply stuff keywords into an article but it does mean that you should make your article comprehensive.

- **Unique content (not duplicated on-site or others sites)**. Duplicated content dilutes SEO page value, whether that's the same content on the same site or a different site. In some cases, sites create duplicate pages simply by adding dynamic parameters to content page URLs for tracking. In other cases, you might have duplicate content because you mistakenly put that content in two places – say on a microsite and the main site. For any duplicate page, you want to point to the "canonical" – the page you want Google to index. The best way is to add a "rel=canonical" tag on the duplicate page pointing to the page you want to be indexed. Most small businesses need a developer to do this but it's something he or she should be able to accomplish relatively easily.

- **Up-to-date**. Content that is out of date (say, from a previous decade) contributes to lower site quality, as it tends to no longer be relevant. That is, unless the searcher is specifically looking for a historical archive of some kind. What many small businesses do is they update content showing a new "update" date in the text to make it clear content is still fresh.

- **Most important content plainly visible above the fold**. For the both the mobile and desktop experience, you want to make sure not to "bury the lead." In other words, put the most important content at the top of the page – with the high-value keyword concepts that the searchers came to find.

- **Excessive JavaScript or Ajax/CSS controls (e.g. accordions and fly-outs) hiding content.** Sometimes the way sites are designed, the content is only visible upon a user hovering or taking an action. That type of content is typically hidden from the search engine and can reduce site quality if that proves to be excessive.

- **Prominent ads and promos that don't overwhelm the page or interfere with user experience.** Perhaps some of your business revolves around advertising on your page. Putting an ad at the top of the page, pushing down the content will affect your site quality. Or, overwhelming the page with ads that take up a lot of real estate. The critical piece here is to balance the user experience with the revenue generation from ads.

- **Use of high-quality images and video.** High quality beats low quality in Google's eyes so make sure images and video aren't grainy, pixelated or blurry. Some websites, for example, stretch images (a no-no) to fit a particular space rather than simply cropping and resizing, which is preferred.

- **Fast-loading pages.** As we discussed in the website section, speed is critical to website performance and for SEO. In addition to the Google PageSpeed Insights tool, you can also use Gtmetrix (gtmetrix.com) or YSlow (Yahoo's browser extension to analyze the speed of your website).

- **No broken links/404 errors.** When companies move or remove certain content on the website, that can create broken links for website visitors – a poor user experience. One thing you can do is to take your site through a SEO audit, (https://marketingniceguys.com/professional-website-seo-audit-and-content-plan/) which will identify broken links you can fix immediately.

Other SEO Concepts to Know

- **Semantic markup.** You can boost your visibility in Google by putting your site information in a structured data framework (semantic markup). Sites such as Schema.org provide a model for semantic markup for all kinds of businesses and industries – everything from recipes to movie ratings to categorizing images and videos. Semantic markup allows Google to easily pull data for display in search results, and hence, Google will prioritize ranking sites that do so.

- **Local Search**. About half of all searches on Google are local. For those businesses that focus on a local, geographic audience, here are a few things that you can do to improve your local ranking.
  - » Get your business listed on Google My Business and other local directories, yellow pages, local Chamber of Commerce, etc. Of all the items on the list, a full and complete Google My Business listing should be your number 1 priority.
  - » Make sure your name, address and local phone number are be displayed throughout the site.
  - » Provide hours of operations and maps and directions.
  - » Use the primary business name, category, city and state in prominent tags such as titles, H1/H2, URLs, link text, meta descriptions, image ALT text and filenames.
  - » Encourage customers to provide reviews and ratings (quantity beats stars) on authoritative guides such as: Yelp. In particular, focus on the top business/category/place queries and sites such as: Urban Spoon, Google Reviews, HealthGrades, etc.
  - » Use Schema.org's Local Business (schema.org) LocalBusiness semantic markup.
  - » Upload high-quality photos of the inside and outside of the business as well as photos of the products offered and people who work there.
- Redirects. A redirect will route website users to a page's new location. There are two types:
  - » **301 (Permanent) Redirects.** These are the preferred method because they pass SEO equity from the old location to the new location. Redirects should lead to a highly relevant match for SEO equity to transfer.
  - » **302 (Temporary) Redirects**. These do not pass SEO equity and discourage the target page from indexation. These 302 redirects are used during site downtime etc.

- **404 Errors**. The errors themselves have no direct bearing on SEO, as they could simply be caused by an individual who comes to the website domain and types the wrong URL. That said, broken links (which will trigger a 404 error on your site) do need to be fixed. One tip: Make the 404 error page interesting and useful – have links go to key pages so individuals can easily find what they're looking for.

- **Robots.txt files**. Your developers should be familiar with a robots.txt file, which tells a search engine which pages on your site to crawl or not to crawl. For example, many companies use a robots.txt file to keep search engines from crawling low-value pages such as internal search results pages or premium content kept behind a pay wall.

- **Crawl budget**. The number of website pages a search engine will crawl per day is based on that website's crawl budget:
  - » Think of it as your "credit line" with the search engine: The more the engine likes/trusts your content, the more time they devote to crawling your site. So....
  - » Don't waste your crawl budget on low-value pages -- such as search results pages or old/archived pages – have them not be crawled. (see Robots.txt file above)
  - » Increase your crawl budget by improving page-load speed

  If it takes 1 second for a bot to crawl a page, at 86,400 seconds in a day, that's about how many pages can be crawled in a 24-hour period. Big sites have millions of pages.

- **AMP pages**. AMP stands for "accelerated mobile page." Creating AMP versions of your content is helpful so that particular content pages load super-fast on mobile devices. It's not necessary to create AMP for all pages (in particular, not necessary for landing pages) but it's really useful for content articles. Sites that do this will rank higher in mobile search.

- **XML sitemap**. A dynamically generated map of your site (not visible to site visitors) that highlights the top content and landing pages for search engines. It helps for SEO purposes as it provides an improved crawlability for your website. If you're curious, the sitemap visible to your website visitors is called a HTML sitemap.

PATIO for SEO

Let's do a quick walk-thru of how to approach SEO operations, from planning to optimization.

Planning & Strategy

First, determine the goals of SEO (for example, year 1, then year 2, etc.). Typically, most companies identify anywhere from 25-50 key terms at a time that they: a. Want to rank for, and; b. Have the resources to make the necessary SEO adjustments. So, for existing pages, try to aim to do those in year one. Remember, SEO changes can take from 6 to 12 months before they take effect so what you're essentially doing is investing in the long-term health of the business.

Second, adapt the personas you created (the core challenges and behaviors), and see what other areas of opportunity there are for you to take on and try to rank in those topics, getting additional eyeballs to your site. What's the plan to create content around those challenges and pain points? Does it make you alter which keywords you had thought to take on?

Lastly, it's important to figure out your areas of focus. No one has unlimited resources. So, figure out where SEO fits compared to other things you have to focus on or fix. SEO is often put off because of the longer-term nature of how it works, but it's often a critical component of driving lead generation and revenue in the end.

Approach

Based on your plan, you have to set the approach, which includes:

Doing the keyword research upfront. We haven't covered keyword research in great depth so far, but it's a critical aspect of understanding your audience. What is the keyword volume in certain topical areas? A few questions to ask yourself:

- What are the terms that drive the most traffic now?

- What are the terms with the biggest potential? (This might not mean the biggest traffic driver, but the most relevant in-market audience). What are the terms you want to be ranked on?
- Where are your competitors beating you at this?
- What are trending terms?

What many companies do is use a combination of free services and paid competitive search platforms to do research. While we have our own keyword research tool at Marketing Nice Guys, we'll cover more of these paid/free platforms in the tools section.

Developing the content approach (we'll talk more in the content section). This includes the new landing pages you might need – or understanding if the focus requires enhancing the existing pages.

Tools & Tactics

As mentioned, a number of companies do keyword/competitive research that can inform your SEO approach. Here are a few that can help in this area.

- SEMRush: https://semrush.com
- SimilarWeb: https://similarweb.com
- Moz: https://moz.com
- iSpionage: https://www.ispionage.com/
- Answer the Public: https://answerthepublic.com/
- Check My Links (Chrome extension): https://chrome.google.com/webstore/detail/check-my-links/ojkcdipcgfaekbeaelaapakgnjflfglf?hl=en
- Keywords Everywhere (Chrome and Mozilla extensions for looking at keyword search volume and competitive data): https://keywordseverywhere.com/

For tactics, here are a few that you can employ:

- **Set the workflows that optimize SEO and copyrighting on page**. We will also cover this in the content area but it's critical to make sure your keywords are embedded into different aspects of the page (as pointed out above) and that there are no grammatical errors.

- **Determine the off-page tactics (social, link-building etc.)** We've discussed link-building approaches already but think about this in terms of the resources you have available. Where are you going to post? How are you going to reach out to other websites?

Implementation

Based on your plan, content approach, and the tools and resources you have available, it's time to implement. Much of what you can do here focuses on the on-page optimization, though as mentioned, there are several off-page tactics that you can also execute. One tip: Attention to detail probably matters most of all in SEO. That's because you have to make sure you're consistently inserting the core keywords into URLs, headlines, body copy, title tags, images, image URLs, meta descriptions, and other areas of the page. Follow your checklists and make sure all the items are covered EVERY TIME you publish.

Optimization

For the 25-50 terms you focused on, have you improved positions? Has the competition made strides in these areas? How can you do on-page optimization better? What are audiences doing if they do, indeed, land on your pages from organic search? Are they sticking around? Clicking through to other pages? Consider enhancing those – adding social or paid media promotion to drive more traffic – and even adding a press release for additional exposure. Most of all, keep optimizing pages that are important to you until you get on page 1 and become the top result.

Finally, with SEO stay patient. There's no magic bullet for it except to do the hard work day in and day out focusing on the above fundamentals. It's not sexy but getting to page one for particular searches is a big deal and obviously ranking first on page one is even better.

CHAPTER 5

Content Marketing

Tell of us if this sounds familiar: You read an article and suddenly announce: "We need a podcast!" or "We need to get into video!"

Suddenly, you and your staff spring into action developing new content without any rationale behind it. It's an all-too-common scenario that happens at companies of all sizes. Sometimes that works out OK. But in other cases, it's complete disaster. We've put together some basic rules that can help you avoid that scenario and guide the content marketing efforts for any small business.

Start with your audience challenges. As mentioned earlier, too often we see content being developed by companies without them having researched their audiences first.[3] This includes understanding basic areas such as where people currently go on the website, what they search for, what their ambitions or goals are, and what challenges and pain points they face. Knowing the latter is particularly important before you develop any content because ultimately, engagement is about relevance. In other words, for content to resonate with potential or current customers, you have to show empathy for their situation. It's a cliché to say "put yourself in the customers' shoes," but that's exactly what you need to do in the case of content. Let's look at PATIO for Content Marketing:

PATIO for Content Marketing

Planning & Strategy

When companies think about content marketing, they often take the Nike approach – they "just do it." But having a plan is critical to successful content

---

[3] https://marketingniceguys.com/what-are-personas-why-audience-research-matters/

marketing efforts. According a recent study by the Content Marketing Institute, 69% of the most successful organizations have a documented plan of some kind. It makes sense. The more you give some thought upfront to your goals in content and where it fits in the overall scheme of your digital marketing, the more you'll be able to focus on driving those key performance indicators that you set to see how you're doing. What are the elements of plan? We suggest starting with these 4 areas:

- What's the goal of content marketing? Where does it fit in the larger context of all the marketing I do?
- What resources will I allocate to it – both staffing and dollars for creation/distribution? Outlining the frequency of production is a key piece here too.
- Who am I targeting and where – what part of the funnel? What does the audience research tell me about the type of content I can produce? Who am I creating the content for?
- After defining the goals, how am I going to measure progress toward the overall goals? What KPIs should I set? (In Chapter 13, we'll cover some of the common KPIs to consider.)

Many organizations only look at content development from the standpoint of awareness – and it's one critical aspect of an organization's efforts to brand its products and services. If that's your content plan, that's perfectly fine. But don't forget that content can be used at all parts of the marketing funnel, including engagement and acquisition as well as for conversion purposes. If you're a B2B company, you're well aware of the power of e-books and whitepapers to get customers on your email lists. But such downloads also provide data on audiences' interests, which can be further used to segment offerings to them. Webinars are great for acquisition too, making people register for a free event and then putting them on a journey toward conversion. Finally, don't forget about testimonials and case studies from current customers to help convince others to take the plunge and purchase. In business-to-consumer organizations (B2C), many of the efforts on the awareness side can translate into sales, depending on the depth of the buyer journey, but testimonials and other lower-funnel content work well here too.

Approach

After you develop a plan, you have to set an approach with content – both a style and a tone for how you want to engage with customers, as well as select your content types. First, let's talk about a content style. For us at Marketing Nice Guys, we suggest using one of 6 approaches that come from the book, Contagious by Wharton professor Jonah Berger. These six areas form his now-famous STEPPS framework (originally focused on why certain marketing efforts went viral, but they also apply to the characteristics of what makes a piece of content good). The six are:

- **Social Currency**: That which makes your customers smarter, more interesting, or funnier when/if they pass it along to others. Social currency is a big aspect of thought leadership, which is critical for a brand in marketing.

- **Triggers**: Content that triggers a reaction because it is linked to something (If you say: "Peanut butter and..." most people will think of jelly, for example.) Triggers are super clever. Think of the famous Geico "hump day" camel commercial. Even though Geico doesn't have the original video still running on YouTube, people still share that ad on... you guessed it, Wednesday. In other words, Wednesday has become a trigger word, making people think of the Geico camel.

- **Emotion**: Content that elicits an emotional reaction is powerful and can help create a customer's positive association with a particular brand. The emotion can come in form of humor, happiness, even fear and sadness in the right moments. How you create emotion goes back to the original point about doing your audience research, and understanding what drives them.

- **Public**: "4 out of 5 dentists recommend Trident." Customers want social proof that others use your products or services or that others recommend it. So, getting your customers to talk about your products in reviews (a form of lower-funnel content), showing them using it, or getting others to recommend it all provides that proof for others to see. This is where companies can take advantage of user-generated content and other areas to engage customers even more.

- **Practical**: Perhaps the most common form of content, practical content helps people figure out how to do something. It's the reason Home Depot shows customers how to tile a bathroom floor, or why Whole Foods provides recipe suggestions. But practical help can also come in the form of job aids, tools, and other content that helps people get along through the day or do their job better.
- **Storytelling**: The last aspect of STEPPS, storytelling is powerful simply because customers tend to remember stories most of all. Linked to emotional content, storytelling is one of the most popular ways to enable content for your brand. It might be a story of how your product helped transform someone's life, or a backstory about a pitch person that is well-known (think about Dos Equis' Most Interesting Man in the World). Whatever the case, storytelling is a great vehicle for top-of-mind awareness.

Once you've chosen an approach, you then have to pick a tone that fits that approach. Make sure that whatever tone you choose fits your overall brand image. Here are a few options as you think about tone.

- Comical
- Witty
- Helpful/Practical
- Thoughtful
- Playful
- Friendly
- Casual
- Cheerful
- In Your Face
- Excited
- Corporate/Straight Up

As shown above, content can definitely provide both social currency and be friendly or playful in tone but make sure your tone matches the style you've picked. After you've put out a few pieces, take a look at the analysis. Did it meet your expectations? If not, go back and make changes to find the type of content and style that resonates most with your audience.

Finally, you have to choose the **content types**. Here's a list of some of the different types of content you can choose from these days:

- E-books
- Images
- Podcasts and audio
- Webinars
- Blogs
- Video
- Newsletters
- Case studies
- Social media
- Whitepapers and articles
- Infographics
- Reviews and testimonials (UGC)
- Mobile/AR/VR content

What type do you choose? What do you outsource and produce? What do you produce in-house? A lot will depend on your overall plan, including your budget. Some might be more costly – such as full-production video. Some might be more time-consuming, such as an e-book or whitepaper. One key here is to think about what strengths your in-house team has – (do they present or speak well, or do they write well?) The other consideration is how to scale content topics that you take on across different content types for efficiency. After all, if people are interested in a blog on topic X, they will likely be interested in a video on the same topic. Scaling those effort will allow you and your team to save time and resources and cut the production needed to publish.

How to Create Content for Each Stage of the Buyer Journey

One of the things that strikes us about some small businesses is that they often don't realize the power that's available to them to promote their brand (and products and services) through creating content. And even when they do make a commitment to produce it, those businesses might only focus on one content type (say a blog) that helps them drive awareness of the business, but not consider the other buyer journey stages, which are often just as important. We get the reasons why this happens: Lack of time, interest, or even the confidence to be able to execute varying content types. But in the end, the businesses that market themselves most effectively will often be those that consider many different content types, aimed at different parts of the marketing funnel.

How do you decide what to produce and for where?

Certainly, the determination on the type of content format to use for each stage involves quite a few factors. And there is no hard-and-fast rule that says different content types can't be used in different stages of the buyer journey. That said, what follows is a quick guide on the use of the following formats and where each commonly fall in a particular content strategy.

Stage 1 of the Buyer Journey (Top of the Funnel): Awareness and Interest

Small businesses often focus on developing content at the top of the funnel, using the various formats and types to make audiences aware of its brand or its products and services. Here are a few examples of content types used at the top of the funnel:

- Written content (blogs, articles, print magazines). Generally, such written content types fall closer to the top of the marketing funnel in terms of strategy but will depend on the approach as well. That's because most written copy (that's not put behind any sort of registration wall) works best to make people aware that companies have products or services in a particular topic area. By producing such content, a company can demonstrate its thought leadership or the ways it can help solve users' problems on a practical level.

- Visual content (videos, photos, infographics). Like the written formats, visual content types can vary greatly in purpose depending on some of the factors listed above. However, the most common aim for visual content is to help associate the brand of the organization with its products and services or particular topic areas. For example, user-generated photos showing customers with a product are a great way to simply make more people aware that a company has a product or service. Or, videos that a company posts in YouTube might serve the purpose of telling a story that connects a particularly positive brand association with the company. Infographics, meanwhile, can similarly help brand that organization as a company that helps those users solve more practical problems. Typical infographics might include a checklist or a representation of data that makes the user's job easier.

- Audio content (podcasting). Companies that engage in podcasting are generally aiming at a core purpose: Branding themselves as a thought leader at or a provider of practical information. Used by both B2B and B2C companies, podcasting distributed by iTunes and Spotify, in particular, can reach wide audiences and serve as a brand touch point for later, when audiences are ready to buy.

- Interactive content (social media, polls, UGC). It's important to distinguish between two types of interactive content – that which is meant for awareness and developing brand touch points, and that which is aimed at driving lead generation, user acquisition and even advocacy post-purchase. In general, social media, polls and user-generated content serve the former purpose, making users aware that the company has solutions or products in a particular area.

Stage 2 of the Buyer Journey (Middle Funnel): Engagement and Acquisition

The part of the buyer journey that is often the biggest challenge for many small businesses comes in the middle – that is, the engagement and acquisition of potential buyers. It's one thing to make people aware of your brand, but it's another to actually get them to interact with you. Here are a few examples of content types used at the middle of the funnel:

- Written content (whitepapers, e-books, case studies, reports). Typically, the goal of these written content types is to spur to interest and action, but they can also be used to help better determine audiences' interest in different topics. The three types – whitepapers, e-books, and reports – are used more prominently at B2B companies seeking to drive lead generation and sales follow up, hence the middle-funnel activity. A common practice works this way – users put in their information into a form, download the content, and then receive follow-ups through emails and sales calls. Newsletters can also be a useful middle-funnel content type as they can help acquire and engage potential buyers. Once audiences subscribe, newsletters can be utilized to market to the existing customer base with not only content, but also offers or discounts or products to buy. (Note: They're also great for stage 4, in terms of keeping the brand in front of those who have already made a purchase.)

- Interactive content (webinars, Q&As): Webinars and Q&As tend to serve those users who are already familiar with a company's brand or products and services, (though webinars can help users become aware of a brand or product as well). As a result, these content types are often aimed at a middle-funnel type of approach: Webinars, for example, are great for acquiring users into a company's marketing automation system (getting them on email lists). Q&As are also key to help with those who might have questions during both the engagement and consideration phase of the buyer journey.

Stage 3 of the Buyer Journey (Lower Funnel): Decision, Consideration & Purchase

If you do get buyers to come this far in the journey, congratulations! You've helped them to make it to the consideration or decision phase of the purchase process. Here are some content types that are often used at this stage:

- Case studies: Right before a purchase happens, buyers often look for social proof that a product or service works as advertised. That's why having case studies for the consideration/purchase phase of the buyer journey are so critical, as they can help push a potential buyer over that threshold.
- Testimonials/reviews: Similar to case studies, producing testimonials or allowing for reviews of a product provides additional social proof for potential purchasers. In particular, such content also adds an additional layer of trust (especially if you include the actual pictures of real customers).
- Sales collateral: Marketing is often charged with developing the collateral sent out by sales teams or just used on the website for purposes of convincing those who are considering a product or service. Typical collateral might include comparing your company to the competition, a quick case study, or even an infographic that shows a product or service's effectiveness. It could also be a video showcasing the features of a product, which a company seeks to put in front of prospective buyers.

Stage 4 of the Buyer Journey (Retention/Loyalty/Advocacy)

Typically, this is an area that is ignored by many small businesses but shouldn't be, as existing customers will often make repeat purchases or recommend your product or services to other customers.

- Product how-tos: Videos that might be categorized as a lower-funnel marketing activity would include demonstrating how a product works for those who purchase it. This can be extremely effective in creating loyalty to a brand.

- Webinars and Q&As for buyers: While webinars and Q&As can be used in the middle of the funnel, they can also be employed for those who already bought a product or service, helping those buyers take full advantage of the different features or elements. Webinars in particular are great ways to gain feedback from buyers as well.

- Surveys/reviews: Speaking of feedback, companies will also use surveys and reviews to help take the temperature of its existing customer base and get valuable insights into a particular product or service, or even the brand.

Tools & Tactics

Outside of the content management system, which we've covered in discussing platforms such as WordPress, there are other tools your business might need, depending on the industry you're in. A new media business, for example, might also require a digital asset management (DAM) platform, which provides a centralized place for different staff to access photos, videos etc. and understand usage requirements and branding. A DAM also makes it easy to search video and photo assets, defining one-time use assets and/or restrictions. And finally, for digitally purchased products, it allows for digital rights management (DRM) to keep sold assets from being pirated.

Second, many small businesses might consider a content scheduling tool. With the plan and the approach set, a centralized place to manage content scheduling is critical, particularly if you expect to invest in content production. A good content scheduling tool/platform will help you manage launch dates, process status, content type and distribution, distribution channels, funnel goals, and persona targets. It may also help you store goal or UTM tracking. For starters, you can download for free our content scheduler/matrix (https:// marketingniceguys.com/content-marketing-planner-and-matrix-free-download/) to keep track of your promotions. As you grow, you can look at other tools such a Co-Schedule or another software.

Third, depending on the content types you'll focus on, you might also consider the following:

a. Podcast distribution (Libsyn)
b. Video hosting platforms (Brightcove, Vimeo)
c. Webinar/Meeting Software (GoToWebinar, Zoom, WebEx)
d. Chat/Chatbot integration (Social 27)
e. Desktop video recording (Camtasia)

Implementation

Obviously, content requires you produce it and distribute it. How you do that, whether that's writing it, drawing it, photographing it, recording it, videotaping it, or using another medium, each area has its own particular best-practice process steps. If you do it in-house, you can save money especially if you or a member of your team has a particular talent, but it also may be worth hiring a professional if you don't. Marketing Nice Guys has ongoing content development (https://marketingniceguys.com/marketing-consulting/) services that can help you in this area if you need. No matter who does it or what area it is, a good rule of thumb for most digital content types is to follow the 3 S's: Keep content searchable, shareable, and snackable.

- **Searchable.** Make sure content is relevant to audiences – and search engines. Know the keywords that have an impact when creating content. As outlined in the SEO section, repeat those keywords in headlines, links and images, URLs. Develop a strategy to use inbound links from your social strategy (improve SEO).

- **Shareable**. Social media share icons should be visible on every piece of content. Why not have your users help you? The footer should on every page of the website should also include the links to the organization's presence on those social platforms.
- **Snackable**. Short, easily accessible content that doesn't waste users' time getting to the point, or is easily consumed via mobile.

In addition to the production side, we suggest implementing a few of the following:

- **Developing a SEO and copy-editing workflow.**

  There's often an urgency on the part of marketers to "just put content out there." But doing so can often mean sloppiness in terms of SEO best practices, which are really critical to putting your content in front of the most eyeballs. We at Marketing Nice Guys recommend setting up a workflow, where you can walk through a SEO checklist of items (https://marketingniceguys.com/one-page-seo-checklist-for-copywriters/) to make sure the pages you publish have those high-value keywords embedded in them. We won't rehash what we covered above with SEO but obviously content and SEO go hand in hand. For other resources, you can download our free SEO Glossary (https://marketingniceguys.com/glossary-of-seo-terms/). The other consideration for SEO is of course, grammatical copy. A lot of grammatical mistakes – typos, or even strangely constructed sentences – will lower site quality and impact rankings.

  In addition to such on-page efforts, it's also key to make sure your content is pointed to from both within your website and from external sites. Those efforts can all be part of the workflow to ensure you are giving your content as much opportunity to be discovered by potential and current customers.

- **Distribute it and track it**

  If you think about all that goes into producing a piece of content, why develop something if you don't have a plan to distribute it? You might be surprised at the number of companies that produce content that no one sees because they don't distribute it to the right channels – or promote it often enough. If you spend the energy to produce the content, you should promote it – on your website, in email, in social, and even with paid media. That's right, paid media. Many companies promote content in paid search or paid social because it gets people to their website. That's a key hurdle in any digital marketing endeavor. Once they come to your site, it's up to you to then make it engaging so they continue to see more content or click around to your products and services. But when you don't do step one, sales become that much more of a hurdle, even if you do have the best products.

Second, it's critical to track and measure your content efforts. Adding tracking links to allow you to know the effectiveness of your promotions is a critical next step. In this case, we'd advocate for using a marketing automation or attribution tracking platform that will help you understand customer behavior. However, if you don't have an existing platform, you can add these tracking parameters onto URLs so at least that you know which promotions drove clicks to your site. An easy way to do this is to take an existing URL and go to a site such as Google's Campaign URL builder: (https://ga-dev-tools.appspot.com/campaign-url-builder/)

So, a link for a piece of content such as this: https://marketing-niceguys.com/cmos-dont-last-long-why-a-learning-culture-matters/ would become something like this: https://marketingniceguys.com/cmos-dont-last-long-why-a-learning-culture-matters/?utm_source=social&utm_medium=facebook&utm_campaign=12-01-21 from a post on Facebook for the day of December 1, 2021. In Google Analytics, such a post would show up uniquely from the main content URL.

What Does Good Content Look Like When It's Implemented? (A Real Estate Example)

To give you an idea of what good content looks like when it's implemented, we drew examples from an industry (real estate) to show you each of the areas of STEPPS that we outlined earlier. Realtors are basically small businesses that have to do a lot of marketing on their own without much support from the parent company/broker.

Social Currency

In the real estate context, here's one we came across on TikTok — that brass and copper handles are toxic to mold viruses. Something we didn't know! But now, we have a bit of information that we can pass on to other people that make us seem smarter. And because we learned it from realtor Marcus Leigh, he is now our authority on it. From the looks of this video, he produced this pretty easily with a mobile phone, a stabilizer, and a little bit of good lighting. Something you can easily do as well.

Why It Works: This particular video had almost 45,000 likes on TikTok. There are several reasons why we believe this one was really effective in marketing his business:

- He appears in it. Anytime you can put yourself in a social video, you're likely to increase the amount of engagement.
- He provided the kind of information a lot of lay people don't know. That's one of the keys to social currency.
- He uses hashtags to spread the word and he distributes it appropriately to TikTok.

Triggers

In the case of real estate, what a lot of realtors do is create an association between themselves and some other concept, such as high-end selling or the realtor behind luxury homes. In social media, this can as simple as the use of a consistent hashtag that reminds people of that particular realtor, or it can be a consistent brand presentation. In this case of Alex Goldstein, the equation of luxury homes in Florida with himself.

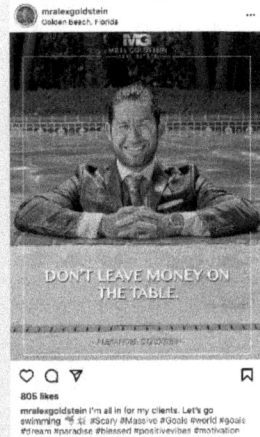

Why It Works: There are several reasons why we believe this one was really effective in marketing Alex's business:

- Design and branding. Note the attention to detail in terms of posting with a particular look and feel that fits his company's brand (the gold implies not only his name but wealth). Such a design can be easily done in the tool Canva that we had mentioned earlier.

- Every picture he takes and promotes in social from a content perspective includes him at some luxury home that he's sold, further cementing in people's mind that he is the man to help sell your luxury property.

- Use of consistent hashtags: #scary #massive #goals #paradise. Alex's focus is about money. That's his narrative. And he makes no excuses for that because he knows his audience cares about that too. Which brings up another point: Establishing narrative consistency is key throughout all your marketing in that it eventually provides that trigger in people's mind that you represent something.

Emotion

Any time your marketing can include emotional content (things that make
people happy, laugh, or even angry) can trigger a more powerful reaction.
Here Florida realtor Jamie Seneca engages audiences with a funny video of her
walking through an empty home imagining furniture, coat racks, and utensils
are actually there.

Why It Works: With 70,000+ views on YouTube, she clearly tapped into
something. What exactly was that?

She connected with the audience through a sense of humor. Other realtor home tours clearly take a more serious approach, but she took a risk here
and it paid off. People now might trust her a bit more because she revealed a
personal side of herself.

OUR PROVEN PROCESSES AND EXPERIENCE.
YOUR GOALS.

$75 Million	100+	100% of Asking Price
$70 Million in Real Estate Sold	Homes Sold	Homes Sold for 100% of Asking Price

TALK TO US ABOUT SELLING YOUR HOME

We've Helped More Than
70 Los Angeles Area Families
Just Like Yours

GET IN TOUCH WITH US

ⓩ Zillow	Google	facebook
★ ★ ★ ★ ★	★ ★ ★ ★ ★	★ ★ ★ ★ ★
38+ Reviews	15+ Reviews	11+ Reviews
4.9/5	5/5	5/5

Public

Real estate professionals also use a number of techniques to reinforce why they are the ones to go with at that decision stage. Ratings and reviews and data canhelp provide that "public" aspect of STEPPS or social proof that others trust a particular realtor. Here's an example of what LA realtor Cindy Nguyen does:

Why It Works: In the decision-making stage of any business process, people wrestle with these kinds of decisions. Trust is a big aspect of what you want to convey as a business – and one way that real estate professionals do that is this type of content on their websites. (As we discussed in the SEO section, if you do focus on a local areas, make sure to create a Google My Business Listing and have a process for more reviews.)

Practical

This is probably the most common type of content that's used in almost every industry. When you provide practical help to someone you automatically become a source of authority. This is certainly true in real estate. Content types that often have practical information, include: blogs, whitepapers/downloads, videos, podcasts, and also webinars. Here's an example of what Keri Shull, a realtor in the Washington, D.C. area did to attract home buyers – put on a home-buying webinar.

Why It Works: Because Keri Shull is helping people with practical information (how to save money when buying a first home), she automatically becomes the go-to authority for those home buyers. Because she puts the webinar behind a registration, she is also able to acquire new potential home buyers to her email marketing list.

Storytelling

People remember stories. That's why they're so effective from a marketing standpoint. Many real estate professionals put their content in storytelling form, typically a client success story. In this case of realtor Renata Briggman, she tells the story of staging a home in the Washington, DC, area.

Why It Works: Renata does a few things well here, in addition to putting this in story format:

- She focuses on a topic home sellers care about. In doing so, she underscores the narrative that she is the realtor to help best stage a home for a home seller in the Washington, D.C. area.
- She reinforces the locality through naming not just the city (Arlington, VA) but also the neighborhood (Woodbury Heights), so she comes up high in local search results.

Conclusion

Hopefully, these examples provided some ideas of what you can do in your own industry and business circumstance.

Optimization

Finally, with content, you should measure your effectiveness. If you remember in the goals at the beginning, it's important to set key performance indicators (KPIs) along the way toward your content goals. These KPIs measure your progress toward a particular goal and will likely include the actual goal itself. So, for example, you might set an overall goal for a campaign to be $100k in revenue. The KPIs would include that $100k goal but also indicators along the way such as: 500,000 pageviews on your content, 10 percent increase on your pages per visit or any other metrics that you look at to make sure you're making progress toward the overall goal. And it doesn't always have to be about revenue. Some content goals are merely awareness-focused, so you might want to measure unique visitors, click-throughs from email or social, or the number of people who come to your website from different sources.

Take that data that you measure and then figure out if you need to adjust. In order to do better, you might need to change your planning and strategy, approach, tools & tactics, and/or your implementation. With any digital marketing effort, it's important to keep testing different areas – a critical aspect of meeting or exceeding the goals you set.

CHAPTER 6

Video Marketing

Video is a major aspect of content marketing hence we'll spend a bit more time on this one in detail. According to research by Cisco Systems, video consumption is currently responsible for about 82 percent of all Internet traffic. If you think about it, that's a huge number. That means, regardless of the business you're in, your customers in one form or another are likely consuming video.

Not convinced yet? Consider these additional stats:[4]

- Video in an email leads to a 200% to 300% increase in the click-thru rate
- Including video on a landing page increases conversion by 80%
- After watching a video, users are 60% more likely to buy a product online

So, how do you get started? We suggest walking through our PATIO framework, which will help you determine the right types of video, as well as other considerations such as pre-production, production, post-production, distribution and more, based on your budget and resources.

PATIO for Video Marketing

Planning & Strategy

When you're in the planning phase, consider these four areas, similar to any content type.

---

[4] Hubspot. http://blog.hubspot.com/marketing/video-marketing-statistics#sm
.00013z8jdfvhvcnxvm9lo063ukll0.

- **No. 1: Where does video marketing fit in the larger plan of all the marketing I do? And what's the end goal of the video(s) I want to produce?** According to a recent survey about video marketing and goals surrounding, 46 percent of marketers[5] suggest that customer education is the most important. Other areas: increase brand awareness, online engagement, number of leads generated, conversion rates, sales revenue, and website traffic. The type of video you produce likely won't help you achieve all those things. So, concentrating on a particular goal will help you focus your efforts on each video. That said, not every video has to be the same approach with the same goal – in other words, you may want to produce different videos at varying stages of the buyer journey with different goals. That's where giving some thought about this upfront is key, as well as considering how much budget you want to allocate to this.

- **No. 2. What kind of budget do I have?** Paying for all the costs of a production crew can be expensive. For a full-day shoot, most crews charge anywhere from $5,000 to $6,000 per day. That doesn't include pre-production efforts or the cost of editing the video during post-production. Depending on the complexity/length of the video and the amount of on-screen graphical elements, post-production costs can also drain budgets. So, it's critical to make sure you set a realistic budget upfront. As a small business, with money often tight, you might ask: Is it worth it? The answer is: Yes, as long as what you produce is compelling and appropriate for the part of the buyer journey you have as your goal. To give you an example, perhaps you recall the original video for DollarShaveClub, called: "Our Blades are F***ing Great (https://www.youtube.com/watch?v=ZUG9qYTJMsI&list=FLZRPQxkK0f_Ajzh5LgmreHg)." Shot for reportedly less than $10,000, it went on to launch the brand and gain tens of millions of views online. We'll break down more of why this worked when we talk about the approach to your video.

---

[5] Envato. https://envato.com/learn/video-marketing-guide/video-objectives/

- **No. 3. Who am I targeting with the videos I produce? And where in the funnel?** This is where you go back to your personas and audience research you did. In some form or other, the most effective videos speak to customer challenges, pain points, or issues for each part of the buyer journey. Similar to the content section, make sure to think about the STEPPS processes here, which we'll cover for video below in the approach.

- **No. 4. After defining the goals, document how you're going to measure progress toward the overall goals by setting up KPIs.** As mentioned, the end goals are the user behaviors you want to see. The KPIs are the steps toward that goal that are indicators that the user is moving toward that end goal. A couple areas here:

  - » Use benchmarks. Any previous performance for video that you've done that is relevant.

  - » Put it in a plan. Why put this upfront? Because you want to see how you're progressing toward a goal. If you're not meeting a particular goal, say for a set number of views, then what are you going to do to increase those? What other distribution methods do you need?

Approach

Similar to other content, you have to figure out the type of video, as well as the STEPPS approach and tone we covered earlier. First, let's cover video type. Here are a few of the many options you have as a small business:

1. **Demo videos.** These videos demonstrate how a particular product works. Usually, they highlight cool or great functionality. These don't have to be expensive to produce and can be done rather simply. A great example: BlendTec's "Will It Blend?" (https://www.youtube.com/watch?v=K-Wqw5SpITg8) series where the company blends all kinds of items including iPhones. It's a great example of humor, as well as showing how powerful the blades are. It's also purposely done to make it seem as a low-budget type shoot, and likely didn't cost a lot to produce either. If you don't have a physical product or you have a software product or service, it's possible you can use a screen capture software such as OBS Studio or Camtasia, while

you do a voiceover or accompanying video that guides the viewer as they watch your screen.

2. **Brand videos.** These videos are typically focused at the company-level rather than the product level and are meant to showcase the core beliefs or tenets of the brand. The goal of these isn't necessarily to sell a particular product but to create a brand association with the customer, so they remember the company when it comes to purchasing a particular product or service type. These videos don't necessarily have to be high-budget affairs but at the very least require a very good videographer and post-production editor.

3. **Product promotional videos.** These videos aim at promoting a particular product. They're not quite the same as a demo video, which walks through specific functions, though that can be the focus. Well-done product promotional videos can capture more the emotion or feeling of owning a product or service, and not just showcase the function. Given they are conceptual, these videos can often cost a bit more budget wise.

4. **Expert interviews.** These videos are done to associate the interviewee's expertise with the company or brand, typically around the area of thought leadership or social currency. They can be shot multiple different ways: a. With a single individual on camera, looking at an interviewer on the side; b. With two (or multiple people) on camera having a discussion, usually shot with at least two cameras; c. The recording of a conversation online through a webinar software such as Zoom, WebEx, or GoToMeeting.

5. **Educational or how-to practical videos.** Companies will often help customers solve practical questions or challenges they might have. An example might be a hardware store showing customers how to replace a faucet. Or a grocery store showing people how to make a particular recipe. The videos are often aimed at those potential customers who are looking for in-market solutions. By providing the videos, the company is helping to solve customer problems, and hence becomes the authority in that particular topic, as well as the go-to source for customer purchasing needs.

6. **Animated videos.** Sometimes, a company wants to tell a particular story through animation. In the past, this area was exclusively the area of

graphic video designers who could produce a particular type of animated feature. And that's still mostly the case today, although there is software available for a layperson to record and produce a basic animated video on his or her own, through products such as Doodly.com, which we like a lot.

7. **Case studies.** These are videos that tell the story of how a product or service transformed or helped change a customer's life for the better. They can be done interview-style, through a re-enactment or through a variety of other means. Great for lower-funnel customers considering a purchase, these videos will often be produced by professional crews.

8. **Live videos.** With the advent of social media and HD-quality video from mobile phones, live videos are a natural extension for companies to engage with audiences. The decision to choose this type of video is really dependent on the industry you're in – are customers going to tune in to watch a live video in your particular area? Though this can be done for very little cost, most live videos done by companies also rely heavily on having engaging on-air hosts.

9. **Talking head videos.** As opposed to an interview-style video, talking head videos are typically just one individual speaking directly to the camera, though also sometimes looking off-camera as well. Similar to interview-style videos, the purpose of these videos is to establish the connection between the talking heads' words and the authority or thought leadership of the company. Usually, a crew is involved in these videos with a specific background chosen, or done on a green screen.

10. **Comedic videos.** If you do have a particular concept in mind that and also some budget to hire local actors you might want to think about a comedy skit. Comedy is memorable and can create a positive brand association for any company. As opposed to other types of videos, comedy skits require a bit more pre-production work, such as writing a script, rehearsing with actors and other considerations.

11. **Webinar videos (archived).** Many companies have realized the benefits of hosting webinars on particular topics, drawing in interested customers to their email lists. Most webinar platforms – Zoom, WebEx, or GoToMeeting can easily record your presentations in a MP4 (video) format, meaning you

can then post them on YouTube or other sites as videos for customers to access.

12. **Testimonial videos.** Typically, just short interviews of a customer talking about a product or service, these are incredibly powerful for the lower-funnel, in-market audience to convince them to buy a product or service.

13. **Social videos.** Using only a mobile phone and maybe an app or two, you can take existing or stock video footage and easily put together a video on your own. Two tools we love here: Canva (www.canva.com) which has stock video and lot of other design and graphic elements and apps such as Boosted by Lightricks (boosted.lightricks.com), which you can download on your phone to produce templated videos quickly and easily.

The type of video you create is going to be heavily dependent on the budget. But here are a few guidelines that we hope can help you. We've split video marketing budgets up into chunks under 3 core areas.

- Larger budgets (more than $50,000).
- Mid-size budgets ($10,000 to $50,000)
- Smaller budgets (0 to $10,000)

Outside of a brand video, we'll make the assumption that you'll want to produce more than one of the others this coming year. There's no hard and fast rule that says, for example, that a particular type of video always costs X amount of dollars. Can you do it cheaper in some cases? Of course. Mobile phones can work well, as long as you have decent audio, lighting, and an appropriate background. That said, here are some general guidelines as you think about various video types:

Videos that generally need larger budgets (more than $50,000)

- Brand videos
- Product promotional videos
- Comedy skits

And of course, if other videos can be done on smaller budgets, they can be done here too.

Videos that can be done for mid-size budgets ($10,000 to $50,000)

- Expert interviews
- Educational/how-to practical videos
- Animated videos
- Case studies
- Talking head videos
- Demo videos
- Testimonial videos
- Comedy skits

Videos that can be done with smaller budgets (under $10,000)

- Demo videos (also here)
- Live videos
- Webinar videos (you just need an existing platform)
- Testimonial videos (but lighting and audio needs to be really good)
- Social videos

STEPPS for Video

Next, try to determine the STEPPS approach. Do you want your video style to lend itself to a particular type of video? Again, there's no hard and fast rule that says you can't produce an emotional demo video for example, but here are some typical ways marketing video styles lend themselves to each video type:

Social currency

- Brand videos
- Expert interviews
- Talking head videos
- Webinar videos

Triggers

- Comedic videos
- Product promotional videos
- Live videos

Emotions

- Product promotional videos
- Live videos
- Case studies
- Comedic videos

Public

- Demo videos
- Live videos
- Product promotional videos
- Case studies
- Webinar videos
- Educational/how-to practical videos
- Animated videos
- Testimonial videos

Practical

- Demo videos
- Educational/how-to practical videos
- Webinar videos
- Product promotional videos
- Animated videos
- Live videos

Storytelling

- Brand videos
- Case studies
- Product promotional videos
- Animated videos
- Talking head videos (if the expert tells a story).
- Testimonial videos

We can't emphasize enough that it's really up to you to choose the video type and then match that type with a style that meets your needs. It may be your creativity can come up with something other than what is typically done. That's great. But hopefully, the above allows you to at least get a sense of the options and the way they are often employed.

Finally, let's talk about the funnel approach that's generally used for each video type. Again, there are no set here, but generally this should give you an idea of the ways such videos are used:

Top of the funnel (awareness)

- Live videos
- Brand videos
- Comedic videos
- Expert interviews
- Talking head videos
- Social videos

Mid-funnel (acquisition & engagement)

- Product promotional videos
- Educational/how-to practical videos
- Demo videos
- Webinar videos
- Animated videos
- Social videos

Lower funnel (decision, purchase, advocacy)

- Educational/how-to practical videos
- Case studies
- Demo videos
- Testimonial videos

Tools (Pre-Production and Production)

We'll further break down budgets and the tools (and crew) you'll need in each in order to be successful in this section. In this portion, we'll cover the pre-production and production aspects of video. Once again, we'll separate this out by budgets available.

If you have a larger or mid-size budget, you might engage with a professional crew for your videos. Generally, on any professional shoot, here are some of the common things you'll see a crew bring:

1. Cameras: 2, HD-quality
2. Tripods and camera stands (unless it's a handheld shoot)
3. Audio (choose between lavaliere mikes, boom mikes, handheld)
4. Lighting (typically three-point lighting, with a key light (strong source), fill light (opposite side) and back light (behind the subject)
5. Teleprompters (if necessary)
6. Encoder/switcher (if livestreaming)
7. Miscellaneous: Green screen/backgrounds, crossbar kits, extension cords, tape (lots of tape)
8. Makeup

Much depends on the complexity of the shoot as well. As for crew members, here are some of the roles that are typically required at minimum:

1. **Producer:** As a small business, you will typically fill this role in being responsible for the shoot.
2. **Writer:** Does the scripting. As a small businessperson, you can save money if you draft the script.
3. **Director of photography** (also called the "DP," who operates one of the cameras)
4. **Second cameraman:** Operates camera 2.
5. **Audio technician:** Decides on the type of mike and is responsible for the audio quality of the shoot.
6. **Teleprompter operator:** You don't necessarily need a professional here if you have an in-house operator. However, we'd recommend you get one because you'll want someone who can pace the words along with a speaker.

7. **Makeup artist:** If you don't need one, you should remind the crew to at least bring anti-shine makeup that the director of photography can apply

8. **On-air talent:** Individuals who will be on camera. If these are professional actors, they can cost up to $500 per hour or more.

You might ask why you need to know this as a small business? After all, isn't this the crew's job to put this together? To a certain extent, it is. But remember crews will charge for the amount of equipment and personnel they have to bring. So, if you can bring your own makeup artist, if you don't need a teleprompter, if you can write the scripts yourself, you can save money.

What if you do it yourself on a lower budget? The equipment you'll need for self-produced video will depend on the type of video you've selected above. For example, with live video or a demo video, you really might just need your mobile phone and a selfie stick/stabilizer of some kind. We recommend a product such as the Smoove Video Stabilizer (https://smove.video/), which can help you keep a consistent shot as you film yourself. Alternatively, as mentioned earlier, you can produce professional looking video with tools such as Canva and an app on your mobile phone such as Boosted by Lightricks.

For the post-production/editing process with phones, you can use a software specific for iPhones such as iMovie. For Android devices (and iPhones), there are several options as well here including FilmoraGo, AdobePremiere Rush, Video-Show, PowerDirector, and others. We won't get into the actual editing process here but each app should have basic instructions available in YouTube or other places to help guide you.

Outside of livestreaming on a phone, you can also shoot great video in front of your computer (ideal for virtual interviews, webinar recordings, a demo video for software walk-throughs, or filming your own in-house experts). With this type of video recording, we suggest a few things (you can find them on Amazon) here that will help:

- Portable green screen, $160
- Ultra HD webcam, $199
- A Blue Yeti USB microphone, $129
- A selfie ring light, $46

Additionally, for walk-through/screen recording you'll need a software to capture your onscreen behavior. For this, we recommend OBS Studio (obsproject.com/), which you can download for free and record your onscreen video as well as screen capture. Other options include Camtasia (now iSkysoft), (www.iskysoft.us/lp/filmora9-video-editor.html) which allows you to create and edit video quickly.

Tactics (mid-level and higher-budget shoots)

As a small business, it's critical to try to save money where you can. Here are some tips for ways to do that if you end up using a production crew:

Pre-production tips

1. **To save some money, write the scripts yourself.** Writers can cost $75 to $250 per hour.

2. **As much as you can, select a room or rooms where you can control the light and sound.** If it's outside, it's likely going to have more variables and you should ask the crew for the best location, lighting and time of day. Make sure to test the audio equipment and surrounding environmental noise.

3. **Rehearse/start on time.** If professional actors need to rehearse, so does your on-air talent. The fewer the takes, the less footage you need. And also, the less time to edit, which can save lots of money in post-production. Also, don't forget to start on time.

4. **Framing.** Make sure the lighting and the camera angles are what you want. Ahead of time, it's good to give the director of photography a view of the mood you're going for.

Production tips

1. Watch the shoot or double as the director. Note any takes you really liked. Remember, you own the production so make sure you get what you want. Re-shoot any bad takes.

2. Once you get a good take, move to the next take. Then go back and re-shoot other takes if you want. The reason for doing this is really cost. If you end

up shooting too many takes, you might not get to all the filming you need done and, hence, your costs increase if you go beyond the set timeframe for the crew.

3. Shoot and add b-roll if it's just a "talking head" or interview. B-roll is essentially background footage that can help visually diversify what's onscreen for the viewer. Listening to one person talk without cutting in other footage can make a video monotonous. The b-roll can be one of the interview subjects walking down the hall with someone or another take that mixes in an example or a graphic about what the individual is speaking about.

Tools (Post-Production)

For any sized production (small-to-mid-to larger) that isn't done on a phone, you'll want to go through some sort of professional post-production – the process of editing video to a final released product. Unless you have in-house post-production capabilities, we recommend that you use the same crew to help you do this. Whatever route you decide, there are a finite set of tools to accomplish video editing. The most common in this area are Final Cut Pro (apps.apple.com/us/app/final-cut-pro/id424389933) and Adobe Premiere (www.adobe.com/products/premiere.html).

So, what's the role of a post-production editor? They will edit the footage, add opening/closing screens, lower-thirds, music, and any motion graphics or animations. Cost for post-production can vary wildly. In a general range, an editor typically runs from $75 to up to $150 per hour or more. Editing a one-minute video can take several hours or more depending on the amount of footage.

Tactics (Post-Production)

As a small business, you can also save time and money in the post-production process with these helpful tips:

1. Provide the editor with the logos or other company assets they need upfront. It helps to have a transparent logo made (ones can be used on a light or dark background).

2. Work out the calls to action you want at the end of the video.

3. Make sure to spell the names correctly if using on-air talent in the lower-thirds.

4. Be vigilant – "cut the fat." Make sure any video gets to the points quickly and in a compelling fashion.

5. Choose the right music. Post-production editors sometimes choose the music without consulting you so make sure it fits the mood you're looking for. You also can't use copyrighted music.

6. Ask your post-production editor to cut a :15 and :30 second commercial of the video/campaign as well. This can be used for promoting the video or the brand/product/service in YouTube ads or other social media.

Implementation

Assuming you have a finished video product, the key here is to distribute it. As mentioned in the content section, developing a video and not promoting it is not only waste of valuable resources, it's also a waste of money. Let's talk about "organic" distribution first. That is, something you post yourself as a business and don't spend money to promote it or boost it. Among the common areas to distribute video include the following platforms:

- Your website
- YouTube
- Organic social channels (Facebook, LinkedIn, Twitter, Instagram, and TikTok)[6]
- Email
- Paid media (social, display, search, native video ads)

In the following section, we'll talk about each one. However, first, you should decide on a strategy as to where your video will be hosted. Many small companies host their video on YouTube (because it's free) and you can easily embed YouTube players on your website pages through WordPress or another CMS. (YouTube has 2 billion monthly active users so it's likely your customers are on this platform.) This probably makes the most sense for small businesses rather than investing in a video delivery platform – such as Brightcove – which you would only use if you intend to have members-only videos or impose some sort of access restrictions, like a video on demand product.

---

[6] Note for TikTok – we'd recommend you shoot specific video on a phone in particular to fit the platform, especially given its unique nature. For those wondering about Snapchat, it's not quite so friendly to small businesses as of this writing and most distribution here is paid distribution with at a budget level that goes beyond what most small businesses can afford.

Setting Up Your YouTube Business Channel

From Google: https://support.google.com/youtube/answer/1646861?hl=en

Follow these instructions to create a channel that can have multiple managers or owners.

You can use a Brand Account to create a channel that has a different name but that's still managed from your Google Account.

1. Sign in to YouTube on a computer or using the mobile site.
2. Go to your channel list.
3. Choose to create a new channel or use an existing Brand Account:
   » Create a new channel by clicking Create a new channel.
   » Create a YouTube channel for a Brand Account that you already manage by choosing the Brand Account from the list. If this Brand Account already has a channel, you can't create a new one—you'll just be switched over to that channel if you select the Brand Account from the list.
4. Fill out the details to name your new channel and verify your account. Then, click Done. This creates a new Brand Account.
5. To add a channel manager, follow the instructions to change channel owners and managers.

Once you've set up your channel, it's super easy to add videos. (You'll see a camera with plus sign in the top right on a desktop or just a + sign in mobile at the bottom of your channel.) If you've made the decision to host on YouTube, you'll want to then add the player for each video to your existing website. If you use WordPress, you can generally copy and paste the URLs or the embed code (which you can copy from your YouTube page) into your site to make the player render.

As you implement on YouTube, here are some additional SEO best practices. Remember, YouTube is the second largest search engine in the world (behind parent Google) so it's critical to make sure your videos are visible and searchable. A few tips:

- **Write Longer Video Descriptions:** This seems contrary to common wisdom, but the more YouTube knows about the video through use of targeted keywords, the more confidently it can rank your video in results.

- **Think About Ranking in Google and YouTube:** Ranking in YouTube is great, but ranking your video in YouTube and Google is better. Google gives YouTube videos an edge in some results – figure out what those keywords are, by examining what videos are showing up in each search engine and what meta data is being used.
- **Share Video Library Liberally in Online Communities:** This will hook your video up with the type of quality, high-retention views that YouTube likes to see.
- **Encourage Subscribing:** If people enjoy watching your video, expect it to top YouTube search results. Ask for others to subscribe in the video itself. Here's a quick primer on creating a subscribe button in your videos.

  1. *If you don't have a button already created, search for "YouTube subscribe button images" and you can download a free one there*
  2. *Save to the image to your desktop*
  3. *Go to YouTube Studio link. (You can find it by hovering over your business profile image on the top right and clicking it.)*
  4. *Click on customization*
  5. *Click on branding*
  6. *Under Video Watermark, click "Change" or "Upload" to upload a new image.*
  7. *Select the image, and save*
  8. *Then select when you want the button to appear. We recommend at the end of the video*
  9. *You're done! The watermark will flash at the end of the video and notify users to subscribe.*

- A keyword-rich playlist gives YouTube deeper information about your video's topic. And like we saw with your description, more text-based content = more views.
- **Employ Semantic Markup (Schema.org):** Just like other content that is practical or helpful, it's good to use semantic markup to highlight data

that a search engine such as Google can pull and display. Making it easy for Google to do that with structured data is important for rankings. If you need help, your developer should be able to tackle this relatively easily. Check out Schema.org's requirements for video: schema.org/VideoObject

- **Provide Transcriptions/Closed Captioning for Your Videos:** This is key so that search bots can crawl the text.

And if you create a channel there, you should try to feed it with regular content. If you have subscribers, they will be alerted to any new content you post. Finally, a few more tips:

- Use engaging thumbnails. The more engaging the image, the more likely users are to click and watch. If you use the YouTube Studio app, you can change out your thumbnail pretty easily to a few different screenshot options or a custom thumbnail if you like.
- Provide Links Back to the Site Embedded Within Video and Subscribe Buttons: Even though YouTube is generally top-of-the-funnel, it never hurts to provide links to particular products and services back to the web site.

If you think about a successful small business on YouTube, one example we can give you is retailer Vat19: www.youtube.com/user/vat19com. As of this writing, they have 8.2m subscribers and billions of views on YouTube, all on the basis of creating fun videos around their products. What made the videos successful? Engaging, funny (emotional) content that is shared widely.

Listen to what founder Jamie Salvatori said several years ago in an interview: "The hardest thing to do in the world is to get people to come to your website. We've probably tried everything. It's just a question of how well those things work and how much you have to pay for them. Right now, our most effective way to get people to our site is via our YouTube channels and our videos."[7]

The one thing to emphasize here is Vat19's commitment to the channel and producing content on a regular basis. As we dive into social media in the next section, this will become a running theme.

---

[7] https://www.practicale-commerce.com/Vat19-com-Thrives-in-2011-Recap

Distribution on Your Website

A few areas to consider when embedding videos onto your website. Assuming you have followed the steps above, videos embedded from YouTube will help boost your SEO. But just make sure the video content matches the page you're on:

- **Home page.** A compelling home page video about the company or brand will help improve engagement of those coming for the first time. Videos are great introductions to who you are as a company.
- **Landing pages.** The SEO for topical landing pages can be boosted with the right videos as well. One thing to also look into here are the video galleries, particularly for video testimonials, case studies or other video types. (Many WordPress themes have functionality which allow you to build them onto a landing page.)
- **Article pages.** Embedding videos into an article is generally a great strategy as the article content will be boosted from an SEO standpoint by the video description and content you've put in, say YouTube.
- **Product pages.** As mentioned early on, embedding video into product pages or landing pages increases conversion by 80 percent. That should be reason enough to produce compelling product video, even if it's a simple demo of how the product works.

Distribution to Social

Now that you've set up the video distribution in YouTube and embedded the video into your website, let's talk about distribution in social channels. For now, we'll save the discussion on TikTok for the Social Media chapter. As mentioned earlier, TikTok marketing requires a specific type of video (generally shot on a mobile phone). Meanwhile, Snapchat is really a pay-to-play vehicle for businesses, and remains the realm of large advertisers. If you can distribute video there and have the means, you should do so. But for the purposes of distributing video in this section, much of the advice below will cover the big four social media platforms: Facebook, Twitter, LinkedIn, Instagram that small businesses tend to use.

First, should you upload and embed video into the social platforms or point to your YouTube or your website page? We've seen evidence that uploading makes sense for a couple reasons:

1. You can engage customers immediately with your content and they don't have to leave the social platform they're on;

2. Even in cases where a goal might be website traffic, we've seen uploaded video perform just as well as a link to the content off the platform. In other words, people will both watch a video and click through. That said, if your goal is to drive YouTube views or subscriptions, we can't blame you for linking off to those sites as well. (Note: With Instagram, you generally upload your video to the platform anyway as there are limited opportunities for outbound linking.)

Second, as with any social media you post, encourage sharing. One of the techniques used by very savvy marketers is they ask their audience to share the video. You might recognize these techniques: "Share this with a friend who needs to see this." "Retweet this to friends" (also, in case you didn't know, spelling out retweet is 12x more effective than just asking for "RT" – and with character limits being less of an issue in Twitter – you should spell it out). But either way, the point is ASK for your followers to share your content.

Third, monitor the engagement. If you're not seeing a good amount of views or traffic from your video promotion, think about adjusting the descriptive copy or headline. Sometimes a language change on a simple headline can increase engagement several fold.

Email Distribution

While most email providers won't allow you to send video embedded within an actual email, you can point to web pages with the video on it. As mentioned, videos promoted within emails tend to increase engagement and click-throughs because recipients are curious about the contents. A few tips here:

- Point to your website landing page rather than a YouTube channel (unless you're specifically trying to grow YouTube as a goal). We prefer the website for those already on your email list, simply because it allows more access to other content and your products and services.

- Use a really great thumbnail image for the video so people will want to click through.
- What types of emails? Newsletters work great for video distribution and engagement, as do product-promotional emails where you can send people to a product page with the video on it.

Paid Video Distribution

Sometimes organic distribution on YouTube and other social networks isn't enough to get in front of the minimum viable audience you seek based on your goals. So, there are options for you to enhance the viewership of your video through paid distribution. The options might include paid search in Google Ads, native video ad distribution through a programmatic ad network – Google has its DV360 programmatic ad platform, for example for those with larger budgets. Or, you can advertise your video on YouTube. Many small businesses aren't so familiar with Google Ads and we'd recommend that, if you are going to try it yourself, you work with a specialist in this area, as you can easily waste money on ads if you don't know what you're doing. *Note: Marketing Nice Guys provides services that can help you in this area, including full-service paid media setup and management (https://marketingniceguys.com/marketing-consulting/) as part of our Marketing Consulting practice.*

Regardless of whether you do it yourself or hire someone, here are some basics you should know before you go into buying ads. YouTube has many paid media options:

- Search ads (similar to Google.com where the ads run to websites off of YouTube);
- Standard banner display advertising;
- Pre-roll (before the video)
- Mid-roll (during the video)
- Post-roll (after the video) advertising.

If you're thinking of promoting video, you might consider a few things first:

What sort of return do you hope to get? Unlike organic distribution on most platforms, in which the cost is really about effort and time, when you start paying for distribution, you're outlaying actual money. As result, it's good to understand the overall goal of the video or videos you're producing and set the key performance indicators or KPIs that will help you analyze whether or not you met your goal based on the amount you paid.

Second, make sure you set a goal that's commensurate with the video type and fits the buyer journey. What we mean by that is if you're producing a video in which the goal is awareness – or more top of the funnel – the goals should reflect that (video views, impressions, % of the video completed etc.). If the video is produced for lower in the buyer funnel – let's say it's a product testimonial or a case study which will be targeted to users who are already familiar with the brand, you might have other metrics that would include website click throughs or even purchases or form submissions. Understanding what success is will be the key.

For YouTube, it's a good idea to develop a couple short ads based on your original video that you can place in front of other videos watched on the platform. If you have some budget, and you're using a crew, as mentioned, ask the post production editor to create a :15 second and a :30 second commercial about the video that you can run on the platform.

Next decide on the ad format, placement, and targeting. YouTube has something called TruView ads, which are based on performance and other options. You can also choose whether to run your :15 second or :30 second ad at the beginning, middle, or end of other videos. Finally, think about the targeting: The more targeted you can get with your audience the better and more effective your ad will be to help you reach your goal. Here are a few ways you can target on YouTube:

- **Behavioral.** Reaching consumers with content who have demonstrated specific interests online such as searching for vacation destinations or expressing interest in getting a quote on a new car.
- **Retargeting/Re-marketing.** Serving content to people who have previously visited a marketer's site.

- **Dayparting.** Reaching consumers at a certain time and/or day of the week.
- **Geographic.** Reaching users in specific geographical locations (country, state, city, DMA, or ZIP code).
- **Demographic.** Reaching certain customers in a particular group. For example, one content channel might be more frequently visited by women, by Hispanics, by people age 18-24, or by people who earn $50K to $75K a year.
- **Household.** Reaching individuals, households, or sites based on user registration data.
- **Purchase-based.** Reaching customers based on products they've purchased.
- **Technographic.** Reaching users by connection speed, operating system, browser type, device type.
- **Look-alike modeling.** Reaching audiences who exhibit similar characteristics to current customers.
- **Keyword Targeting.** You can use keywords that will help match your ads to the video content. This works just like contextual targeting on the Display Network, and applies to both YouTube and the Display Network.
- **Customer List.** Upload a customer list and target those individuals as they use YouTube.

Launching a Video Ad

As mentioned, we suggest working with an expert on deploying your ad. However, if you want to try a few yourself, we'll walk through a quick scenario with you here. For example, let's assume the following: You have fitness training course that targets people ages 20 to 50, and you want to let them know about your brand from an awareness perspective. Say a top-of-the-funnel type promotion.

In order to run YouTube Ads, you need to log into Google Ads. If you don't have a Google Ads account, we'll show you how to set one up later in the paid media section. (As mentioned earlier, let's assume that your video has been produced and uploaded onto YouTube.) Here are some basic steps:

- Upon login, you will need to create a campaign and the first step is to choose the campaign goal. Here you can choose various options. But if it's a top-of-the funnel goal, let's assume the goal is video views/impressions.
- Next step, select the type of ad you want to run. There are several options available here.
    » The "Skippable in-stream" subtype helps reach viewers on YouTube and across the web with skippable in-stream ads optimized for efficient impressions.
    » The "Non-Skippable in-stream" subtype helps you reach customers with your entire message with non-skippable in-stream ads.
    » The "Bumper" subtype helps reach viewers on YouTube and across the web with bumper ads optimized for efficient impressions.
    » The "Outstream" subtype helps you to get more people interested in your brand with video ads designed to reach people on their phones and tablets.
    » The "Ad sequence" subtype helps you tell your product or brand story by showing people a series of videos in the order that you define.

Let's choose a bumper ad, which is a 6 sec non-skippable that shows before the videos and is recommended by YouTube for brand awareness.

- Next, let's enter in the campaign information:
    » Start date
    » End date
    » Bidding – Video campaigns on YouTube use the CPM (Cost per Thousand Impressions) or CPV (Cost Per View bidding methods). A view is counted when someone watches 30 seconds of your video ad (or the duration if it's shorter than 30 seconds) or interacts with the ad, whichever comes first.
    » Location: For our example we will only target the United States. However, you can pretty much target any place in the world on YouTube.

- Next select, let's select the Audience:
  - » Affinity audience: Fitness and Health Buff
  - » Keywords: Fitness training related keywords
- Finally, let's create the ad:
  - » Select the video
  - » Add descriptions, headlines, and the calls to action.
- Hit launch and you're done!

That's a simplified walk-through of the process but hopefully it gives you a basic idea of how placing a video ad in YouTube works! We can't stress enough that you will want to have an expert implement these for you as you'll also want to monitor the ads' performance and optimize based on the results.

Optimization

Alright! So, you've done the video, posted it, and distributed it out to your audience. Now, we're going to go over analysis and optimization. One of the cardinal sins of many businesses is that they spend so much time developing and pushing something out, they don't bother to look at how well the video does. Let's review what we talked about at the beginning of the chapter: Setting the Key Performance Indicators (KPIs) based on that goal. These are measurable indicators that provide the evidence that you're moving in the right direction toward that goal. Typical video KPIs include things such as:

- Total video views
- Completion rate
- Repeat visitor rate
- CTRs to product or lead pages
- Revenue lift
- Total revenue
- Total ad revenue (if ad supported)

You can also group these into larger buckets if you like. For example:

Overall Brand Exposure. This might include views on video, page traffic, bounce rate, percentage of video completed, shares/social metrics, comments, impressions on video ads or any paid media, click-throughs on video ads or paid media.

Conversions. This might entail analyzing Click-Through-Rates -- or CTRs -- to product or lead pages. Also, this includes looking at any revenue lift since the beginning of a video campaign and total revenue.

Content Approach/Execution. Which content approach did you choose? Did it resonate with the audience? Remember the six are:

- Social currency
- Triggers
- Emotion
- Public
- Practical
- Storytelling

Perhaps the approach was right but maybe the execution wasn't? Think about what you might do again if you could approach this differently the next time, given the data you've collected. What would you do that was the same?

Distribution. Did you hit a minimum number of impressions to get in front of the audiences you wanted? If not, what do you have to do to pump up that distribution? More organic posts? Perhaps additional paid posts? Or, if you've hit your target, perhaps it's worth adding additional channels or dollars to it. This is really where you can optimize on a real-time basis with video.

If you see success in one channel, you can push to other channels as well. Remember, we only started with distribution to a few areas: YouTube, organic social, email, the website, and paid YouTube distribution. There are a number of others you can use as well. Here's one list of distribution channels that covers most content distribution, including video and areas you might further consider as you optimize your distribution efforts. The 3 core areas are paid, earned, and owned:

Paid Channels include areas such as:

- Paid display banner ads
- Search ads
- Social ads (including paid messaging and chats)

- Advertorials
- Native ads
- Sponsorships
- Press releases (through a platform such as Cision)
- Influencer marketing

Earned channels include areas such as:
- Search engine rankings (SEO)
- PR and media coverage
- UGC content ("Shared" content or user content)
- Consumer social media posts
- Forwarded Emails

Owned channels include areas such as:
- Websites
- Messaging (notifications through apps)
- Microsites
- Content newsletters
- Social media (accounts)
- Mobile apps and alerts
- Emails

Targeting. Based on the data, think about the following: Was your target audience correct? Did the approach resonate with the audiences' challenges, pain points or need for entertainment? What can you tell from comments, likes, shares or other data?

With video, it can be so labor intensive that it's hard to optimize and adjust your video content based on feedback or other data you receive on it. Plenty of marketers have launched something, then asked the production team to go back and re-do it based on feedback. Primarily, however, the analysis you do based on answering the questions above can help you inform your next video project. The key, as with most things in marketing, is to be laser-focused on what an audience wants. But hopefully, this has allowed you to get the ins and outs of what you need to get started with (or improve) your video marketing.

CHAPTER 7

Social Media

It's often said that social media is one of the biggest conundrums for many businesses. The reason is that having followers doesn't always equate to having customers. Add on top of that the challenge of gaining followers in social for many small businesses, and it becomes even more of a vexing issue. What resources/staff should I put into the effort? Is it worth it for my particular business? Which social platforms should I be on? And then, even if I take the plunge to create an account on a platform, how do I create enough content to not inadvertently create a ghost town on my channel?

Are there success stories? Of course. Some businesses are built entirely on their presence in social. What's the secret? For the most part, it's the willingness to commit to creating relevant and engaging content in the channel and continuing to build a following by using various tactics. For small businesses, who don't have a lot of resources to spare, the question then becomes: How important is the social component to your overall business success? For example, if you sell B2B, do you really need that Snapchat or TikTok account? Probably not. But, maybe your presence on LinkedIn or Facebook becomes more of a priority. If you're a B2C seller or you have a retail presence or other type of business, you might think about TikTok or Instagram, YouTube or channels that can help you boost your brand and following.

While we'd love to tell you there's a secret formula to it all, unfortunately, we can't. Much depends on your industry, your content, your marketing voice/tone, and frankly, your willingness to engage with current and prospective customers on that platform. However, what we can do is cover some of these core social channels and a few the best practices to employ in each. Remember, though, much of it is about your commitment to each channel that you create a business account on.

Let's start with our core foundational framework, PATIO. For social, the framework will help you break down the decision-making process and understand the operations required for your social efforts. One thing unique about social media is that, while there are similar activities you do consistently across all of them, the PATIO framework will often vary by channel. There are exceptions to this: In terms of tools (especially scheduling tools), some of them will be the same (and we'll list a few of them broadly below). In addition, for the 'O' in PATIO (Optimization), we're going to cover that as a whole as well, because many of the principles apply across all the different channels. We'll do that after we've discussed all the separate social platforms. Before we get there, however, let's think about the planning and strategy that you have to do for social media generally and cover the tools that work across many different platforms.

PATIO for Social Media (Overall)

Planning & Strategy

Like content and similar areas, it's critical to have an overall plan of attack in social. Here are few questions that you should try to answer upfront:

1. What are the overall goals for social? If you're a B2C business or a retailer of some kind it might be within your expectations to drive direct sales revenue. If you're a B2B business, more realistically, you might think about social driving awareness of your brand and/or your product and services. Setting the right goals will help you stay committed to the various social platforms should you decide to dive in.

2. Where should you allocate resources (personnel)? To which channels? One thing to keep in mind is that if you're going to commit, you have to be willing to dedicate time and resources to whatever channels you decide to engage on. One of the big mistakes that brands can make in social is that they create accounts and then don't fill them with anything. And it's not just text copy content. You might need design, or photos, or videos to

continue posting and creating. And then you'll have to be active (posting, responding, social listening, etc.)

3. What's the emphasis on paid social? What role does paid distribution play in the overall scheme? What budget should you allocate versus other paid channels? Many platforms (such as Facebook) are actually disguised pay-to-play venues, even though businesses do have opportunities to post organically. That's because nearly all platforms limit the reach of organic posts such that even a company's followers might not see them in the user feed. Hence, using paid social to distribute content needs to be looked at here as well. You don't need a ton of money, depending on your target audience and your goals, but you should have an idea about what you'd like to accomplish. We'll talk more about paid social at the end.

4. What are the KPIs based on the goals? How do you know if you're successful? This is where setting the key performance indicators will help you, as well as any previous benchmarks for performance (if you have them). The KPIs tell you how you're progressing. So, if the overall goal is to drive $50,000 in revenue from your social media, your KPIs would include that end goal but also might include indicators such as social ad impressions, click-throughs, landing page views from the ad. Keeping track of those things will give you insight on where there is potential fallout. Do you need to increase the impression goals to meet the overall? Do you need to adjust any paid media ads? Do you need to adjust or optimize the landing pages? The more data you look at, the more you'll be able to pinpoint how to best optimize as you go.

Tools

For the Tools portion of Tools & Tactics, the ones you'd use to implement social media are pretty standard across all. So, we won't repeat them for each platform, but if you are operating across multiple platforms, it's probably worth investing in a social scheduling and management tool of some kind. The benefits include:

- Scheduling and posting outside business hours
- Managing your social media platforms in one place

- Making it easier to maintain content
- Allowing for consistent tracking and data collection
- Engaging in social listening, developing better AI (sentiment analysis) of what your customers might be saying.

Here is a list of the various scheduling tools you can consider.

- SmarterQueue (includes social listening)
- Loomly
- Sprout Social (includes social listening)
- Hubspot (part of a larger MAS, includes social listening)
- Kenshoo
- SlackSocial
- Hootsuite (includes social listening)
- Buffer (includes social listening)
- IFTT
- Mention (include social listening)
- Social Oomph
- TweetDeck
- Tweepi
- Social Flow
- SocialBro
- CrowdBooster
- Post Planner
- Laterbro
- AgoraPulse
- MeetEdgar
- Schedugram
- Oktopost
- Shoutlet
- Spredfast

With that out of the way, let's dive into the details for each main social platform.

Facebook

Regardless of whether you're talking B2C or B2B marketing, Facebook remains the 800-lb. gorilla in the space. With more than 2.7 billion active users, it's highly likely that you'll find your customer base on the platform. The hard part for most businesses, though (outside of certain publishers), is that Facebook throttles down the organic reach of most posts from organizations, so they aren't seen by the majority of followers. As of this writing many believe the organic reach is roughly 2 to 4 percent on average. Yes, so, 96 to 98 percent of what you post organically may not appear in the feed of your followers. For small businesses inevitably this means looking at the platform as a pay-to-play space, where you can organically post to reach some people, but you might boost your posts (or buy an ad) to put content in front of your own followers and beyond. On the positive, Facebook is still inexpensive for small businesses in that spending a few hundred dollars a month can get your brand in front of thousands of potential customers, depending on your target audience and industry.

Planning and Strategy for Facebook

First with any of the channels, figure out where Facebook fits in your overall strategy. We'd suggest that, because of what we mention above, the platform is really perhaps best for B2C companies promoting a product (especially impulse purchases) and for B2B companies in terms of content marketing. Though B2C companies have a successful content marketing strategy on Facebook too. Here are some general questions you can answer as you develop your Facebook strategy:

- **What's the goal of your posts?** Is it to promote your product? Engage your audience? Is it an extension of your content marketing strategy in terms of distribution? Is it to promote your brand? Or drive people to the website? Is the goal to eventually get them to your subscriber list? Finally, what does success look like? Make sure to set realistic goals and KPIs as many small businesses go into Facebook with resources expecting it to drive sales immediately and end up being disappointed. Our recommendation is to focus on creating those customer touchpoints through content – helpful or practical content can work great here for small businesses. And then use Facebook ads to consider boosting of content or creating ads aimed at conversion or lead generation (depending on your customer base.)

- **Does it align with your content strategy and approach?** It's important to integrate your social posts with your content marketing strategy – and promote the type of shareable content that aligns with your overall content strategy. So, if your approach to content is to provide thought leadership and social currency, your posts of Facebook should reflect that.

- **What resources do you have to create assets?** Facebook, like other social media, requires organizations to be able to access photos, videos, and text (blogs or articles), or other unique content that you can use to help sell your brand and your products and services. And it's important to regularly produce that content for your audience, as most platforms reward brands for being regular content machines. When you're planning, make sure to take this into account and don't start a social media account without the ability to fill it regularly.

Approach for Facebook

As mentioned above, if you commit to doing Facebook and establish your strategy of regular content, it's likely that your business will need to boost your posts/ pay for an ad to distribute the content further, which we would recommend. A few areas that may seem obvious but are critical to your success:

- **Maximize fan growth by offering unique value.** We would recommend scaling your content to the extent you can – in other words use blogs, videos, or other assets and promote them across all platforms. That said, it's also important to make sure that content fits with what your audience on Facebook expects so that they share it with others to help you grow your fanbase.

- **Use high quality images/video and reflect the brand in terms of voice and humor.** The more engagement a post receives, the more likely Facebook's algorithm will share it with others. So, creating unique content posts that have value is the primary goal. In this case, humor works. But make sure it's brand appropriate. Videos typically work well here, too.

- **Use the 80/20 rule for content versus straight product promotion.** Putting out one product promotion after another generally doesn't fly, and it's typically better to focus on helpful or interesting content. That said, if you have a retail business or some sort of impulse-based B2C product for purchase, you can focus on a paid strategy delivering ads on Facebook. Otherwise, for organic posts, you'll likely do best with a content-focused approach.

- **Employ Facebook to drive your website traffic.** Though it's not considered an "inbound link" from a SEO standpoint, links from Facebook to your page are generally helpful to make audiences aware of your content and provide the indirect benefit of getting traffic to your page, which increases the likelihood others will link to you from their own websites.

- **Boost content with ads. Depending on the context and industry, lower funnel ads may work here.** Facebook officials will tell you page fans still matter for paid posts because Facebook offers discounts on ads that can be delivered with a social context (basically showing a user that one of their friends also likes the brand featured).

- **Add a customer service component.** Use posts/feed/comments as a sounding board for products/services and a way to enhance the relationship with customers. If customers ask a question, answer it.

Tactics for Facebook

A lot of your "organic" success in Facebook will depend, frankly, on the type of small business you have.

- **Publishers.** If you're a publisher of that can produce viral-type posts for a broad audience you're much more likely to have Facebook promote your content both to your followers and, even others who the platform determines might be interested through its other discovery feeds. That's because its algorithm is based on views, shares, and other criteria that reward engaging posts. One need only look at Buzzfeed and the work it has done in social to see an example of a company that has done this well. That doesn't mean you also can't boost or promote posts on your own but, in such viral cases, Facebook will do the work for you.

- **For retailers – or those with e-commerce businesses that go direct to consumer.** The platform can work well with a mix of content (on the organic end) and product promotion/boosting on the paid end. If you are a bit larger-than-average organization, it also pays to do customer service (answering customer queries etc.) and social listening if your posts are getting engagement.

- **Sole owners / proprietors.** If what you're ultimately selling is you and/ or the services you provide, social media (including Facebook) was made for you. That's because all the platforms lend themselves well to personal videos or other content you produce about yourself. And because you might appear in the videos or your content is primarily about you and your thoughts, it tends to get viewed more. To put it bluntly, people on Facebook want to know about other people, so any "hey-look-at-me" post that reveals more about you will be generally valued by Facebook.

- **For B2B businesses.** We suggest developing content for organic posts, along with a mix of boosting of content in paid ads, as well as products/ services to the right audiences. There are exceptions here of course, but the goal of most B2B companies' posts should focus around awareness and visitor traffic. Facebook can deliver lead generation in particular cases but it's also wise to keep expectations in check as most B2B purchases aren't the of impulse variety that often work on the social network, and therefore the higher-funnel touchpoints should be the goal.

- **Time to post and post frequency.** According to a recent study by Hootsuite/We Are Social, the best times to generally post on Facebook to get the most visibility and engagement are 9 a.m., noon, and 3 p.m. And the best days are Thursday, Friday, Saturday, Sunday. That said, if you're a B2B business, we've found that posting the middle of the week, Tuesday, Wednesday, and Thursday can work really well too. One thing you can do is to check to see your Facebook analytics as to when you audiences tend to be online. For most small businesses, we would recommend posting at least 3 times per week or more.

Implementation for Facebook

Now that you've set your plan, approach, and tactics, you have to now make those posts a reality. A few things that help if, as a small business, you don't have a ton of resources in this area:

- **Think About Great Quality Images or Develop Design Templates for Social:** A big thing to keep in mind is that Facebook like other social media is still very much a visual medium. You need to have access to great quality images or at least branded templates that you can use. If you look at most photos by those who have large followings in social (let's say celebrities or social media influencers), they are generally using professional photography or they have a sense of the visual elements they're capturing if they do it themselves. As a small business, you might not have access to professional photography or don't invest in that for what your business is. However, it's still key to think about how you approach your visuals. You can find great free stock images at places such as unsplash.com or pexels.com. Canva, which we've recommended earlier not only has photos, but also templates for infographics, lists, and other ways to create a great visual identity. You can also do posts of quotes/text and in those cases, it might be good to have a design team create a few templates for you with your brand on it ahead of time. It will allow for you to present a consistent brand identity in social and will be easy for your social media specialist or manager to update. The other tool we love is one called Mematic (a mobile app) where you can add your brand logo to existing images, along with text, to create fun memes.

If you're linking to a blog post, it helps if the images on the website are in OpenGraph protocol, basically a structured data format. This way your photos/images can be brought into Facebook seamlessly when you post. This will allow the image to be clickable to the blog itself.

- **Schedule Your Posts:** We provided a list of the tools above, but you should definitely take advantage of the ability to schedule posts (for not just the week but weekends as well if that applies), cross-post on different channels, track performance, and monitor engagement.

- **Develop a Workflow That Includes Copy Editing:** As a small business, you may not have a copy- editing department, but typos and copy errors, as well as text errors in the design, can kill the engagement of a social post. In general, a good guideline is to have at least one other individual review the post ahead of time for both voice and copy quality/grammar.

- **Think About Boosting Content or Purchasing Ads for Retargeting:** As mentioned, Facebook limits organic reach. Hence, your regular posts may not be reaching even all of your followers. So, one thing to think about is to boost your posts to guarantee impressions in front of targeted groups. The good thing about Facebook is that it's relatively inexpensive. The other alternative is to create ads. In the latter case, we recommend ads based on retargeting to focus on your best opportunities. (It's the process of putting ads in front of visitors who visit your site – or who are registered with you. It can be done through uploading lists manually or through a Facebook pixel-embed on your website.) We'll cover Facebook ads specifically closer to the end of this chapter.

Instagram

If Facebook is the 800-lb. gorilla in the space, its brother Instagram must be at least 600 lbs. In recent years, Instagram has become the favored platform for a lot of marketers big and small. That's because it's primarily a visual medium. On the average post, there aren't a ton of opportunities to click through because outside links generally aren't made clickable, except for the main link on your company home page or when you engage in advertising. As a result, it's almost its own self-contained world, where companies use those opportunities to brand themselves in front of the 1 billion or so users as of this writing.

The audience demographic is particularly skewed toward the 13-34 age group, a key target for many small businesses.

Planning and Strategy for Instagram

Similar to Facebook, it's important to figure out where Instagram fits in your overall strategy. For marketers, Instagram tends to be an awareness/top-of-the-funnel channel in terms of focus. That's because, outside of paid ads, (which allow website click-throughs), organic posts are meant to be engaged within Instagram itself. So, one goal is typically putting your brand in front of your followers and extending the reach through various tactics. This goes for both B2B and B2C companies. Here are a few considerations to keep in mind as you develop your Instagram strategy:

- **How will Instagram help me visually brand my products and services?** The emphasis here is on visual. Do you have a particularly visual product or service you're selling? Many attractive influencers, for example, simply sell themselves on Instagram because the platform naturally optimizes for good-looking individuals. But outside of those more extreme "small business" examples, ask yourself if there are opportunities to promote the surroundings you work in (connecting those nice surroundings with your brand)? Do you have tips or helpful practices for customers that can be delivered through video or photos and text? Do you have visual content that's funny or emotional that your followers will share with other to grow your brand reach?

- **Instagram requires you align your content strategy.** Like Facebook, Instagram may require at least some dedicated resource that can help you create social posts on your own, but it helps if those posts are part of a larger content development strategy, as images should reflect the brand. This is where it also helps to have a design-oriented individual involved.

- **What resources do you have to create visual assets?** Even more so than Facebook, Instagram requires organizations to be able to access great photos, videos, and/or infographics. And, similar to Facebook, it's important to regularly produce that content for your audience, as most platforms reward brands for being regular content machines. When you're planning, make sure to take this into account and don't start a social media account without the ability to fill it regularly.

- **What does success look like?** How will you grow your followers? In other words, what will constitute success for you in terms of engagement? With Instagram, as mentioned, it will likely focus more on top-of-the-funnel KPIs – awareness, likes, shares, follower growth – rather than simply a sales metric from an organic perspective. Unfortunately, many small businesses don't have a large following on Instagram. As a result, a lot of work may go into posts but you may not see a huge return because not many people will get to view what you're posting. It's important to include tactics and content posts that will get attention. Which we'll cover next.

Approach for Instagram

The approach to Instagram is similar to Facebook – but because the platform isn't exactly the same – a bit different.

- **You have to create unique value.** As a small business, it's much more efficient to scale content – use the same photos, videos, infographics other visual assets – across all platforms. That said, Instagram may require its own approach because it has particular requirements all its own – everything from photos sizes (portrait is generally better, landscape images will shrink to fit to a square size), to the fact that you can't embed links to websites so blogs and other types of content don't work there.

- **Use high quality images/video.** We hate to keep restating this but poor images don't cut it anymore.
- **Use the 80/20 rule for content versus straight product promotion.** If you have physical products you can show, it's fine to do so in a promotion to make people aware you have it. That said, unless you're in the jewelry business, not matter how much a visual delight your products or services are, it might be you want to focus on other content "for the 'Gram." Again, there's no hard and fast rule here about product promotion but you should know your audience and what they are most likely to engage on.
- **Create ads and think about your 'influencers.'** Depending on the context and industry, lower funnel ads may work here, especially if you're in retail or a B2C type business where impulse purchases are the norm. For B2B, there are also ads that can drive lead generation so it might be worth it depending on the industry as targeting on Instagram (which is owned by Facebook) can be quite exact. One other thing to think about – influencers. We're not talking about Kim Kardashian here (although if she supports your product, you should by all means encourage her to do so). What we are talking about here are everyday influencers who might have a larger following that already use your products and services. Getting them (either through payment or goodwill) to give you a shout-out on Instagram (with them showing your product or service) can give a boost to your efforts to drive additional conversions and revenue.

Tactics for Instagram

Similar to Facebook, a lot of your "organic" success in the platform will depend on the type of small business you have and the type of content you're willing to put out.

B2C businesses. Small retailers can do really well with products and services that can be represented in photos or videos in a super-visual manner. For these businesses, we recommend using professional photography or really high-quality video.

B2B businesses. We suggest developing engaging photo and video content for organic posts, along with a mix of boosting of content in paid ads, as well as products/services to the right audiences. There are exceptions here of course, but the goal of most B2B companies' posts should focus around awareness and the upper-funnel marketing touchpoint. Like Facebook, Instagram can deliver lead generation through ads in particular cases but it's also wise to keep expectations in check as most B2B purchases aren't the of impulse variety that often work on IG, and therefore the higher-funnel touchpoints should be the goal.

Take advantage of various Instagram post types. Some companies don't do enough in terms of using a mix of photos and video, or even using Instagram Live and Stories, which are great to have the brand appear at the top of the app. Also, consider uploading longer videos at IGTV.

Reels. Launched in Aug. 2020 to take on TikTok, these are 3-to-15 second videos filmed in portrait mode on mobile devices only. Brands can't take advantage of music like individuals can but these might be interesting for walk-throughs, how-tos, or implementations – other than showing the latest dance trend. Instagram has been showcasing these quite a bit since launch.

Time to post and post frequency. According to a recent study by Hootsuite/We Are Social, the best times to generally post on Instagram are generally 8 a.m. to 9 a.m. on Mondays and Thurs. Posting more content on off-work hours is great too. For most small businesses, we would recommend posting at least 3 times per week or more.

Use hashtags (#___). One of the advantages of Instagram is that a user can follow hashtags in his or her feed. So, for smaller businesses that don't have a built-in audience aware of their brand, one way to get them to discover your content is through adding popular or specific-focused hashtags in a deliberate manner. The hashtags can help people discover your account and the great content you feature on your pages.

Follow and interact with your followers. Similar to what we say with Twitter (below), following your followers and commenting and liking can boost support for your own posts. And keep your brand in front of them.

Implementation for Instagram

Like Facebook, implementation involves a few core areas.

- **Getting access to quality images, video or infographics.** On Instagram, if you don't have a process to produce these on a regular basis, then you either have to invest in it or use free stock photos we mentioned in the Facebook section. (You can find great free stock images at places such as unsplash.com or pexels.com. We recommended just crediting the photographer when you use an image.) As mentioned earlier, Canva is also great to create photo, video and graphic content for Instagram. Finally, a tool we also use is Mematic (a mobile app) where you can add your brand logo to existing images, along with text to create a funny meme. One additional note: If you have a comedic sense about your business, these can work really well on Instagram.
- **Schedule your posts:** Similar to Facebook, you should definitely take advantage of the ability to schedule posts (for not just the week but weekends as well if that applies), cross post on different channels, track performance, and monitor engagement.
- **Tagging other users:** In addition to using hashtags regularly, one way to get posts out in front of more people is to tag them in a photo (using the @__) and also in the text description. This will allow them to be alerted to see it and comment or share it with people too.
- **Purchasing ads for retargeting.** Like Facebook, Instagram can be used to retarget individuals that have visited your website. Again, the best

part about Facebook and Instagram, is that showing ads to prospective customers is relatively cheap and the targeting is quite specific.

Twitter

Twitter is an odd social media outlier in many ways for businesses, and not just small businesses either. At one point, Twitter fell out of favor significantly with marketers as spending had dropped on the platform, user growth stalled, and it became known as troll haven. Since 2016, it has rallied a bit, as a more significant voice (particularly in political areas) with about 340 million users. It also can be great if you, as a small business, do something related to big live events (Super Bowl, Oscars, NBA All-Star Weekend, the Grammys etc.) The hardest part for small businesses is that, to do it well, it takes resources and a lot of ongoing commitment to engage with customers there (at least in the organic sense). And unless it's part of your brand, it can be tricky to avoid controversial subjects or discussions there, which can alienate potential customers quickly.

Planning and Strategy for Twitter

Similar to other platforms, it's critical to develop your strategy for Twitter. A few things to think about:

- **Can you justify the ROI on your efforts?** One reason a lot of small businesses aren't on Twitter is that it takes some resources to both create posts and ultimately engage with customers in conversations. Many of the enthusiastic conversations that are had on the platform aren't ones that a normal small business would want to engage in, unless, again, that's part of the company's brand. Twitter also takes monitoring. If you have a brand on Twitter and you somehow get involved in a negative conversation, it can spiral out of control quickly. Some might argue it's better to have a presence (so that you can respond) but it really depends on your small company and what business you're in. Similar to Facebook and Instagram, make sure to also have your goals outlined upfront for what you hope to achieve.

For most small businesses, you'll want to look at a few core metrics of success:

» Follower growth

» Engagement (retweets, likes, comments etc.)

» Direct revenue (mostly in the case of ad buys)

Mostly, make sure to be realistic when setting your KPIs.

- **It does a play a role in SEO.** One tip we always give small businesses is to promote any new website pages they create (like a blog or a new landing page) into Twitter first. That's because Google will index Twitter to discover new content and pages. From a SEO perspective, it doesn't count as an "inbound" link to your page, as we mentioned, but it does help in getting the search engine to at least find your new page.

- **Engage in a conversation with your audiences.** If one thing you sell as a small business is your intellectual capital – for example, thought leadership as a consultant etc. – Twitter can be a productive place for you to engage with followers to promote your brand.

Approach for Twitter

Similar to Facebook and Instagram, your content strategy and approach should play a big role in what you post on Twitter. A few unique things to the platform include:

- **Give feedback and monitor your reputation.** Similar to FB, this is an opportunity to learn from customers and improve your relationship with them. Definitely use Twitter for customer service.

- **Stand for something positive or humorous.** If you do decide to go on Twitter, it's important to create a positive atmosphere around your brand and avoid controversial topics. Using a content approach that involves emotion or a sense of humor can work here too.

Tactics for Twitter

Similar to Instagram, there are specific tactics you can use to try to grow followers. A few of them include:

- **Using hashtags.** Twitter is actually where the use of the hashtag (#)

was first popularized. For people looking for various topics, it can be really useful so that others discover your content and then retweet it. You should also consider creating original hashtags that are funny or memorable.

- **Try to create a thread.** For some of your posts, why not expand on 280 characters you get in one tweet (it was originally 140) to add other tweets onto your original. This is what's known as creating a thread, where you have a running commentary on your original post. That means people can engage with your original post, your 'comments,' or any number of add-ons you make on the same topic. For example, you can take a blog that you've written and breakdown the various parts within Twitter itself through the multiple-post thread. Here's an example at right.

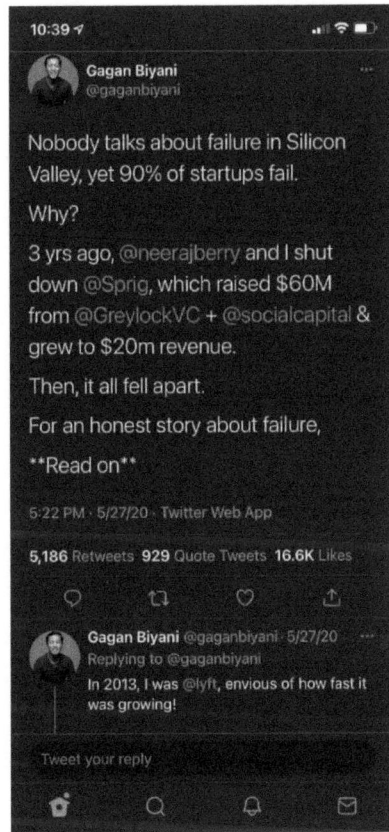

- **Tag others.** If you think something might be interesting to a particular influencer or someone you know in the audience, make sure to tag them with the @__. In same example on the right, you can see an illustration of that.
- **Can you take advantage of 'live events'?** If your business is such that you have a certain relevance to live events, that can help boost your brand's awareness as Twitter is often the platform of choice to talk about what's going on. The Super Bowl, the Oscars are the biggest examples, but it might be a live event on a smaller scale too – the ones that are local to your community.
- **Time to post/frequency.** The best time to post on Twitter: noon

weekdays and 5 to 6 pm. These are the moments around workers' breaks when they tend to check their feeds. Wednesdays tend to perform best. If you're B2C company, posting on weekends can also work really well. For B2B companies, it's better during the weekdays.

- **Consider ads.** In our experience, Twitter ads can show the decent conversion rates compared to other social platforms. Much will depend on your particular industry and the types of products and service you sell, though.

- **Follow and share content from others.** Twitter is unique in that the platform goal is "conversation." Hence, the more you can interact with your followers, following them, liking or commenting, and creating a conversation, the more you'll likely see interaction on your own posts. Yes, there are brands that follow no one (Cartier is an example). But it's important to remember that the brand's fans follow that account because it is already established (and very much aloof.) So, its brand identity is based on not following just anyone.

Implementation for Twitter

When implementing Twitter, the key aspect here is to create compelling copy that fits into the 280 characters allotted. A few other techniques:

- **Ask for retweets.** As in literally spell out "retweet" and ask your followers to share with their followers.

- **Use images and video.** Though it was originally a text-based platform, images or uploaded video make the post more visible in Twitter and will generally improve engagement, unless the goal is simply a one-line quip or funny comment you want to make to your followers. If you're linking to a blog post, it helps if the images on the website are in OpenGraph protocol, basically a structured data format. This way your photos/images can be brought into Twitter seamlessly when you post. This will allow the image to be clickable to the blog itself.

- **Use Twitter to aid content discoverability.** As mentioned above, Google indexes Twitter first to find new content. So, promoting blog content or other pages there will help aid in the discoverability for search engines.

LinkedIn

In general, if you're a small business retailer and sell directly to consumers, there may not be a ton of reasons for your company to have a LinkedIn presence (outside of recruiting), because it is focused on "professionals" and/ or work-related networking and issues. That said, it's not unheard of for smaller B2C companies to demonstrate their community approach or thought leadership here in terms of how you operate your business or your particular mission and vision. For B2B companies, LinkedIn tends to be the main social media platform, especially since a lot of discussion there happens about work – and that includes products and services businesses buy from each other. And with more than 800 million professionals currently using the platform, it's a great opportunity for your company to push both practical content and thought leadership.

Planning and Strategy for LinkedIn

For the purposes of this, we're going to focus primarily on small businesses that sell to other businesses, simply because those are the majority of the cases. That said, the guidelines we have here can apply to B2C small businesses as well. Here are a few strategic considerations as you think about posting on LinkedIn.

- **Practical and thought-leadership content drives LinkedIn conversations.** If you are a B2B company, producing practical content or thought leadership type content should be on your radar already. And distributing such content to LinkedIn is a great way to engage your audiences. The more engaging the content, the more LinkedIn will show it to followers of those that engage. LinkedIn is especially useful for publishers, authors, consultants, coaches, and trainers, who develop a lot of content as part of the normal course of business. In particular, downloadable assets – whitepapers, e-books, infographics – can work great on LinkedIn as a way to acquire new potential customers and gauge topic interest.

- **Create a business account but also post on your personal account.** Many small business professionals are already on LinkedIn as individuals but make sure your business also has an account and create posts on your business account that you can share from your individual account as well. The strategy behind creating a business account is that you can brand your small business (assuming it's not just you and not just your name).

- **For any small business, take advantage of your personal network here first.** Similar to the point above, many small businesses start with referrals from people you know from your individual network. Make sure to use LinkedIn to let your individual connections know about your business. It's a big opportunity to at least begin introducing your brand and getting potential customers.

Approach for LinkedIn

LinkedIn allows for several options for content distribution:

- **Upload or point to your website?** You can post a blog on LinkedIn itself, upload a video, or point to a blog on your site or a video you have on YouTube. It's up to you how you do it. There are pros and cons to each. We at Marketing Nice Guys tend to like to use LinkedIn as a place to help us drive awareness of our content and our services so we prefer to link to our website. That way, people who come to the site can also explore other services we offer. That said, if you're set on engaging with the LinkedIn audience first and foremost, uploading the assets or creating the asset on LinkedIn is the better route.

- **Follow the 80/20 rule regardless.** The goal of most content you post on LinkedIn is the same as other social media platforms: four out of five posts should be content related and you can sprinkle in product or service promotions occasionally. For the most part, though, the goal isn't to sell directly but get your brand in front of potential audiences and become that thought leader or helpful provider of content.

- **The more often you post, the more you're rewarded.** If you can produce regular content, that's great. LinkedIn loves being the place for shared discussions about professional life. Companies that post 20x per month can be rewarded by reaching about 60 percent of followers. For organic posts, that's a lot better than Facebook, which limits organic reach by most companies. You might ask: How do I create all that content? One trick with LinkedIn is to post the same content piece multiple times per day but adjust each post slightly to use different language. You can do this through the tools to automate the scheduling. In other words, once the LinkedIn algorithm decides your post is no longer relevant to show, you have to put it back in circulation for people to see you. LinkedIn will reward this type of behavior.

- **Keep it professional.** Because it's a professional networking site, politics, memes, or other types of non-business-related content are generally frowned upon. If you do use humor, keep it "professional" in that respect too. It's not Instagram or TikTok.

Tactics for LinkedIn

- **Ask your own followers (as an individual) to follow your business account.** Many individuals, especially those who have been on the platform a long time, have thousands of personal followers. As of this writing, LinkedIn allows individuals to invite up to 100 of those followers a month to follow your business account. And it renews every month. This is a great way to get the business in front of your network.

- **Create your own group.** But monitor it. Some companies create their own discussion groups that can help engage audiences in particular topics. But make sure to monitor those who join and the posts in it as you want to regulate anyone who comes in and simply posts promotional content for their own purposes.

- **Consider using LinkedIn Ads.** Compared to other services, LinkedIn can be pricey from a cost standpoint to advertise, but we think a few tactics here can help. We've found LinkedIn to be decent for executive audiences if they fall within your audience targeting. It's also not bad for testing account-based marketing (ABM) approaches where you can reach different individuals at the same company each with a different message about how your product or services best works for them. We've found other ad types – InMail promotions – can be pricey, unless super-targeted and often end up making the audiences angry for the spam.

- **Post times and frequency.** Best time to post is around 5 to 6 pm. Midweek -- Tuesday, Wednesday, and Thursday. LinkedIn tends to have super-low engagement on Friday night and Monday. As mentioned, if you're a B2B company, the more frequent you can post, the better.

Implementation for LinkedIn

A few things to also keep in mind as you're doing LinkedIn posts.

- **It's OK to tag others, but only do it if the post is directly relevant to them.** For example, if you mention a company or an individual in a piece of content you're posting about, it's OK to tag them in it. But it's not like posting in Facebook, Twitter, and Instagram where you can try to tag individuals or companies more broadly. We would recommend being judicious here.

- **Use hashtags.** Similar to other social networking sites, it's great to use hashtags. In fact, it's encouraged by LinkedIn that you do so. You can help the discovery of your posts that way.

- **Use images and video.** Similar to other platforms, images or uploaded video make the post more visible in LinkedIn and will generally improve engagement. If you're linking to a blog post, it helps (again) if your images on the website are in OpenGraph protocol, basically a structured data format. This way your photos/images can be brought into LinkedIn seamlessly when you post. This will allow the image to be clickable to the blog itself.

Pinterest

If you don't have a business that sells primarily to women, we'd suggest you stop here and move to the next social media platform. If you do, keep reading! Pinterest is a social media platform that acts like a bulletin board – a place to share useful lists, fashions, design ideas, recipes etc. Topics span just about anything you could think of, but perhaps because of its original nature, it remains about 75 percent female. Hence, the companies that do best in front of the roughly 444 million users tend to be retail – and tend to focus on women.

Planning and Strategy for Pinterest

Pinterest is a unique platform so we can't emphasize enough that it has to fit your business focus and audience profile. As you craft the plan, here are a few tips:

- **Create content to engage first, but always think lower-funnel purchase.** Of all the platforms, Pinterest is one of the best at generating revenue from pin clicks to websites, especially directly to e-commerce related products. Pinning an image of a particular product – let's say it's a couch or shoes, or a handbag – and linking to buy it should be an aspect of your small business strategy if you are a retailer.

- **Think about an audience engagement strategy for pinning others' content or ideas and having others do the same with your content.** People share or steal other pins on Pinterest all the time. Which is fine. But make sure you then don't forget to include your brand or URL on the pins themselves. That way if someone else pins your pin you can make sure everyone knows where it came from.

- **Be prepared to engage with others on the platform, follow them or other companies related to yours.** Remember, Pinterest is a social media network which means it's about sharing content – yours and other people's, particularly inspirational pins or other content. Make sure whatever you pin and share fits your brand.

- **Consider the design resources or visual needs.** If you haven't accounted for procuring the visual assets, it may be necessary to develop them specifically for Pinterest if you're really serious about engaging. To start, there are many places you can go to get free Pinterest design templates, particularly if you're short on resources. Canva, as we suggested previously, has tons of these templates.

Approach for Pinterest

Once you have a strategy, which we would recommend center around e-commerce for small businesses, here are a few things to consider on the approach.

- **Create topical boards aligned to your taxonomy.** Basically, boards are collection areas for pins on a similar topic. For these, we would recommend the board creation follow your content or product taxonomy to keep it consistent.
- **Keep it fun and practical.** Because (for many small businesses), the focus is retail, we would error on the side of keeping your pins fun, motivational, or helpful in a practical sense. Lists are great, recipes, helpful infographics all work here. That's not to say that serious subjects aren't posted but it has to fit your brand and company. And remember the target audience is still likely to be women looking for practical ideas, or potentially looking at design, fashion or other boards. Think moms and young women as a core audience here.

Tactics for Pinterest

With the strategy and approach set, here are a few other areas from a tactical standpoint:

- **Keep it vertical and visual.** An estimated 85 percent of Pinterest views are mobile, so portrait images for pins work better than landscape. Also, the visual is the main attraction here, so make sure it's compelling.
- **Plan for seasonal buying far in advance.** If you're thinking about Black Friday that last weekend in November, make sure to make the most of it in October, etc. Also, planting the seed for spring fashion ideas might

need to be happen in late winter. Pinners tend to plan far ahead.

- **Target potential customers with ads.** Pinterest targeting can be built around keywords, interests, location, age, and other demographics.
- **Post times and frequency.** The bottom line: pin consistently. Pinterest recommends pinning something once per day to ensure you reach a wider audience. Best time to post: Saturday and Sunday midday. Worst times: During the workday but after hours isn't too bad.

Implementation for Pinterest

When it comes to finally producing and posting the pins, here a few recommendations:

- **Use boards to connect with Pinners.** One idea here is to showcase other Pinterest users who use your products and services. Or create a DIY board or tips on how to use your boards and topics. The goal is you want people to get inspired by the pins you have in each board.
- **Make sure to create robust descriptions.** Pinterest allots up to 500 characters of space for a pin description, while only the first 50 characters of which will appear on most user's newsfeeds. But pins themselves can show up in Google, especially if others point to them or they are popular. So, make sure to use SEO-friendly tactics to embed those high-value keywords.
- **Consider headlines and text overlays on your pin.** This is both to reinforce your message and where you can insert your brand name.
- **Make it easy to shop and add UTM tracking.** You should generally add UTM tracking anytime you post something in social media so that if someone clicks back to your website you can trace it to, in this case, Pinterest. Because Pinterest is such a lower-funnel referral engine for so many websites aimed at products and services for women, it's good to add the tracking to URLs so that you can know which visits came from your Pinterest clicks. The easiest place to do this is Google's UTM builder (ga-dev-tools.web.app/campaign-url-builder/).

TikTok

We would be remiss for not mentioning the rise of TikTok, as it can fit as a content distribution vehicle for some small businesses. In 2019-21, TikTok came out of nowhere to become a big force in social media, upending the industry. (Its rise caused Instagram to add a new video type called Reels to its existing service.) Originally focused on super-short videos, TikTok in essence overtook a big portion of the 13 to 30 age group. If your business is focused with this demographic, and you have to ability to produce interesting short videos, we would encourage you to dive in. There are lots of ways you can develop creative videos for potential audiences here. But one note: Outside of also posting the same video on Instagram, what you create here will likely be used only for TikTok so make sure it's worth your investment and time for video production, even if it's likely just you or an employee producing it with his or her phone. One thing in its favor: As of this writing, TikTok now has 100 million users in the U.S. alone.

Planning and Strategy for TikTok

The great thing about TikTok is that videos posted here can generally be done without a film crew. Most indeed are simply candid ones uploaded by individuals who do everything from their phone. But small companies who want to take advantage of the platform and haven't had much experience on it should watch other TikTok videos to get a sense of the video types and particularly tone of what others do. A few different ways to think about strategy:

- **Doing it yourself.** Posting your own video content is great. Keep it aligned to your brand and message but make sure it's right for TikTok and not simply a video you'd post on LinkedIn. Generally, the two don't cross much. There are some exceptions.

- **Using influencers or having followers use your products and services.** One way to strategically think about TikTok is to let others speak for your brand. Having influencers post a video of them using your product or service, or encouraging user-generated content from your followers is potentially another way to think about it.

Approach for TikTok

While we can't dictate what you ultimately choose for a content approach on TikTok, we'd simply reiterate that you should watch and model approaches that you see that work on the channel. If we had to generalize, most small companies keep the content on the light side – fun, engaging, but also can be informative. That doesn't mean you have to do a dance video, but heavier or serious topics probably should be avoided, unless there's an emotional storytelling component and it fits your brand. A few other suggestions:

- **Follow TikTok trends.** TikTok has started a number of new trends in social media and if you can find a way to jump one of them (and it fits your brand), that's great. Watch for trending hashtags too.
- **Blend in product/"salesy" content sparingly.** On the platform, there is a general disdain for advertisements so make sure to establish your credibility as a content source first before going straight to product promotion. You can do it here and there but keep the focus on the audience and creating engaging content. The exception might be retail or fashion. You can also have followers do a video using your product.

Tactics for TikTok

- **Reach out to influencers.** On TikTok, there are a set of influencers who have great ability to sway younger audiences with content, probably more so than your average, middle-age celebrity. Several platforms offer influencer searches – Grin, #Paid, CreatorIQ – where you can connect and find popular TikTok influencers.
- **Strive to create compelling video.** This may go without saying, but if your video isn't compelling, funny, interesting, engaging, or helpful, users will move on.
- **Frequency.** Like other platforms, the more you post, the more the platform will reward you. But that means creating a lot of regular content (and usually just for TikTok), as it's not typical to use the content outside the platform, except, say, on Instagram.

Implementation for TikTok

A few implementation tricks:

- **Use hashtags.** Like other social media platforms, TikTok organizes topic discovery around hashtags. If you click on the Discover search icon at the bottom of TikTok, you'll see a list of trending hashtags with examples.

- **Comment on followers' posts and interact.** Like other social media platforms, if you're going to do it, you should dive in fully. Take the time to craft meaningful responses.

- **Use TikTok effects.** TikTok gives you additional options for a post that includes its own "effects" – on-screen stickers, icons or other additions under categories such as "Beauty," "Funny," "World," "Animal," "Interactive," and "Editing." One cool feature includes a green screen effect, which allows you to select an image of your choice to replace the video background.

Snapchat

A Note on Snapchat

Small businesses, especially those that sell to the 13-to-30 demographic, often ask us about Snapchat, the social media platform that also saw a revival during the pandemic of 2020-21. The issue with Snapchat, however, is that its model is generally built around businesses paying to play. It's also heavily focused on larger advertisers with bigger budgets who are interested in doing more unique implementations. Snapchat is definitely an innovator, for example, in using augmented reality in advertising. For that reason, though, it's not generally seen as an avenue for smaller businesses. So, until that changes, we'll leave Snapchat out of the mix for the time being.

Optimization for All Social Media Platforms

First, a word about optimization. As we said at the beginning, it's important to understand which channels you want to focus on for your business. If you find you can't fill the channel with regular content, that could be a problem impacting your performance right there. Most of the platforms reward regular organic posting and if you're only doing it once per month, you likely won't get a ton of distribution. A few other tips here:

- **Analyze for likes, shares, comments, click-throughs, conversions.** There are really two ways to measure engagement:
  - » **Within the platform itself:** Obviously, you'll want to look at which posts received the most likes, shares, or comments. Generally, with most platforms, shares and comments are what drive virality. In other words, the social platforms love when a post drives a discussion so the latter two (shares and comments) are perhaps the most important metrics.
  - » **Those that click-through to your website and/or convert:** Again, we would keep your expectations in check for organic postings driving lots of sales. It really depends on the platform and what you're ultimately selling. That said, you should keep track of it.

- **Replicate the best posts.** After you've analyzed the best posts and take some time to understand why they work so well, you'll want to replicate that approach for future content. If you ask any successful social media guru, this is what they focus on – whether they notice it's a particular topic, a way to write or craft the post, a storytelling component, or other patterns they pick up on.

- **Test and try new things and look at the community to see what works.** Great social media accounts never stop evolving. They watch other accounts, trends, and evolve the approach based on audience feedback. If you watch closely, they also run occasional trial balloons, where they might push something a bit different. It's all done in the name of continuing to improve engagement.

Paid Social Media Ads

Most of what we've covered above is the PATIO framework for organic social media, which you really should establish first before simply diving into ads. But, as many small businesses come to realize, there can be limits to your ability to even reach your own followers through organic posts. Hence, some turn to advertising. For most small businesses, it can be tricky running your own ads, if you're not familiar with the ins and outs of each social media platform. For example, Facebook will update its ad options continuously, so one ad type that might be available now may give way to another within a year. The same goes for other social platforms. Also, the targeting varies as each social media platform has different data on its users. That's why, for most small businesses, we do recommend **hiring an agency like Marketing Nice Guys that specializes in social media targeting and strategy** (https://marketingniceguys.com/marketing-consulting/), even if your overall spend isn't quite so much in the beginning. That's because an agency can help guide you on the best ad types and strategies whether you're thinking about:

- Photo ads
- Video ads
- Collection ads
- Slideshows
- App installs
- Product carousels
- Retargeted ads
- Email or messaging ads
- Account acquisition

And that's just a small sample of what's available. Each platform above has wildly different options and ways to reach audiences too. An agency can help you also decide where your money (and on what platform) your money is best spent. Finally, a good agency will also make sure your targeting and ad optimization strategy aligns with your business and the expectations.

If you don't have the budget to spend on an agency, you can definitely try to do it yourself. We do suggest giving yourself some time to get up to speed on a few areas, and asking the following questions:

- What's my overall goal for social advertising (brand awareness, website visits, conversions)?
- What are the various ad options on each platform?
- What type of audience targeting is available? (Demographic, psychographic, location, topic, profession/title etc.)
- What are the ad optimizations by objective (link clicks, landing page views, impressions, conversions) are commonly used?
- What are the assets required for each – photo/video requirements, text/character limits?
- Are measurement/analytics available?
- Does the platform allow for retargeting? What are the minimum traffic requirements for that?
- What metrics will I use for success?

As mentioned, each platform collects different data on its users/members. You could literally write a book – and people have – about each platform and how to best use it for advertising. For the purposes of our efforts here, we're going to provide a quick example of what's available on Facebook and its network from an ad perspective. And then we'll dive into four areas to consider upfront if you're a small business.

Facebook/Instagram/WhatsApp/Messenger

The nice part about Facebook is that it's generally inexpensive for small businesses and owns Instagram, WhatsApp, and Messenger so you can go to a centralized place for advertising on any of those four: https://www.facebook.com/business/. One popular strategy for small businesses is to cross-post the same ad on, say, Instagram and Facebook because it's more efficient (and easy). For WhatsApp and Messenger, some small businesses use these services to respond to customers. So, they will set up business accounts on one or both where customers can contact them. For the latter, another strategy here involves running ads to those accounts, primarily to notify existing or potential customers they have set up an account to answer queries. Facebook does provide a lot of helpful information for small businesses here as well: https://www.facebook.com/business/small-business/free-tools. While we won't get into all the small details about implementation of ads on Facebook, we'll dive into a few key areas you should try to pay attention to starting out (or ones you can discuss with the agency you hire). This should give you at least the basics about what's available to you on the platform. We'll cover:

- Ad types
- Ad targeting
- Ad optimization by objective
- Retargeting

Ad Types on Facebook

As of this writing, Facebook provides eight ad types on its platform.

- Photo Ads (which run in users' feeds)
- Video Ads (which run in users' feeds)
- Stories (which run in between Facebook user stories)
- Messenger Ads (which run on FB Messenger inbox)
- Carousel Ads (which run in users' feeds)
- Slideshow Ads (which run in users' feeds)
- Collection Ads (product showcase type ads which run in users' feeds)
- Playable Ads (particularly for game app installs. Allows people to visually see an example of the game through video. Runs in users' feeds.)

What ad types you ultimately choose are going to be based on the assets you have available, but mostly your marketing funnel strategy and the business you're ultimately in. In our experience with small businesses, carrousel and collection ads work great for those with e-commerce stores, assuming you have great shots of various products. For other small businesses, particularly B2B ones, we've seen video ads work well, sometimes with better click-thru rates than photo ads. But you'll want to test to see how your performance fares.

Ad Targeting on Facebook

No advertiser blasts ads to all 2.6 billion users on Facebook. (That would be quite expensive.) You must target your audiences more specifically. Here are the options available as of this writing, from Facebook itself:

- **Locations.** Target ads to people based on locations. (https://www. facebook.com/business/help/285255905140138) You can select country, state, province, city, congressional district, zip and post codes. Most objectives let you target worldwide (type in "worldwide"), by region (for example, "Europe"), by free trade area (for example, "NAFTA," the North American Free Trade Agreement) or by app store availability (for example, "iTunes app store countries").
- **Age.** Target ads to people within an age range.
- **Gender.** Target ads to women, men or people of all genders.
- **Languages.** Target ads to users of certain languages.
- **Detailed Targeting.** Include or exclude people from an audience based on criteria such as demographics, interests and/or behaviors.
- **Connections.** Include or exclude people from your audience based on connections to your Pages, apps or events. (https://www.facebook.com/ business/help/1819812758298988?id=176276233019487)
- **Custom Audiences.** Custom Audiences are select audiences of people you already know that created from information you provide or from information generated on Facebook's products. You can create Custom Audiences from a list, the Facebook pixel, the Facebook SDK and engagement on Facebook.

Note: You can also use Custom Audiences to create lookalike audiences. A lookalike audience is an audience that we create based on a Custom Audience source that finds other people on Facebook who are the most similar to the people in the source.

Detailed Targeting includes:

- Ads they click
- Pages they engage with
- Activities people engage in on Facebook related to things like their device usage, and travel preferences
- Demographics like age, gender, and location
- The mobile device they use and the speed of their network connection

Again, your targeting is going to be based on the type of business you have, if you're location specific, and whether you're a B2B or B2C business. One thing to consider above is Facebook's "lookalike audience" option, which can help you get in front of potential customers who "look like" your existing list of, say, current website visitors.

Optimizations Available by Objective on Facebook

With any ad, you also have options to use Facebook's AI engine to help you optimize performance. You can optimize by the following options per Facebook itself:

Brand Awareness

- Ad Recall Lift - Serving ads to maximize the total number of people who will remember seeing your ads.

Reach

- Reach – Serving ads to the maximum number of people.
- Impressions – Delivering ads to people as many times as possible.

Traffic

- Landing Page Views - Deliver your ads to people who are more likely to click on your ad's link and loading the website or Instant Experience. (Pixel)
- Link Clicks - Delivering your ads to the people most likely to click on them. (Note: This is different from landing page views as people who click, don't always follow through to the landing page. We do recommend landing page views as the optimization method, if you choose between the two.)
- Daily Unique Reach - Delivering your ads to people up to once a day.

Engagement

Because Engagement can refer to many actions, choose the type of engagement you'd like to focus on in the Campaign level, then get more specific.

- Impressions - Delivering your ads to people as many times as possible.
- Post Engagement – Delivering your ads to the right people to help you get the most likes, shares, or comments on your post at the lowest cost.
- Daily Unique Reach - Delivering your ads to people up to once a day.
- Page Likes - Delivering your ads to the right people to help you get more Page likes at the lowest cost.
- Event Responses - Delivering your ads to the right people to help you get the most event interest at the lowest cost.

App Installs

- App Installs - Delivering your ads to the people most likely to install your app.
- Retention - Delivering your ads to the people who are more likely to open your app on day 2 (24 - 48 hours) or day 7 (144 - 168 hours) after install.
- App Events - Delivering your ads to the people who are most likely to take a specific action at least once.
- Value - Delivering your ads to people to maximize the total purchase value generated and get the highest return on ad spend (ROAS).
- Link Clicks - Delivering your ads to the people most likely to click on them.

Video Views

- ThruPlay - Delivering your ads to help you get the most completed video plays if the video is 15 seconds or shorter. For longer videos, this will optimize for people most likely to play at least 15 seconds.
- 2-Second Continuous Video Views - Delivering your ads to get the most video views of 2 continuous seconds or more. Most 2-second continuous video views will have at least 50% of the video pixels on screen.

Leads

- Leads - Delivering your ads to the right people to help you get the most leads at the lowest cost.

Messages

- Replies - Delivering your ads to people most likely to have a conversation with you through messages.
- Leads - Delivering your ads to the right people to help you get the most leads at the lowest cost.

Conversions

- Conversions - Delivering your ads to the right people to help you get the most website conversions.
- Value - Delivering your ads to people to maximize the total purchase value generated and get the highest return on ad spend (ROAS).
- Landing Page Views - Delivering your ads to people who are more likely to click on your ad's link and load the website or Instant Experience.
- Link Clicks - Delivering your ads to the people most likely to click on them.
- Impressions - Delivering your ads to people as many times as possible.
- Daily Unique Reach - Delivering your ads to people up to once a day.

Catalog

- Conversion Events (Suggested Option) - Delivering your ads to people more likely to take action when they see a product from your catalog.
- Value - Delivering your ads to people to maximize the total purchase value generated and get the highest return on ad spend (ROAS).
- Link Clicks - Delivering your ads to the people most likely to click on them.
- Impressions - Delivering your ads to people as many times as possible.

Store Visits

- Daily Unique Reach (Recommended) - Delivering your ads to people up to once a day.

- Store Visit - Delivering your ads to people more likely to visit your business locations.

Similar to Google, Facebook's AI engine stores a lot of data on its user base. Depending on your goal, you'll want to optimize for those who are most likely to do the behavior you specify and it can help you better target your ad dollars.

Retargeting on Facebook

With retargeting, you can remind people about the products they've browsed and/or purchased on your website, mobile app, or on Facebook Marketplace, and Instagram Shopping. The goal would be to put relevant ads in front of people to see products or similar products to what they saw visiting those areas. One thing Facebook notes is that, as iOS 14 (Apple's privacy notification changes) gets adopted, the accuracy of retargeting audiences may be degraded. Here is more from Facebook on retargeting:

Requirements for retargeting

- Facebook pixel/app events: You need a Facebook pixel implemented on your website, and use standard events to report which product IDs from your catalog are being viewed, added to cart and purchased. If you want to retarget people in a mobile app, you can set up app events. If you're not sure how to set up a pixel or app events, consider reaching out to a website or app developer.
- Catalog: You need a catalog to use dynamic ads. If supported, you can use an existing data feed from one of Facebook's integrations (for example, Shopify). If you don't have a catalog, learn how to create a catalog.

Retarget an audience

To retarget an audience with dynamic ads:

- Go to ad creation and start creating your dynamic ad. When you select your audience, choose Retarget ads to people who interacted with your products on and off Facebook.
- Choose a retargeting option:
  - » Viewed or Added to Cart But Not Purchased: Promote products from your catalog to people who viewed or added those products to their cart.

- » Added to Cart But Not Purchased: Promote products from your catalog to people who added those products their cart.
- » Upsell Products: Upsell products from your catalog to people who viewed products from your product set.
- » Cross-Sell Products: Cross-sell products from your catalog to people who viewed products from your product set.
- » Custom Combination: Promote products from your catalog to a Custom Audience based on how people interacted with your products. If you choose this option, you can select the audience interactions taken by selecting inclusions and exclusions. For example, you could include people who added products to their cart in the last 45 days and exclude people who purchased products in the last 45 days.
  1. Enter the number of days where the action occurred for your retargeting option.
  2. (Optional) Select **Show Advanced Options** to add a Custom Audience or Lookalike Audience to your targeting.

What iOS 14 Means for Small Businesses Advertising

If you haven't paid attention recently to the war going on between Facebook and Apple. It's understandable. Two tech giants going to war over privacy can seem, at best, an esoteric topic has little to do with the running of your business. But if you get into the details, there are potentially some large impacts for those small businesses that advertise on social networks. We'll talk about iOS 14 from the perspective of advertising on Facebook, primarily, since that social network is a popular outlet for many businesses. But the changes that have rolled out will also apply to any social or ad network that has the capability to track your activity across destinations outside its own.

First, What Is the Big Deal With iOS 14?

Starting with iOS 14, the update to the company's operating system for iPhones and iPads, Apple will require that all apps in the App Store show a prompt to its users on iOS devices, asking them for permission to track them outside the app. That seems like a good step for individual privacy (and that's where Apple wants to position itself, as the privacy champion.) However, for small businesses looking to better target customers with ads, it can be a big setback. For any app that small businesses now want to advertise on, your ad targeting in essence, will likely degrade because you will no longer have data on a whole pool of users.

Why might you ask?

Because most everyday iPhone users are expected to opt out of app tracking. The current expectation is that roughly on 10- to 15-percent of users will allow the app to track them when asked the question in the popup. (See right)

To illustrate what this affects in practice, let's look at Facebook advertising as an example. First, Facebook, (prior to iOS 14), collected something known as an IDFA (Identifier for Advertisers) – basically, a unique identifier for mobile devices that is used to target and measure the effectiveness of advertising on a user level across mobile devices. With the recent change by Apple, Facebook announced they will no longer collect this IDFA (www.facebook.com/business/news/preparing-our-partners-for-ios-14-launch). This change in posture will likely impact Facebook's ability to understand behavior of the user of that particular mobile device outside of its app, affecting future targeting capabilities and conversion tracking.

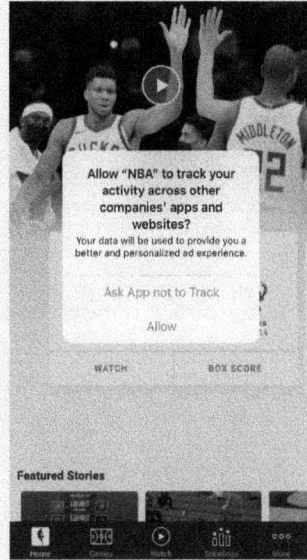

To do Facebook ads, small businesses also embed a Facebook pixel on their website. The pixel allows Facebook to track activity of its user base outside of the app, particularly if someone clicks from Facebook to your website. The pixel can also track individuals who just come to your website through desktop or your mobile web browser. Because Facebook can match those users who visit your site with its own Facebook user data, it can help small businesses target those website visitors with ads in Facebook (something known as "**retargeting**."). Similarly, Facebook tracking helps small businesses better understand conversions. So, if you do a promotion in Facebook and an individual clicks to the website and coverts, Facebook can capture that data. But let's say a user comes from the Facebook mobile app and he or she has opted not to allow the Facebook or Instagram app to track them. Those individuals, say, click a link shared to their news feed and go to your small business website. Suddenly, there's a "black hole" of data. Because of the iOS 14 update, Facebook can't track an opted-out user's activity on the websites clicked from its social media platforms. Hence, that activity cannot be used for retargeting, targeting, and conversion tracking.

Doesn't iOS 14 Only Affect Mobile App Tracking?

Yes, it does only affect mobile app tracking. Apple doesn't run the internet so if a customer does visit your website on a desktop, or visits on your site a mobile browser that's not "default Safari," then a platform such as Facebook can potentially still pick up that data. (Safari automatically disables cross-site tracking of 3rd party cookies, which you can adjust if you want to be tracked.) The problem, of course, is that most of the users who visit Facebook use its mobile app. Roughly 80 percent of users on Facebook report only using the application on their mobile phone. Hence, if Facebook is not able to effectively track user behavior and a large pool of Apple iPhone users who suddenly opt out, which most believe will happen, the ability to target based on this data will become more limited. It will also result in inaccurate reporting for conversions as well as more ineffective remarketing efforts. That means your ability to create more super-personalized ads to audiences may be impacted greatly. That translates into more wasted spend.

What Can You Do If You Rely on Facebook Targeting and Retargeting?

And it's not just Facebook. Any app that you advertise on that tracks activity across the web will be affected by the change. Note the NBA image, for example, which offers advertising on its app, as well. If you are a small business that relies on Facebook ads and targeting there are a couple things you can do.

1. **Collect more first-party data and keep users logged in.**

    The change with iOS 14 is significant in that it signals a shift away from third party data (such as a Facebook pixel on your site) to first-party data collection. First-party data collection is when you legitimately collect data on visitors within your own website, getting them to register and sign in. When individuals register and sign in, analytics platforms have the ability to collect data on that registered user and, in essence, do footprint tracking on where they go on the site and what they buy. Data such as this can be collected in a spreadsheet (email) and uploaded to a platform such as Google or Facebook to retarget individuals in those platforms that have visited your website.

    Second, some sites (such as banking or shopping sites will log you out after a particular session). If you don't have to log a user out, our suggestion is that you don't do it. If you look at sites such as Facebook, which are masters of data collection, they will keep you logged in on the site until you actually log out. Or if you clear your cookies.

2. **Develop more content, particularly downloadable content.**

    In line with point no. 1, content marketing becomes even more important in two respects. First, in terms of data collection. Content downloadables such as whitepapers, e-books, or even webinars and news-letters can help you capture data of potential users and you can market to them in other ways, using email and other means. Second, as the programmatic and display advertising world fumbles to see where everything shakes out post-iOS-14, as a small business, you can still reach individuals by producing great content that draws individuals to your website.

3. **If you still want to do Facebook, a few additional tips.**

First, in terms of optimization approach, many small businesses (or agencies that run ads for them) might use Facebook's AI engine to best target for those most likely to convert. If you still do this, we recommend excluding iOS devices and in the near term and focusing on Android devices only in mobile. It's not a long-term approach but at least in the near term you can test to see how well those campaigns perform. Another approach here might involve adding UTM tracking links to your campaigns where you could match a conversion or sale based on a traffic bump from a particular social network promotion – a way to rely less on the Facebook tracking pixel. Lastly, you might try a lead ad campaign, where you could, again, generate contacts that would go into your first-party data collection. For the most part, top-of-the-funnel awareness campaigns shouldn't be affected too much, as you can still use Facebook's own first-party data for that.

Note: There is still much to be learned about the full impact of Apple's iOS 14, what percentage of users have opted out of tracking and what it all means going forward for the small business advertising industry. But suffice to say, it's important to start shifting gears if you haven't already, as the change is already upon us.

In Facebook and other social platforms, data suggests that retargeting (that ad that follows you around), works. People are more likely to click and engage with the ad because they are already familiar with the brand (typically having visited the website before). As mentioned above, you'll need to set up a Facebook pixel on your website, which you should do for all the major social platforms, as well. (Of course, note that with the mobile iOS 14+ changes, the data might become more inaccurate.)

As you can see, there are a lot of options, and we haven't even gone into the details about making sure your creatives (photo, video text) fit the right Facebook specs, which you can find here.[8] Remember to consider your overall goals, as well as the resources it will take to produce the assets for any ad, and how you'll measure and analyze performance.

That's just an example of one platform (albeit the biggest). Each social media channel, as mentioned, has some unique differences in ad options, targeting, and ad optimization. But there are also many similarities. And if you're not sure, we're happy to help you. Just contact us about any platform at contact@marektingniceguys.com and we'll respond.

One alternative here for do-it-yourselfers is to find services (such as a Marketing Help Desk that we offer) that will simply provide guidance or help review your campaigns, but at an hourly rate. In the end, it's really about focusing on your return on investment and making sure the dollars you spend have the biggest impact on your marketing performance. At the very least, we hope this has given you at least additional insight into what you need to know as a small business in social.

---

[8] https://www.facebook.com/business/ads-guide

CHAPTER 8

Email Marketing/ Marketing Automation

Marketers love email. According to a recent survey, it was voted to be the top ROI driver of all marketing channels (59 percent to 21 percent for social media, the nearest competitor). It also continues to be a great way to communicate with customers and prospects, and build brand awareness.

But email marketing isn't what it was even 10 years ago. Today, sophisticated small businesses do a lot more than just send a newsletter or occasional product offer out to subscribers. Technology allows for these businesses to track incoming leads, automate marketing "journeys" to them, and collect data on site behavior that can trigger other emails. You may occasionally hear the term "marketing automation," which refers to the ability to automate a lot of marketing processes rather than doing every step manually. An example might be the following scenario in which someone downloads a whitepaper from your website and you send them a series of automated emails below:

- 1st Email: Thanks for downloading our whitepaper/learn more about our services
- 2nd Email: You might be interested in this blog on this topic
- 3rd Email: If you need help in this topic area, we have services to assist you
- 4th Email: Let us know if you need our services, here is our contact information

In other words, in the ideal world, you wouldn't want to manually send these emails to everyone who downloads a whitepaper. You would want to automate those processes upfront.[9] This is one reason why choosing an email/marketing automation system (MAS) that fits your goals is critical. After all, if your MAS can't do some of the things you need it to do (or see your competitors doing), you might be missing a big opportunity to engage or convert your customers. And, as you consider your needs, it's important to first think about your overall strategy. So, as we have with other sections, we'll start with Planning & Strategy as part of our PATIO framework. This section will inform not only how we do our emails but also what platform we'll choose.

PATIO for Email

Planning and Strategy for Email

Before you choose an email/marketing automation provider, you should consider your strategy first. Here are a few questions to ask yourself as a small business, as you think about email.

1. **What role does email play in your overall digital marketing strategy? Again, what's the goal of your emails? Content engagement? Website traffic? Conversions? What part of the funnel?**

   In most cases, you've already acquired the individual subscriber to your list using a valid method (purchase, registration, download etc.).[10] At this point, most customers probably know you, so many small businesses use email to engage or convert their customers (mid-to-lower funnel approach). So, as you think about buying a platform or executing a strategy, it's key to understand what you're trying achieve from the email itself. More sophisticated tools allow for better automation and targeting to those who demonstrate some intent to purchase. However, if your goal is to achieve ongoing engagement, you may not need a more expensive automation tool.

---

[9] Email is only one aspect of marketing automation, but a major part.

[10] We don't recommend buying new lists these days if you can avoid it, as it can amount to spamming potential customers, something that can get you in trouble with both your email provider and privacy regulations. If you do buy lists, we can recommend other options for you.

2. **What do the staffing resources look like? Do you have someone to manage this area?**

Like other channels, email requires someone to manage your sends on an ongoing basis. After all, even if you decide to automate emails, you still need someone to set that up and monitor the success of the campaigns. Plus, you'll want to develop manual email sends as well. And like other channels, you might want to think about design resources for images or other visuals you might need within the email as well. This is true for B2B or B2C emails. Staffing itself isn't a big consideration of your platform choice as systems generally charge for the number of subscribers versus system users. But if you do have multiple staff using a platform from different teams (example sales) and doing more complex campaign workflows, you likely will want to opt for a more sophisticated platform.

3. **Do you have a sales team and/or need Integration with your sales CRM?**

If you have a separate sales team, you may want to consider which emails are sent from marketing and which are sent from sales. How do you want them automated from each? Or, at least coordinate your messaging so that great sales prospects can be put into, say, an automated sales email journey, and not be bothered with broader marketing emails. Alternatively, the other question to ask is how you want to connect your marketing automation platform to your CRM, or do you want more of an all-in-one solution (see the hybrid options below). If you want to manage more complex campaigns, with more sophisticated workflows and triggers, a simple email platform may not be for you.

4. **What can you realistically see doing in email this year? Are you using the capabilities of your current email platform or any email platform?**

Many small businesses don't even set up basic segmentation and automation so we'd recommend tackling that first before embarking on any advanced data collection. But if you've already set that up, a good next step is that think about what data is available for you to collect and then whether you have the capabilities to store that data within your current email/marketing automation platform. If you don't, it may be time to upgrade. One thing to consider: Don't overbuy a platform if you're not going to use it for many of its capabilities. We see this all the time with small businesses that spend a lot on an email platform when all they really needed was, say, Mailchimp.

5. **Segmentation and targeting: Who will receive the emails and how will you define the segments?**

   Similar to the point above, if you haven't segmented audiences by acquisition type or topic interest, we would encourage you to do so. The days of sending email blasts (the same email to everyone on your list) is probably fading because, to the extent you can, you'll want to personalize these to improve engagement. Segments are great way to do this. What segments can you create? Here are a few examples:

   - By demographics
   - By geography
   - By purchase history
   - By open rates
   - By clicks
   - By type of purchase
   - By web site activity
   - By job title
   - By organizational function
   - By social engagement
   - By acquisition type

   The more advanced lists or combinations of those lists that you need will mean you'll want a more sophisticated platform.

6. **How will you acquire new people to your list? What kind of data do you want to store?**

   The goal of your email program isn't just to convert those who are currently on your list to a purchase of some kind. It's also to acquire new people to your list so you can continue to expose them to regular promotions and content from your brand. Many small businesses acquire new potential customers to their lists through newsletter registration, webinars, e-books/whitepaper downloads, and other events (offline and online.) To the extent you can, we would make sure the acquisition method is stored within your marketing automation platform/CRM so you know how you acquired them. That way, you can personalize an email journey or a set of manually sent emails based on the acquisition source. As far as a platform goes, most basic email providers and hybrid email/CRM systems provide forms and even landing pages you can use. Or they can connect to the forms and landing pages that you use on your website. The big difference between the two is the data that can be acquired on different users and stored. The more sophisticated systems allow for more advanced, automated data collection on areas outside email, which can be key if you need it to see a more robust, customer picture.

Choosing a Platform Based on Your Unique Needs

Once you understand your strategy, then we believe you can dive into selecting the right email/marketing automation platform for your needs. A lot of small businesses, for example, might choose a provider such as Mailchimp or Constant Contact when they start out because: a) They're inexpensive and; b) The goal isn't to do much beyond sending a newsletter or an occasional product offer to customers. And they're great platforms. You can also automate some email processes if you take full advantage of the functionality. But if you want to do more than that, you might need a different system. Here are three levels of email platforms we see. For most small businesses, the first two areas will likely work just fine, but you have to select the one that fits your overall goals.

In the follow section, we'll provide a look at a basic email platform (Mailchimp) versus a mid-tier/hybrid email/CRM (ActiveCampaign).

Basic. (e.g. Mailchimp)

Many choose an email platform such as Mailchimp when they're just starting out as a small business. Again, consider your strategy above as you walk through the pros and cons that we list below.

Pros

- **Inexpensive.** Starting at $51 per month for 2,500 subscribers, it's fairly inexpensive and stays comparatively that way the more subscribers you have.
- **Easy to design and use.** Not a complicated interface and design and most small business owners can do this on their own.
- **Landing page builder.** You can design landing pages with forms relatively easily in Mailchimp or use a tool such as Zapier to connect website forms in, say, WordPress to Mailchimp.
- **Basic automation.** You can automate some processes in Mailchimp such as abandoned carts or an email journey to someone who downloads a whitepaper etc.

Cons

- **Lack of a CRM.** While Mailchimp does say it has "CRM" capabilities (it can store user data and provides access to e-commerce and other reports), it doesn't have full capabilities for linking other marketing activities to sales, managing deal pipelines or doing anything more complex. It can connect to Salesforce (https://mailchimp.com/help/connect-mailchimp-for-salesforce/) if need be.
- **List management.** In Mailchimp, lists are mutually exclusive (mailchimp.com/help/create-audience/). – In other words, you can't include contacts on different lists in the same campaign. That's fine if all your lists are individual, distinct business opportunities but it gets unnecessarily complicated if that's not the case.

Mid-Tier/Hybrid. (e.g., ActiveCampaign)

Systems such as ActiveCampaign, for example, double as a quasi-CRM, which means they can collect site visitor data or other activity (say in social) for better targeting of emails. (It also can connect to larger CRMs such as a Salesforce if need be, too.), let's look at ActiveCampaign here.

Pros

- **More advanced automation.** Compared to a Mailchimp, ActiveCampaign can do much more sophisticated email workflows that you can automate. For example, you can create triggers based on lead scoring functionality or website activity. You can also do more with segmentation, tagging and storing data.

- **More advanced list management.** Unlike Mailchimp, the same campaigns can be sent to users on multiple lists. You can segment subscribers via tags or custom lists – processes you can also automate. Furthermore, ActiveCampaign offers lead scoring, which can be a powerful tool for helping small businesses decide to send the right email to the best prospects.

Cons

- **More expensive.** At $129 per month for the professional package with 2,500 subscribers, it's a higher monthly charge than a Mailchimp. And this is usually where it becomes a barrier for some small businesses to migrate to.
- **If you don't need all the advanced automation, it may not be as cost-effective.** While we'd always recommend businesses take advantage of as much data as possible and automate as much as they can, the truth is, some businesses may not need a fancier setup. And they may just need basic email capabilities, which Mailchimp can do and more.

Sophisticated. (e.g., Hubspot, Marketo, Salesforce Marketing Cloud)

By definition, these email platforms are intended for enterprises and usually aren't used by smaller businesses. They tend to be more expensive marketing automation platforms, designed for organizations that have many subscribers (hundreds of thousands to millions). And for companies that have teams that work in the platform. Many of these can also be somewhat complex for the end users, and harder configure. As such, for small businesses, we're not going to recommend any in this area, though Hubspot might be the one exception, given its relative ease of use and comparative pricing for certain types of small businesses.

Approach to Email

After you've settled on the right email system and established a basic email strategy, you should think about your approach – kind of the "how you do it" aspect of any email operation. Here are a few areas to consider:

Make Sure to Automate Your Emails

Emails sent in response to subscriber actions (downloading content, subscribing to a newsletter, visiting a page, purchasing, etc.) or attending an offline/online event (webinar or conference), have been shown to be the most effective in terms of open rates, click-thru rates, and conversion. Yet, so few companies employ them well. That's because it takes time to set up the "trigger" and segment audiences within your CRM or marketing automation platform. But investing in that today can pay off in the future. Consider the following stats for triggered messages:

- Opened at a 25% rate versus 14% for non-triggered
- Have a CTR of 13.5% versus 1.2% for non-triggered
- Have a conversion rate of 4.2% versus 3.9 percent for non-triggered[11]

Here are a few ways you can set up triggered emails and texts within your marketing automation system:

- **Welcome series:** Welcoming people who are new to your list.
- **Anniversary emails:** Recording when you started a relationship with someone can be super helpful keeping your brand in front of them and having them re-up for your services. You can also send discounts or offers based on that.
- **Alerts and reminders:** For those companies that collect mobile numbers or have apps, this is a great way to keep customers engaged, by setting up offers and triggers based on account types or other subscriber information.
- **Re-engagement series:** Occasionally, you'll have those on your list who haven't engaged with your emails, say, for the last year. In those cases, you'll want to suppress any non-performing email accounts. But before you do, setting up a triggered email to re-engage those individuals (who

---

[9] eMarketer, 2018.

haven't opened after a particular period) can be helpful. The ones who open or respond can remain on your list, while those who don't, can be left off regular emails, helping you avoid becoming spam for ongoing outreach.

Consider What Email Types You'll Use

Part of any approach to email involves understanding what types of emails to send and deciding which to employ. Here is a sampling of different types that often work well for small businesses.

- **Offers.** These are emails that might involve product or service offers such as "Get 25% Off ____! Or, "Get a Free Trial."
- **Sweepstakes.** ("Enter Now and Win $5,000.") These are often used by companies to continue engagement and gather additional data on customers around a particular topic.
- **Product information emails.** These are emails that promote single-products, catalogs of multiple products, and are focused on driving e-commerce-oriented revenue in particular.
- **Brand or Company Information.** Sometimes, companies will send emails not focused on selling but more on promoting the brand. Maybe it's a particular cause or campaign embraced by the company or in line with the company mission.
- **Newsletters.** One of the best ways to engage customers on your existing list, newsletters can alert recipients to practical information, thought leadership, and also new products and services. Typically, they are sent once per month.
- **Co-marketing.** Sometimes referred to as chaperoned emails, these are emails sent by another organization on your behalf to their list. Typically, you have to pay for this, but it's a way to get your products and service in front of others outside your existing list. (Or conversely, you can offer to send emails to your list on behalf of other organizations for a fee as well.)
- **Lead-based.** Companies use email to generate registrations (leads) for events such as content-based webinars or product demos. Or

companies also send out emails in response to a lead that already has been generated, such as those that respond to an inquiry (e.g., requesting a price quote).

- **Dedicated sends.** Dedicated sends are emails to a specific group – say those registered for an event, or a set of community followers who, say, joined a group in the past month.
- **Event invitations.** As a small business, maybe you want to invite individuals on your list to a new grand opening or unveiling. Maybe you have an exclusive online event for your best customers, for example.
- **Form submission kickback.** ("Thank you for submitting your information.") Many forms – even those not connected to a dedicated marketing automation platform – can send an automated email to a particular user. In general, we do recommend automating this with a triggered email from your marketing automation platform when possible.
- **Triggered emails.** As mentioned earlier, triggered emails are simply automated emails that can be sent based on behavior (form submission, a new newsletter subscriber, an abandoned cart, product purchase, etc.)

Once you decide on the types you want to send, you have to set up the right segmentation on the back end and think about the next area, the 3 Ts of Email: tone, templates, text.

Tone

Email is like any other form of "content" in that it has a particular approach in terms of messaging that represents the company. Here are a few different approaches to tone you can take:

- Comical
- Witty
- Helpful/Practical
- Thoughtful
- Playful

- Friendly
- Casual
- Cheerful
- In Your Face

Templates & Text

Most email templates will vary by email type, but a few guidelines for small businesses might be in order.

1. Choose a template that visually conveys the content in such a way that's it's easy to scan.
2. You may want a designer to help with the images and implementing a design approach if your standard, out-of-the-box email platform doesn't offer decent choices.
3. Make sure that the email template carries your brand in a visually appealing way, typically your logo but also the visuals themselves.
4. Don't use a ton of text. Some text is fine but the goal of most emails is to tease the recipient enough to get them to click through. Too much text creates an overwhelming experience.[12]
5. Calls to action matter. Having a clear call-to-action (button, in particular) that stands out against the template can make a difference between someone clicking and someone not. Some examples of different call-to-action button text:

   For Purchase

   - Shop now
   - Shop now. Get 50% off.
   - Yes! I want one.
   - Order now
   - Claim your discount
   - Get the style you want

   For Content

   - Learn more
   - Read on

---

[12] One trend in newsletter these days is to write it as a blog. If you decide to go that route, that's fine, if the goal is simply to engage people on the list within the email itself.

- Download the e-book/whitepaper
- Read the full story
- Get the app
- Watch now (video)
- See her story (video or text)

For Events

- Register now
- Reserve your seat
- Book your ticket
- I'm coming!
- Count me in!
- Book now for the early-bird
- Sign me up!
- Save my spot!

For services

- Book your appointment
- Start your free trial
- Upgrade now
- Make me a VIP

That's just a small sampling of the types available to you. Definitely make sure to customize this for your business.

Consider Image Scaling and Workflow

A few areas to consider here:

1. **Scaling images.** In the ideal world, you can choose image you want and you'd have a library of pre-cut images for promotions and a design team that focuses on marketing alone. In the real world, if you even have designers, it's a bonus, but the number and different sizes for your design needs in social, the website, and email alone can be massive, if you think about mobile, desktop and other devices. So...
   - Reusing images is fine.
   - It's important to develop a design workflow so that a single image can be cut for all the sizes – website, email, social, ads -- at one time for a campaign. That will keep your costs lower.

2. **Copy Editing.** Your reputation suffers with typos that go out in headlines or in body copy. Set up a workflow that avoids these common mistakes. For most small businesses, this means typically just having someone else read the copy with an eye toward grammar.

Think About Frequency and Cadence

Finally, the last part of your approach is deciding on the frequency and email cadence with customers. Much depends here on your industry. For example, it's not uncommon for some retailers to send emails every day (sometimes multiple times per day.) That said, it will also be dependent on staffing resources, overall goals, and email types. A few keys:

- Don't overload customers. There's no definitive line but email fatigue is a real issue.
- Develop a schedule with incorporating best practice tactics (we'll cover in Tools & Tactics)
- Retail can generally send more emails than, say, a B2B marketer because people open them in greater frequency, particularly during sales.
- Watch open rates carefully. (More on this in Implementation)

Tools & Tactics for Email

For any small business, a big decision will come with choosing your marketing automation/email platform. And not all of them are created equal, as we describe above.

For tactics, we encourage you to test the best times during the week or even the weekends when your audience might be most receptive to your message. Here is some data from SmartInsights.com on research they've done on open rates for certain types of business-to-business (B2B) and business-to-consumer (B2C) customers:

- **Entrepreneurs/Workaholics (B2B):** SmartInsights found that, because entrepreneurs work around the clock, many have a bit more time to read emails on Saturday and Sunday. Indeed, the company found in its study that open rates were, in some cases double on Saturday and Sunday, and click through rates increased more than 50 percent.

- **'Normal' People (B2B):** For those who generally work 9 to 5 at an office (if you can call these "normal people") the best times to send email to get it opened is generally between midday on Wednesday and Thursday. Also, the company suggested that sending an email overnight to have it opened first thing during the weekday in the morning is not a bad tactic either. Just don't try it on Monday when most office workers are likely focused on catching up.
- **Consumers (B2C):** For the average consumer, a B2C email is received and opened on all days. But perhaps the best day is Friday because that's when many people are ready to shop.

Other data suggest the following in terms of email effectiveness:

- Mondays tend to be the worst day because many people are catching up on work email, getting back into the office (even their home office).
- Tuesdays and Thursdays around noon local time tend to spike in opens as people grab lunch and have a breather to peruse other content.
- The highest clicks, however, often come from companies sending emails overnight and, if it's the right industry (particularly B2C companies), at 6 p.m. during the week.

As mentioned, the critical piece here is to test what works for you.

Social

Make sure to embed social media buttons on emails. We've seen many of these buttons perform particularly well when it comes to email click throughs. (Data suggests that emails that include a social sharing button have a 158% higher click-thru rate.)

Personalization

We can't emphasize enough the need to personalize the experience, regardless of the marketing medium you're using. In email, it's especially important. Here is some data that will hopefully convince you.

- Tailoring subject lines improves open rates by 26 percent. (For example, including someone's name in the subject line.)

- Personalized emails generate revenue and transactions six times higher than non-personalized emails.
- Some 81 percent of consumers say they are at least somewhat likely to make additional purchases, either online or in-store, as a result of targeted emails.
- Yet, 70 percent of brands still fail to tailor their email campaigns.

Obviously, if you have a large list, you can't send one-off emails to everyone so using a marketing automation platform and including, for example, the first name as a dynamic variable in the body copy or the subject line will help you improve engagement alone. Not to mention other ways you can also personalize email through topics and interests, acquisition method, or even past behavior.

Implementation for Email

When it comes to implementing your email program, we'll cover a few things here:

- Setting expectations with customers
- Spam, cleaning user data, purging lists, including (removing unengaged users)
- Mobile
- Subject line/sender name/body copy best practices

Setting Expectations with Customers

These days, customers are concerned about their data and privacy. And they don't want to be inundated with emails from various providers. So, setting some expectation upfront is a great thing. For example, you should always outline for customers (in your privacy policy, registration forms, and other areas of the website) the following information:

- Why they should subscribe/create an account (offers, deals, discounts, insight)
- How many emails they will receive
- When they will receive the emails
- What the emails will be about
- What address and brand/person are the emails being sent from.

If you set the right expectations, you will reduce the chance someone will be surprised by your email and unsubscribe from your list. Also, it should probably go without saying, but never sell customer information or give information to a third party, which would violate privacy rights.

Avoid Becoming Spam

There are a couple aspects we'll cover in terms of "best practices" here. First, when it comes to acquiring lists and then when it comes to sending emails to your existing customers and managing those individuals. In terms of acquisition, many companies still buy email lists and send emails to those who they believe would be prospective customers. You can try this, but the practice is generally frowned upon by most email platform providers because it potentially makes them a spam enabler. So, they might restrict your ability to upload thousands of individuals to your platform. In general, it's a good idea to ensure opt-in for any emails you send (i.e., let subscribers know you'll be sending them a regular newsletter or something else upfront).

You'll also want to make sure you're monitoring email open rates and other performance. If you send out "cold emails," this can depress your open rates and spam filters can often detect a domain sending lots of these emails, and block them. A few other tips to watch to keep your open rates up:

- Send emails from a person's account rather than a sales@company. com. You're less likely to get picked up by spam filter (although many big companies still send them from a single corporate account.)
- Honor requests to be removed from the subscriber list within 10 business days. Most email platforms have a mechanism to remove individuals automatically but if you have a more complex permissions process, just make sure you're not having to remove individuals manually, which can become overwhelming. The current U.S. law requires law requires companies to include the company name, address and an unsubscribe link (usually in footer). For more, see the CAN-Spam Act (US): http://www.ftc.gov/tips-advice/business-center/ guidance/can-spam-act-compliance-guide-business
- If you do business in different parts of the world, you may be subject to other laws as well:

» Europe (GDPR)

» Canada (Canadian Anti-Spam Law or CASL)

» California (CCPA) – affects companies making more than $25m per year and doing business with California citizens.

Each of these is more restrictive in terms of specific marketing opt-ins to protect its citizens against spammers. So, make sure to read up on them if these apply to you.

Cleaning User Data

If you've had your list for a while, it's important to "clean your data." In particular, what many small businesses don't realize is that they can be penalized for continuing to send emails to unengaged individuals. (As mentioned earlier, a depressed open rate can mean that your emails to even your engaged email subscribers can go to spam.) So, for example, if you've been sending emails to those who haven't opened any in 12 months, you should remove them from any active segments. (One tactic you can do here is to put the unengaged individuals into another email journey to "win them back." If they don't respond after that journey, it's safe to say that you can remove them.

Mobile

With almost half of all emails currently being opened on a mobile device, ensure your emails look good on a phone. Today, most email platforms provide "responsive" templates (similar to your website). If you haven't switched over to a responsive template, you should. Another area to look at it would be emails that come from your CRM – automated "thank you for purchasing" or other transactional emails. (Many of these aren't yet responsive.)

Subject Lines/Sender Name

There are only two reasons emails get opened: the sender name and the subject line. Marketers often pay attention to a subject line but sometimes don't think about sender name. In fact, according to a recent Litmus study[13], 42 percent look at the sender name first, 34 percent look at the subject line first, 24 percent

---

[13] https://www.litmus.com/blog/6-shocking-myths-about-subject-lines/

consider the preview text first (this is typically the line in emails that provides some explanation for the subject line). Some tips on the sender name:

1. Generally, many small companies opt to using the company name, but it's OK to use a consistent personal name for, say, newsletters or, for example, in the case of a celebrity. Personal names often do better performance-wise when it comes to getting people to open.

2. Test the sender name. If it's a personal name, test male or female. In our experience, female names tend to get higher open rates. That's not true everywhere but it's worth testing to figure that out what works in your case.

3. Come up with creative ways to do your own company emails: "The team at (Company Name)" which could improve open rates, for example.

   For subject lines, keep in mind the following guidelines:

   - Entice the customer, make them curious about the email contents
   - Create urgency or call to action
   - If you're a retail business, discounts can work ("25% Off All Dresses")
   - Keep it under 45 characters, short and to the point (most are read on mobile!)
   - Preview text should explain or support the subject line but not repeat it.
   - Consider putting the recipient's name in the subject line ("John, we're giving you 25% off")

Email Body

Once people open the email, it falls on your email body copy and images to drive clicks, typically to your website. A few things to keep in mind as you design your email templates:

- Most people read emails in less than 10 seconds so put your most important and compelling information at the top
- Many email clients allow the user to "preview" the email without having to open it
- Include a link in the first one or two sentences in the email -- or clear visual call-to-action.

- Limit Information: Most emails usually have one goal and that's to drive people to the website.
- Bold every link in the email, which will help increase your click-through rate
- Every link in the email should be tracking URL. You'll want to track every email so you know the performance.

Other suggestions:

- **Plain text.** Include plain text versions of email as some people still have their setting to plain only (this is getting to be less the case)
- **Images**
  » Create links for all images that have a call to action, so they go somewhere
  » Each image should have alt text
  » Generally, the rule is less than five in any email so as not to overwhelm
- **Footer**
  » Signature should be consistent with the "from" name in the email
  » Add social media icons here
  » Add the unsubscribe link here
  » Also add your blog, URL, or announcements for upcoming events or products. Links help to drive users to the website, which is the typically the goal.

Personalization

The more that you can create the feeling that you're personalizing an email to someone, the greater likelihood that it will be opened and clicked. For example, even something simple as automating the inclusion of a recipient's first name in the subject line can improve your open rates greatly. (Similarly, putting someone's name in the body copy has also been shown to improve click-through rates.) There are several ways to personalize emails so they get opened, and it's not just based on name. For example, you can choose to target based on:

- Geographic location
- Job title
- Website activity/behavior on the website
- Email engagement

Whatever method you choose, what's key here is to make sure you're storing the right data on each customer/potential customer, and creating the right segments in your marketing automation platform. That way, you can automate and/or manually pull those segments and target the appropriate messages to those audiences.

Here's an example at right of something the Venetian Resort in Las Vegas sent to us during the pandemic. It would've been great had the Venetian only sent this to Essential Workers (hospital staff, grocery workers, factory workers etc.) But instead, they appeared to have sent this email to their entire list – which made no sense given that most people couldn't take advantage of the offer. That's an example of an email blast that only applied to a certain set but wasn't personalized for the receiver.

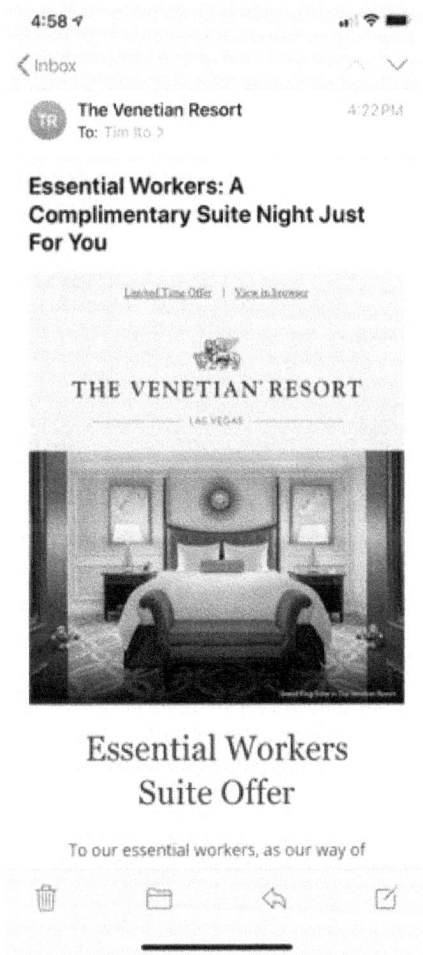

Optimization for Email

If you're going to send email, it's important to measure how well you're doing. Most all marketing automation/email platforms provide the ability to gain analytics about email performance. And combined with Google Analytics or another site analytics platform, you should be able to get most of the data below:

- Total opens/open rate
- Total clicks/click-through rate
- Total conversions/conversion rate
- Conversion revenue
- Total unsubscribes/unsubscribe rate
- Traffic spike (See if there was a surge in traffic (page/web site/target link) the day of and the day after you sent the email.)
- How many leads you received/lead quality

One thing you can do once you collect the data is to compare that with more established benchmarks for your industry. Are beating or falling short in one of those areas? (You can find a lot of industry data by just searching Google for email open rates and click through rates by industry, for example.) A few common areas that the data might tell you to optimize:

- **Send time.** As mentioned above, if you're sending at a time when people aren't opening or clicking through, test it.
- **Subject line/sender name.** If you have a low open rate, you might want to test a different subject line or use a different sender name.
- **Email body copy or images.** If you're getting low click-through rates, it might be due to poor copy, or images that aren't so compelling.
- **Calls-to-action.** Do the call-to-action buttons in your emails make people want to click? Try adjusting the language (or sometimes even the color of the button) to make it stand out more.

A/B Testing

One thing you should also consider doing: A/B testing different aspects of your email to see which one performs better. Typically, what marketers do here is they test 20 to 25 percent of the audience with two (or a few different options). The one that performs best on the test is the one that gets sent to the remaining 80 percent (or 75 percent). The one thing to keep in mind here – you should only test one variable at a time. So, if you're testing, say, your subject line, don't test other elements such as body copy, sender name, or calls to action. By doing more tests over time you can come to better understand what elements of your email perform and which ones don't.

CHAPTER 9:

Paid Search

For small businesses, paid search can be intimidating. Though its premise is relatively straight-forward – showing ads for your business based on certain keywords in search – the implementation of any Google ads (or Bing) search advertising opportunity can be complex. That's because there are a number of best practices to follow in the setup and the execution of any paid search advertising campaigns. And it's easy to waste money if you don't know what you're doing. We do recommend that if you do want to do this yourself as a small business, you should get some training in paid search ads or hire a specialist who has experience running search campaigns. For most, however, we recommended hiring an agency (like ours) that can help you best implement what you want to do. The money you spend on agency can actually save you headaches and costs over the long haul (and actually will be much cheaper than hiring someone full-time).

That said, as a small business, you should understand the basics – everything from how the search auction works to implementing campaigns so you can be informed should you decide to do it yourself (or even if you hire an agency). We'll start out by focusing on the fundamentals, and then move into our PATIO framework for paid search.

Within search, you might notice Google provides retailers an additional opportunity to appear in shopping results (above), which is keyed off the same paid search terms. Google also provides paid opportunities for local companies to have its business listing appear in its local results (typically you see a map and ratings of the various businesses keyed off of a local search, where a company's Google My Business listing appears).

Google   instructional design courses   🎤 🔍

All   News   Videos   Images   Maps   More   Settings   Tools

About 52,800,000 results (0.56 seconds)

GW Education Technology MA | George Washington University | gwu.edu
[Ad] landing.gsehd.gwu.edu/ ▾
Focus on E-Learning, **Instructional Design** & Ed Tech at GW Online. Learn More! NCATE Accredited.
Certificate Option. ESOL & SPED Praxis Prep. Develop a Portfolio.

Instructional Design Courses | Ashford University® Online | ashford.edu
[Ad] onlinedegrees.ashford.edu/Accredited/Affordable ▾
Balance Your Work, Life and School at Ashford University® Online. Apply Today! Student Centered.
Career Oriented. Technology Driven. Apply for Free. 100% Online.
List of Degrees · About Ashford · For Business · Business · Accreditation · Admissions

Paid

Online MS Instructional Design | Improve Learning w/ Technology
[Ad] quonline.quinnipiac.edu/MSID ▾
Empower Digital Learning & Improve Learning Outcomes w/ Technology. Learn More! Live Support 7
Days/Week. 3 Specializations. Nonprofit University. 100% Online. Flexible Career Path. For Working
Professionals. Career-Ready Skills. **Courses**: Educational **Design**, **Design** for Learning.

Explore Instructional Design | Northwestern University
[Ad] sps.northwestern.edu/info-design/master ▾
Prepare for your **instructional design** career with our 100% online & part-time program. Inquire about...

Instructional Design and Technology | edX
https://www.edx.org/micromasters/instructional-design-technology ▾
Our unique approach to **instructional design** focuses on understanding learning theory, blending
traditional **instructional design** models with rapid prototyping and data analytics to create online
courses. You will gain hands-on experience developing and publishing online **courses** using the edX
platform.

Learn Instructional Design: Online Courses, Training, Tutorials, Videos ...
https://www.linkedin.com/learning/topics/instructional-design ▾
Top **Instructional Design Courses**. **course**. Writing a Research Paper. By: Judy Steiner-Williams. 1h 56m
2s. **course**. Elearning Essentials: **Instructional Design**. By: Samantha Calamari. 1h 9m 32s. **course**.
Instructional Design: Needs Analysis. By: Jeff Toister. 1h 25m 37s. **course**. Train the Trainer. By: Ajay
Pangarkar. 1h 5m ...

Google   Japanese matcha green tea   🎤 🔍

All   Shopping   Images   Videos   News   More   Settings   Tools

About 10,200,000 results (0.65 seconds)

See Japanese matcha green tea   Sponsored ⓘ

Tea Bags   Powdered   Up to $25 $25 - $50   Over $50   Nearby

Shopping

Ceremonial Pure   Matcha Tenju-   Biscottea Matcha   Matcha Bear's 6   Organic
Japanese Matc...   Marukyu-...   Tea (Shortbread)...   Bottle Pack   Japanese Matc...
$29.95 $47.43 $6.25 $89.99 $10.31
Full Leaf Tea C...   Sazentea   Harney & Sons...   Matcha Bears   Jet.com
             ★★★★★ (19)   ★★★★★ (9)

Genuine Japanese Matcha | We ship from Kyoto, Japan | hibiki-an.com
www.hibiki-an.com ▾
We are proud of Quality and Value. Check out a High-quality **matcha**. Buy now! $36 or more Free
Shipping. Enjoy the fresh flavor. Genuine **Japanese Tea**. We ship worldwide.
Matcha Super Premium - $98.00 - 40g/1.41oz in canister · More ▾

Amazon.com : Premium Japanese Matcha Green Tea Powder - 1st ...
https://www.amazon.com/Premium-Japanese-Matcha-Green-Powder/dp/B010143FFQ ▾
★★★★★ Rating: 4.4 - 478 reviews
Amazon.com : Premium **Japanese Matcha Green Tea** Powder - 1st Harvest Ceremonial HIGHEST Grade
- USDA & JAS Organic - From Japan 30g Tin (1.06oz) ...

Amazon.com : Organic Matcha Green Tea Powder - Japanese ...
https://www.amazon.com/Organic-Matcha-Green-Tea-Powder/dp/B00DDT116M ▾
★★★★★ Rating: 4.4 - 2,713 reviews
Amazon.com : Organic **Matcha Green Tea** Powder - **Japanese** Culinary Grade **Matcha** - 4 oz (113 grams)

Matcha
Tea

Matcha is finely ground powder of specially grown and processed green
tea leaves. It is special in two aspects of farming and processing: the
green tea plants for matcha are shade-grown for about three weeks
before harvest and the stems and veins are removed in processing.
Wikipedia

Origin: China

Other names: 抹茶, "fine powder tea"

Quick description: Stone-ground Japanese-style green tea

People also search for   View 15+ more

Green tea   Tea &   Mochi   Sencha   Latte
       Infusions

More images

Feedback

Paid Search Fundamentals

First a few terms you might hear in reference to search marketing.

- **SEM (search-engine marketing)**. This doesn't refer to SEO, which we've already covered but only to paid search placements.
- **PPC (pay-per-click)**. Though this latter term can refer also more broadly to other types of paid digital advertising, it's primarily used in reference to search, which is its origin.

Paid search is also part of a larger "paid media" umbrella which can include display advertising, native advertising, social media advertising, video advertising, text ads, and more. We'll cover more paid media in the chapter that follows but we split out paid search in particular because the knowledge set here is so specialized.

Why Do Companies Invest in Paid Search?

Search engine marketing (SEM) typically constitutes the largest share of a company's digital marketing spend. The average company spends about 45% to 60% of its digital budget on paid search. There's one primary reason – return on investment (ROI). The great part of paid search advertising is that you can target individuals, in particular, who show an interest in your brand or intent to purchase a product or service. Advertisers know this by simply researching the terms individuals are searching on.

By purchasing ads on those terms, small companies can vault their brand to the top of the results, making their particular offering more attractive for purchase, especially if their own websites don't rank so highly. In Google Search, the average conversion rate reached 3.8% in 2020, while in Google Shopping, according to recent research by eMarketer, industry conversion rates can range from 1.1 to 3.1 percent. That said, some companies use paid search for other means too – branding and awareness, site traffic, and lead generation, looking to engage customers in different parts of the buyer journey. What you decide will depend on your plan and strategy, which we'll cover more in the pages that follow.

How to Set Up an Ad

Here are the basics for how you set up an ad in Google Ads (for search):

1. **Start a campaign.** Like building a home, a good account structure, including campaign structure, lays the foundation for executing your ads well. Loose guidelines:

   A. Start with the campaign and understand the campaign's goals

   B. Develop ad groups by theme or product line

   C. 7 to 10 ad groups maximum per campaign

   D. 20 keywords maximum per ad group

   Benefits of a good campaign and ad group structure, include:
   - Improving your impression share
   - Not competing against yourself for terms
   - Improving your quality score with improved relevance

2. **Set the location/targeting.** If you're a local business serving customers within a particular geographic area, make sure to set the targeting only for that particular location or area around which you generally gain customers from.

3. **Set audience targeting.** You probably don't want to put your ad in front of just anyone, so it will help to narrow down your audience set by habits, titles, or other criteria you may want.

4. **Set a bidding strategy and daily budget**[14] – How much are you willing to spend on a particular day within that campaign? What do you want to optimize for? Typical bidding strategies include maximizing for clicks, conversions, landing page views etc. In order to do any of the options but clicks, you need to turn on conversion tracking. (We recommend starting with clicks until you get some decent data in the door. We'll cover more about bidding strategies in the PATIO section.)

5. **Set sitelink & callout extensions.** You can do these at the ad group level too, but if you don't, they default to the campaign level. These are the additional links and copy that fill out the ad to make it bigger and more prominent.

---

[14] Note: Your bid will be based on your maximum cost-per-click (max. CPC) bid, -- the maximum amount you're willing to pay for each click on your ad (though the final amount you're charged per click -- your actual CPC -- could end up being less).

6. **Set up your ad group and match type**. This includes:
    - Naming your ad group
    - Identifying the keywords that you want in that ad group. (We'll talk more about this below in the PATIO section of Paid Search.)

    Note: For each keyword, make sure to set the match type when you enter them. As of 2021, Google changed its match types, getting rid of any new broad match modifier types, and now only allows 3 types:
    - **Broad Match (keywords don't need any additional punctuation, so it's the default)**. Broad match allows the ad to show for searches on similar phrases and relevant variations, including synonyms, singular and plural forms, possible misspellings, "stemmings" (such as floor and flooring), related searches, and other relevant variations. (NOTE: Broad match in Google's parlance is "VERY BROAD" so it's important to watch anything you've marked as broad match because you can easily waste a lot of money on terms that don't seem so relevant.) Example: Kitten. Searches that can match: kittens, kiten, kitten photos, cats, etc.
    - **Exact Match** (Requires you to put [] around your keywords [online training course]). Exact match allows your ad to show only for searches that use that exact phrase, or close variations of that exact phrase, and no other words. Example: [adopt a kitten]; Searches that can match: adopt a kitten, adopt a kiten
    - **Phrase Match** (Requires you to put "" around your keywords "online learning"). Phrase match allows your ad to show only for searches that include the exact phrase, or close variations of that exact phrase, **with additional words before or after**. Example: "adopt a kitten"; Searches that can match: adopt a kitten, adopt a kiten as a pet, how to adopt a kitten

Previous to 2021, Google allowed for something called Broad Match Modifier, basically a halfway ground between Broad Match, which was super broad, and phrase match, which still requires the same words to be in the query. But the company will be phasing this out in favor of simply doing phrase match.

Negative Match

Occasionally, you know upfront that you don't want your ad to show for certain variations of a particular keyword. For example, if you manufacture a seasonal allergy medicine, you'll probably want to show up on searches for types of "allergies" such as "seasonal allergies" or "hay fever allergies," "pollen allergies," but you likely don't want to show on "peanut allergies," so you'd make "peanut" a negative match. You can do this anytime in Google. Negative matches are critical to use so you don't waste money on terms that are unlikely to convert.

Types of Negative Keywords

For search campaigns, you can use broad match, phrase match, or exact match negative keywords. However, these negative match types work differently than their positive counterparts. The main difference is that you'll need to add synonyms, singular or plural versions, misspellings, and other close variations if you want to exclude them."

From here, you can apply new keywords, a new negative keyword list, or an existing negative keyword list to your campaigns or ad groups.

How to Add Negative Keywords

1. Sign into your Google Ads account.
2. Click Keywords from the page menu on the left.
3. Click Negative keywords.
4. Click the plus button.
5. Select Add negative keywords or create new list.
6. Choose whether to add negative keywords to a campaign or an ad group, then select the specific campaign or ad group.
7. Add your keywords, one per line. Make sure that your negative keywords don't overlap with your regular keywords, because this will cause your ad not to show.
8. Click Save.

Note: If you're adding negative keywords to a search campaign, you can choose a match type by using the appropriate symbols. If you're adding your negative keywords to a campaign, you have the option to save the keywords to a new or existing negative keyword list and apply that list to the campaign. Check Save to new or existing list, then enter a name for your new list, or select an existing list.

7. **Draft your ad**. Google began making changes in early 2021 to its standard expanded text ads – the three headlines separated by hyphens, along with body copy. Moving forward, it has restricted use of these in favor of what it calls responsive ads, in which an advertiser enters generally 8 or more headlines options, along with 4 body copy options and Google's AI engine pulls ads together that perform the best – one of the many changes recently as it tilts toward greater use of artificial intelligence. Hence, if you draft ads yourself, you will likely do so in the new responsive ads format. Like expanded text ads, you still get 30 characters for each headline and 90 characters for the description. If you'd like, it's easy to use our MNG Search Ads Creation Tool, which you can download for free (https://marketing-niceguys.com/mng-keyword-and-search-ads-planning-tool/). Or, you can drop us a line at contact@marketingniceguys.com and we can send it to you.

8. **Submit the ad**. Google will then review your ads to check for any linking errors or violations of policy. If all is good, Google will make your ad live.

How the Auction Works: Quality Score

Once you draft the and submit it, Google first assigns your ad a "quality score" from 1 to 10, where 1 is the lowest score and 10 is the highest. The higher the Quality Score, generally the less you need to bid to reach the first page. Hence, higher quality ads typically lead to lower costs and better ad positions. 3 factors go into the quality score:

1. The expected click-through rate. What is the likelihood your ad will be clicked?

2. The ad relevance. How closely does the ad match the intent of the query?

3. The landing page experience. How relevant, transparent and easy to navigate is the page for users?

Other relevancy factors might include landing page quality and expected ad performance in a targeted geography.

How Auction Works: Ad Rank

Once you've established your bid and Google has given you a quality score, Google then calculates your Ad Rank, which is simply your bid amount times the quality score. So, if your quality score is 9 and your maximum bid amount is $4.00, your Ad Rank is 36. Google then compares your ad rank to other competitors and decides the order of which ad shows where in paid results. In the above example, if your competitors' ad rankings are below 36, they will show below you. If it is higher, they will show above you.

How the Auction Works: What You End Up Paying

As mentioned, most companies end up paying less than their maximum bid. Google determines your cost using the same factors – though the actual amount of what you pay depends on the (bid and quality score) ad ranking of the person right below you. Google uses the following formula:

- **Your price** = The ad rank of the person below you/Your quality score + $.01.

So, in the example we give above, where you had a quality score of 9. And let's say the competitor right below you earned an ad rank of 27. You would pay $3.01, though your maximum bid was $4.00. That's because 27 (the ad rank of the person below you)/9 (your own quality score) + $.01 = $3.01.

As mentioned, even if you don't eventually run the ads yourself, it pays to know how the Google auction works so you can guide your agency or your staff person in the best way possible for what you want to achieve and you can understand how your budget is being spent.

PATIO for Paid Search

As we've said, for each marketing channel, it's important to think about all parts of the process so you can best understand all the steps required to conduct your marketing operations. And with paid search, it's probably even more critical given you're spending additional money (beyond your own time and resources) to advertise your business.

Planning & Strategy: 4 Key Areas to Consider

In discussing planning and strategy for paid search, we cover the following questions in depth.

1. **What role does paid search play in your overall digital marketing strategy?**

   Again, what's the goal of the ads? Website traffic? Lead generation? Conversions? What part of the funnel? In the case of most small businesses, we'd recommend that you focus on the lower-funnel conversions. Paid search is, after all, the one area where you can see buyer intent much more clearly, based on what gets searched. See the example here when we search "Braze marketing automation platform targeting":

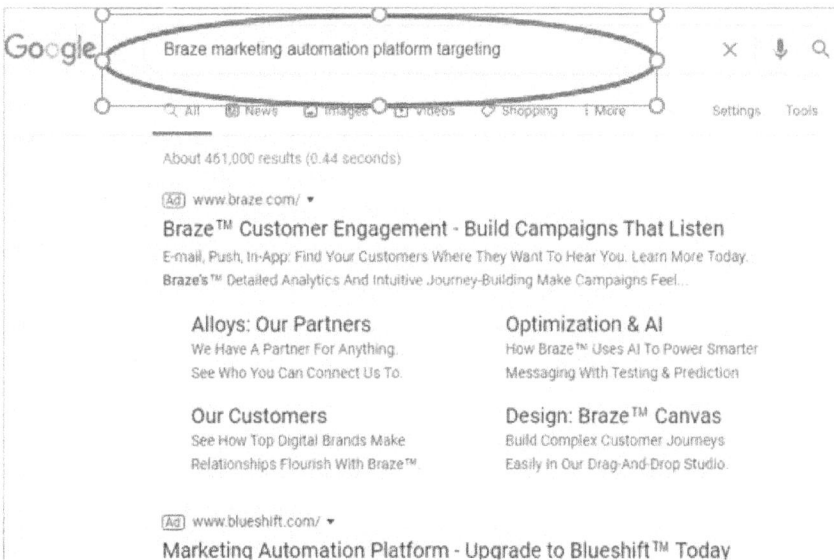

Braze, as you can see, does an ad for its platform off of its own branded keyword. After all, those that tend to type in "Braze" already know the brand and are probably more likely to be at the point of looking at a particular solution, especially if they search for particular functionality. If we just typed "marketing automation platform," for example, we might still be in the research or exploratory phase, months away from a purchase.

That said, you may want to show up at that point as well to push the brand earlier in the funnel. But for many small businesses that lack a big budget, it might be you focus on those with more of an immediate need to buy. After getting some sales in, you might consider expanding your reach.

2. **What's the budget you have to work with?**

A few things to consider as you think about budget. Oftentimes, the big gating factor in getting your ads seen (something called impression share) is due to budget. It can be due to other factors as well if your ad doesn't have a high Quality Score, but having enough money to show up for the terms you're bidding on is critical. Also, another question to consider is: What keywords are my competitors spending their money on? Finally, before you get moving on any particular initiative, it's good to get an understanding of how much the CPCs (costs per click) are for the keywords you're bidding on. You can get a general idea by using Google Keyword Planner in the Tools & Setting menu or using other competitive research tools, which we'll discuss below.

3. **Who to target? What stage of the buying journey?**

In order to best show your ads in front of the right audience, it helps to think ahead of time about what types of individuals you want to show your ad to. It may not be clear until you start doing it too. But let's say, for example, you want to target corporate instructional designers. But you don't want instructional designers who may do it for K-12, for example, as that audience may not be able to spend like companies can. So, you'll definitely want to layer that audience in upfront to avoid spending on clicks from the wrong audience type.

Also, as mentioned earlier, you'll want to think strategically about what stage of the buying journey to target your potential audiences. Maybe, as a company, you need more awareness. If so, thinking about terms that are more in the research phases or even upper funnel searches might make more sense. That said, most small businesses, as mentioned, focus on the lower funnel.

4. **Which KPIs (key performance indicator) matter most to me?**

   Similar to no. 1 (your end goal for paid search), your KPIs should reflect whatever it is you decide. For example, if you use paid search for brand awareness and reach, it might be the KPIs you'll want to measure are simply website traffic (page views and unique visitors) from search. If you focus on conversion-oriented goals, then revenue and conversion volume will be your focus. And settle on what you think is a good ROI after letting your ads run for a bit and after improving/optimizing them. Then use that as a benchmark for future ads. If your ads are underperforming, then you should call a marketing agency (or switch agencies) if you think you can get better ROI.

Approach

Once your plan/strategy is set, it helps to think about how you want to approach a paid search initiative. A few things to consider, which we'll cover here.

1. **Keyword research**: If you're going to spend money, it helps to invest the energy and time to do keyword research the right way. A few things that can help you:

   A. **Tools**. Look at what competitors are buying. The SEO tools we identified earlier such as Moz, SEM Rush, or SpyFu can help you determine that. Also, the Keyword Planner within Google Ads is an invaluable free tool to help you understand the basics of how much a keyword costs per click. Note: It's not always super accurate in reflecting the actual cost once you get into the auction but meant more as a guideline.

   B. **Data**. Go back to your personas (Chapter 1) and understand the challenges and pain points. Look at the Google Analytics traffic on the site and what search terms people are using on your internal search appliance. And then, try some common variations.

2. **Match types**: One thing we always recommend to clients just starting a paid search initiative is to take a wide-to-narrow approach. What we mean by that is, upfront, even with the best keyword research, you might not be able to sniff out all the potential variations individuals use to search when

thinking about terms related to your business. Starting more broadly in terms of match types, then narrowing with more exact match and phrase match, and eliminating the irrelevant terms through negative match will help you. Note: If you don't actively manage match types, you will end up wasting lots of money and destroying ROI. It's ok to spend to learn, but if you don't apply the learning, you'll be wasting money.

3. **Bidding strategies**: Adopt and test bidding strategies that best meet the goals you have set. Google will push you into more automated "smart" bidding strategies but before you go there, we recommend, for two reasons, managing it manually first: a. So, you can learn how the processes work and give yourself a good baseline in terms of performance and; b. With many of the bidding strategies Google might push you toward, you may not end up optimizing your campaign as much as it will often encourage you to spend a lot more money. That said, here are a few ways to optimize. The following options below are taken directly from Google:

5 'Smart' Bidding Strategies Per Google (Focusing on Conversions)

» **Target cost per action (CPA)**: *If you want to optimize for conversions, you can use Target CPA to help increase conversions while targeting a specific cost per action (CPA).*

» **Target return on ad spend (ROAS)**: *If you want to optimize for conversion value, you can use Target ROAS to help increase conversion value while targeting a specific return on ad spend (ROAS).*

» **Maximize Conversions**: *If you want to optimize for conversions, but just want to spend your entire budget instead of targeting a specific CPA, you can use Maximize Conversions.*

» **Maximize Conversion Value**: *If you want to optimize for conversion value, but just want to spend your entire budget instead of targeting a specific ROAS, you can use Maximize Conversion Value.*

» **Enhanced cost per click (ECPC)**: *If you want to automatically adjust your manual bids to try to maximize conversions, you can use ECPC. It's an optional feature you can use with Manual CPC bidding.*

One note: If you're focused on lower-funnel conversions, one method some agencies use is to start with an automated bidding strategy of maximizing conversions. After a period of time – like a few months – they learn a good CPA and then switch to a target CPA strategy that helps them optimize conversions at the right price.

Two Bidding Strategies (Focused on Clicks)

» **Maximize Clicks**: *This is an automated bid strategy. It's the simplest way to bid for clicks. All you have to do is set an average daily budget, and the Google Ads system automatically manages your bids to bring you the most clicks possible within your budget.*

» **Manual CPC bidding**: *This lets you manage your maximum CPC bids yourself. You can set different bids for each ad group in your campaign, or for individual keywords or placements. If you've found that certain keywords or placements are more profitable, you can use manual bidding to allocate more of your advertising budget to those keywords or placements.*

4. **Branded/Non-Branded Terms and Short-Tail/Long-Tail Terms.** Do you need to buy your own branded terms? The answer depends on a couple things:

    A. Are competitors buying your branded terms? Or are they buying broader terms where your brand might appear in a search? For example, let's say you sell basketball shoes. And your competitor is buying keywords more broadly such as "basketball shoes" – that competitor's ad would show up even if someone typed: "[your brand] basketball shoes."

    B. Does your business depend on traffic to the website? Coca-Cola, for example, doesn't really need to buy its own branded term in Google since it does limited business in online e-commerce and if someone types "coca-cola," they will find the coca-cola website. Also, Pepsi doesn't need to buy the "coca-cola" keyword or its own branded term for the same reason.

For non-branded terms (those terms where your brand isn't mentioned), **our main recommendation is** don't overload on possible keywords.

Focus on those that you believe can have the biggest impact first. Then test. Remove those that don't perform, and add others that you think might.

Finally, test a good mix of short-tail and long-tail keywords. Short-tail keywords are those that are more popular and have larger volume but indicate the searcher is still primarily in a research mode. For example, the term "basketball shoes" is a short-tail term. It's popular, but really just the beginning of someone's search about what's available. Long-tail terms tend to be closer to those showing intent to buy. For example, if I type in "nike lebron 17 red and black basketball shoes," that's a long-tail keyword as I'm likely closer to knowing what I'm looking for. More generally, short-tail terms tend to be good for brand awareness.

5. **Apply conversion tracking**: It doesn't make sense to test a Google search ads campaign and not connect it to Google Analytics. Make sure you've connected your analytics account because it's the only way you can take advantage of different bidding and conversion strategies. Also, don't you want to know how well your ads have performed? Analytics is THE way to learn that.

Tools

We'll split this section into two parts – the actual platforms you need to purchase and display your ads and then other, competitive research tools. First the ad platforms:

- Google Ads. Google is the proverbial 800-lb gorilla in the space and it makes sense to start here because most Americans use it to search the Internet. If you're going to attempt to do this yourself, you can try a few things to get up to speed.
  - » Free Classes. Google offers free classes and a certification in Google Ads that may be worth your time if you can pick up the concepts on your own.

- » One-on-one training with experts. At Marketing Nice Guys, we offer one-to-one individual training on paid search (https://marketingniceguys.com/1-to-1-marketing-training-for-individuals/) that can help you learn the ropes quickly – in a half-day.
- Bing Ads. Don't forget to use Bing as well, which can also be very effective and has similar functions.

As for the competitive research tools, we mentioned earlier a number of companies that help you look at keyword volumes and do competitive research in SEO and paid search. Here are a few that can help in this area:

- SEMRush: https://semrush.com
- SimilarWeb: https://similarweb.com
- Moz: https://moz.com
- iSpionage: https://www.ispionage.com/
- SpyFu: https://spyfu.com

Note: Some of these can be expensive and have different pricing models. However, all of them provide great data, including what competitors are spending overall, how competitors are ranking on particular terms, and what paid terms are driving your traffic and competitor traffic.

Some free tools include:

- Answer the Public: https://answerthepublic.com/
- Check My Links (Chrome extension): https://chrome.google.com/webstore/detail/check-my-links/ojkcdipcgfaekbeaelaapakgnjflfglf?hl=en
- Keywords Everywhere (Chrome and Mozilla extensions for looking at keyword search volume and competitive data): https://keywordseverywhere.com/
- Google Ads Keyword Planner: For keyword volumes and relative costs, don't forget Google's own Keyword Planner, which can be super helpful. Log into Google Ads, then go to Tools & Settings/Planner/Keyword Planner in the menu to access.

Tactics

As for tactics, we've already covered the basics of building an ad. But here are a few things to pay attention to as you think about actual operations:

- Making use of extensions. Note how the extensions (basically additional text copy placements to enhance your ad – shown below) make the ad bigger for better visibility. Also, they provide additional calls to action to get customers to the website.

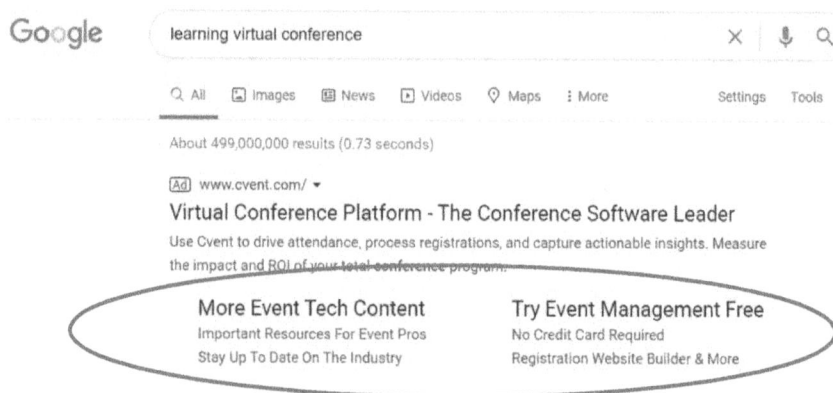

- Optimizing landing pages.[15] To give yourself the best opportunity to not only get the best quality score but also optimizing conversions, it helps to make sure your landing pages are "good." Here are a few key areas to think about:
  - » Relevancy. The landing page content has to be relevant to the search user's query.
  - » Multiple conversion points. It helps if the page has multiple conversion points. In other words, many places for a visitor to convert (either as a lead or a purchase).
  - » Contact information and other details. For example, especially for leads or questions, it should include your store location, phone number, email address, and other relevant details.
  - » Speed matters. We've said it with SEO, but a slow-loading page contributes to a poor experience and a poor Quality Score.

---

[15] For more information, you can check out our blog on this, 6 Elements of a Great Ad Landing Page: https://marketingniceguys.com/6-elements-of-a-great-ad-landing-page/

- Use headlines to create a sense of urgency and a call to action. One thing to keep in mind is that the ad copy will likely be the most critical factor in determining whether an individual will click your ad or not. It helps if you can create a sense of urgency to click. Using language that includes the following will often help improve CTR:
  - » A deadline
  - » Limited-time offer
  - » Supplies inventory "still available" or "in stock"
  - » Buy now/Get now/Access now, etc.
- Remarketing to site/page visitors. Use search to remarket to those who have already visited your site with a headline and language that reflects awareness of your products and services. Typically, you can remarket to site visitors within search, display, or text ads (say in Gmail).
- Layering campaigns. The last tactic, layering, can help you to not waste money on individuals who may not buy from you. An example might be that you are retargeting website visitors who came in from a particular search campaign, say. Not everyone who clicks, after all, may fit your target audience or those who would buy from you – it's well-known, for example, that 15 percent of all Google clicks are actually fraudulent, either by a machine or a mistake. So, to retarget such individuals would be to keep spending the same money on poor conversion possibilities. That's where you can add an additional targeting "layer" – let's say it's a particular job title or demographic that better fits your known audience. In this way, you can keep your spend in check while targeting the right individuals.

Implementation

As you build and create your ad, a lot of paid search implementation involves going through all the steps and making sure, like SEO, you're paying attention to all the little details that matter. After all, if you don't pay attention, you can end up wasting resources and money easily. Here are some examples that show you both good and bad paid search implementations:

Dick's Sporting Goods Example Mid-Funnel

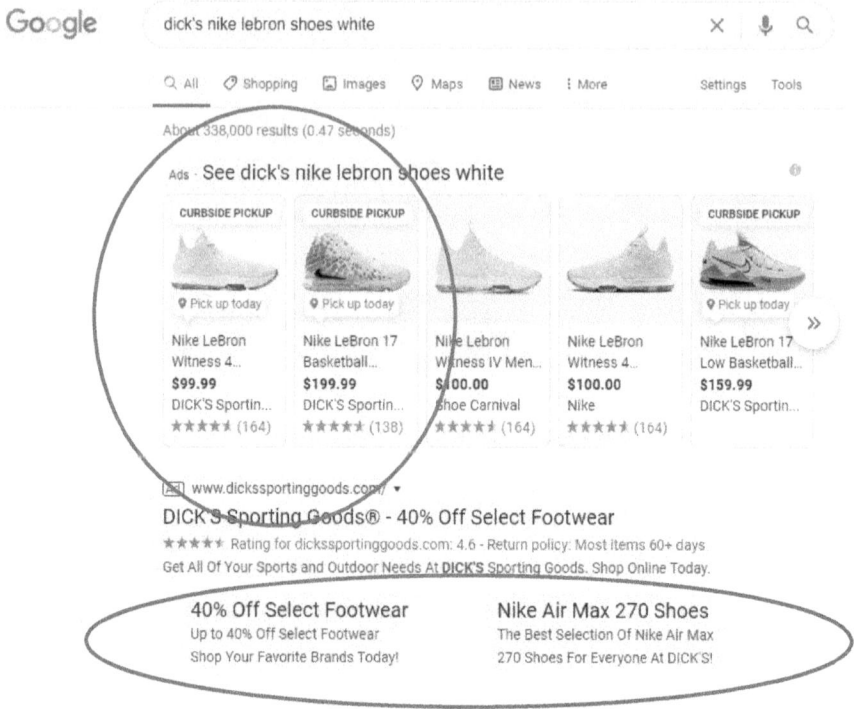

So, in searching for a pretty specific shoe (mid-funnel search), we wanted to see if Dick's had white Nike Lebron shoes. Dick's does four good things here:

1. Puts their inventory into Google shopping, where it gets recognized up high.

2. Used structured data (schema.org) to allow Google to deliver ratings.

3. May have used keyword insertion in the headline (or another technique) to recognize that the user is looking for shoes and target the ad more specifically.

4. Used sitelinks to make the ad bigger.

New York Toyota Dealer Keyword 'Toyota'

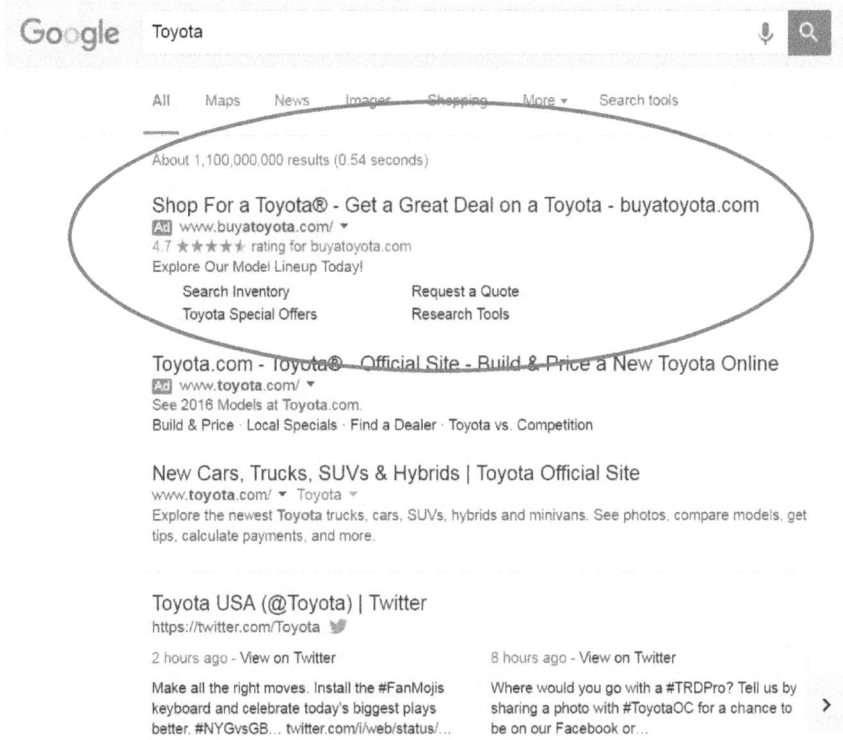

This is a NY Toyota dealer from 2016. They outranked the parent company for those doing a search from the Washington, DC, area. But, think about it. Why show an ad to people in the DC area if you're a New York dealership? A better approach would've been to limit the geographic reach of the ad. Otherwise, the dealer does a nice job. Some strengths:

- Site Links – The dealer makes the ad bigger and give users many more places to click. In fact, it increases CTR probability even when users aren't clicking the site links themselves, meaning a positive lift on the main headline too.

- Calls to Action – The dealer isn't missing a call-to-action opportunity -- the main description line as well as every single site link includes an action-oriented verb, enticing the searcher to click.

Wegman's (Advertising Its Food Delivery Service, but Ends Up on 'Training Delivery'

List of Training Methods - The Human Resources Social Network ▾
https://www.hr.com/en/.../training_and.../list-of-training-methods_eacwezdm.html ▾
Jun 14, 2001 · Many **methods** of **training** are available- each has certain advantages and disadvantages.
Here we list the different **methods** of **training**...you ...

Emerson Learning & Development - Learning Consulting Services
[Ad] change.emersonhc.com/learning/development ▾
Get Advice from the Leader in Learning Solutions. Contact An Expert Today!
Business Strategies · Achieve Long-Term Results · Step By Step Guidance · National Availability
Expert Advisory Services · Learning & Change Experts.

Wegmans Delivered Fresh - Delivery Waived on 1st Order
[Ad] www.wegmans.com/instacart ▾
A whole week of groceries **delivered** to your door the same day. Shop Now.

Searches related to training delivery methods

training delivery methods **pdf**	training delivery methods **in hrd**
training delivery methods **matrix**	training delivery methods **pros and cons**
types of training methods **for employees**	training **techniques for trainers**
training delivery **definition**	**modern** training methods

Goooooooooogle ›
1 2 3 4 5 6 7 8 9 10   Next

Look at what happened when we searched for "Training Delivery Methods" from a few years back. Wegman's, a grocery chain, keyed on the term "delivery," but didn't think about other forms of delivery as a negative. This ad was likely wasting money because it was too broad.

Optimization

Paid search, in particular, requires continuous monitoring and optimization. Few campaigns work if you just "set it and forget it." And especially here, the data that you collect in this instance is critical in helping you optimize performance and ROI. A few areas to look at for optimization:

- Adjusting keywords based on performance: Are you adjusting keywords that are not performing on the strategy goals you need – branding, lead generation, conversion?
- Adjusting campaign structure and budget based on low impression share. One metric to look at is impression share, which is the amount of time you show up for a particular keyword search. If it's low, it's often an indicator of a low budget, poor quality score, or a poor campaign structure.

- Are you cannibalizing your own keywords? If you have the wrong campaign and ad group structure in place, it can be easy to bid against yourself. Check to see you're not cannibalizing your own keywords.
- Keep honing in on when to show up. And to the right people in the right part of the funnel. Use layering techniques to get more targeted. Other tips:
  » If you're B2B, maybe you bid down on the weekends
  » If you're best conversions are in the a.m., maybe heavy up during those times.
- Monitor ROI. With conversion tracking, which we'll go through in the final chapter, make sure it is set up properly, it's key to monitor your ROI. (Remember ROI can also be seasonal so take into account the big seasons of your business.)

CHAPTER 10:

Paid Display and Native Advertising

First, let's start with some definitions, which may help:

What is Display Advertising?

Graphical advertising displayed next to content on web pages, applications, email, videos etc. Also called banners, they come in standardized IAB (Interactive Advertising Bureau) ad sizes, and can include text, logos, pictures, and rich media/video.

What is Native Advertising?

Native advertising is a form of digital advertising that "matches the form and function of the platform on which it appears." (Wikipedia). Typically, native advertising comes in the form of content/articles that mirror the content and articles of a publisher's site. (In other words, these are the ads that look a publisher's actual organic content – one reason they are effective.)

What Is Programmatic Advertising?

Basically, advertisers buy into an exchange – their ads are placed and served to customers based on data that the exchange knows about a particular website visitor. The exchange works with various publishers. Computers and algorithms make the ad buying, placement and optimization of ads more efficient, putting the right ads in front of the right audience across any number of sites.

The majority of ads you see these days are programmatic of some sort (social, display, native, video).

A programmatic ad buy works in the following way:

- Advertisers request their ads be shown to certain types of users based on data.
- Programmatic networks match the advertiser's request with those users they have across many different sites to show the right ads to the right individuals.
- Individual publishers can participate in the exchange by giving access to user data (through a supply-side platform), and they a get % of revenue. (Originally, this was the way for publishers to sell remnant inventory, using a third-party network.) Those with their own user data can also essentially "sell" that data to a programmatic network, allowing them to get a share of revenue anytime one of their unique users is shown an ad (even on someone's else site) based on the data provided.

What Is Connected TV and OTT?

Connected TV (CTV) refers to any TV or screen that can be connected to the internet and access content beyond the normal (linear) offering from a cable provider. Examples include: **Roku, SlingTV, DirectTV on Demand, Amazon Fire Stick, Apple TV, Chromecast. Etc.**

CTV **includes ads bought programmatically** and shown on computer/ mobile streaming, or over-the-top (OTT) devices. If you hear the term OTT advertising, it refers to the ads that appear only for devices like smartphones and tablets or computers (not on the actual original programming on a television, which is known as linear TV.

With CTV, there has been an explosion in advertising demand just in the last few years. For the most part, this has been dominated by ad purchasing from larger companies, which have both the means to produce different video ads and ad budgets to make it work. However, more recently, we've seen additional opportunities for small businesses to advertise at costs that fit their budgets. For example, we have advertising running for clients on platforms such a

Brandzooka, which specializes in programmatic-based ads for CTV/OTT devices. (One note: You'll likely still need to work with an agency as many of these platforms still cater their business to companies like ours.)

Digital Out of Home (DOOH)

Suppose you go to the gas station and see a digital ad at the pump. Or you go to a bar and it's an ad you see on the trivia machine. It's a burgeoning market for particularly marketing agencies who want to target geographic areas. Demand in 2020 got hit hard by the pandemic, but it's expected to come back to life again once Covid-19 eases. How does DOOH work? As an example, let's say I want to target military personnel for an offer, say, near a local military base. A DOOH platform will be able to identify gas stations, bars, etc. in the area that can be a potential opportunity. On top of that, I can access data from mobile usage and the proximity of military personnel's phones to a particular gas station or bar and know individuals fitting my target audience have visited there. Hence, the ability to target granularly is what makes DOOH especially attractive. Like Connected TV opportunities, this area tends to be the realm of large businesses who can afford the budgets and can create the media assets. However, it's an opportunity to keep in mind for your small business as you develop further.

PATIO for Display and Native (Programmatic) Advertising

Understanding what's available to you is one of the first aspects of digital advertising. And that goes for search, display, native, Connected TV, DOOH, or social. Realistically, most small businesses (due to budgets or constraints around media production) can focus only in a few areas: search, display/native (some programmatic ads), and social. For most, Connected TV and Digital Out of Home probably aren't in the cards, however there are options through ad agencies such as ours, as most demand-service providers (DSPs) will work with agencies but not businesses directly. Since we've covered search and social already, let's talk about display/native in the context of our PATIO framework, starting with planning and strategy.

Planning & Strategy for Display and Native

First, let's start with the following questions you need to consider as a small business when thinking about advertising. (If they seem familiar, it's because they are the same general questions for any advertising channel.)

1. **Should you do it yourself or hire an agency?**

   Similar to search advertising, many small businesses will hire an agency (or some sort of expert) to help them when it comes to display and native – or any other form of programmatic advertising. That's because the campaign setup, the ad copy and creative execution, the targeting, and the ad optimizations can get a bit technical if you don't know what you're doing. That said, there are several tutorials available online if you just want to dip your toe in and learn more. If you are the type of do-it-your-selfer who loves learning about how things work, you can get started on your own or even become an expert at it. The big question should really be both your time horizon (how much time do you have to learn?) and how you spend your time and where this fits in your priority as a business owner. Thinking that through can help provide you the answer.

2. **What role do display and native ads play in your overall plan? What's the end goal of the ads? What part of the funnel is your focus?**

   With most display and native ads, the goal we recommend you generally set for these should be top of the funnel awareness (except for say, remarketing which might hit more of the middle of the funnel or even lower). Most display ads and native ads are simply meant to make the target audience aware of a company or keep a brand top of mind. They aren't designed to convert. Let's say that again: *They aren't designed to convert.* Many small businesses mistakenly go into advertising thinking that placing a single banner will suddenly get the cash register ringing. But that's not really the role of such advertising. If you think about it, display ad click through rates are roughly .08 percent (even for the best placements), which means out of every 10,000 people, 8 people will click on the ad. That's not great if you're seeking conversions. (Native ads are much better averaging .80 percent – or about 80 people for every 10,000 who see the ad.) Neither of which, however, really should be strategically aimed at making potential customers convert on the spot. They're much better suited for companies that have a longer-term horizon, establishing their brand, registering an additional touchpoint needed on the road to an eventual sale.

Let's take this USA Today ad from the Department of Veterans affairs about Suicide prevention. The goal of the ad is probably two-fold: Awareness of the issue – and getting people to sign up to pledge to the cause of helping veterans. Like many display ads, click-thru shouldn't be expected in great volume. The signups may not be as prioritized here as they are for other digital marketing channels as it's really about making more Americans aware.

3. **What's your budget allocation for display/native? Versus overall budget?** Another way to ask this question is to consider your conversion horizon. A lot of small businesses we know want conversions now, and as mentioned above, display advertising (or even native) tends not to be the best, immediate-term conversion mechanism. Display advertising is often likened to billboard advertising on a highway in that goal is much more about making people aware of you and your brand/products/ services than it is necessarily about generating clicks or conversions. So, when allocating budgets consider how much you want to think longer-term about establishing your brand through channels such as display.

As a result of the way most audiences react to display advertising, you as a small business advertiser will often be charged based on the impressions of an ad – what's known as a CPM – a cost per 1,000 impressions. Depending on the type of inventory and the targeted audience, your CPM could range anywhere from a few dollars to $100 or more. Typical banners still cost around $25 to $30 for every thousand impressions.

4. **Who are you targeting? And at what stage of the buying/conversion process?**

As mentioned above, display and native ads tend to be used most in the top of the marketing funnel, meant to keep your audiences aware of your brand or your products and services. It is true that display ads can be used to convince customers to buy today – but conditions have to be generally right for that to happen: 1. Either customers are already aware of your brand and you retarget them (show ads to those who have visited your website), or; 2. Your product or service is retail-based and can be considered an impulse-type buy.

5. **What KPIs are you planning to measure success?**

Advertising is tricky for small businesses. Here's an example of why that's the case in more concrete terms: Let's say you show an ad to members of your target audience. It gets a certain number of clicks, maybe on the low side of what you're expecting, and no one converts directly from that ad. But then, say, a week or so later, many of those same individuals you showed the ad to, search for your company in Google. Those searches do in fact lead to conversions. Could you attribute some of that conversion to the original display ad? Of course. And more sophisticated marketing attribution platforms will help you to do that.

But if you just looked at your display ad performance in isolation, you'd probably be less than convinced of its value. After all, you'd be paying for the impressions, some clicks, but no conversions. That's where we often stress to small businesses that ads are part of a system – and some of that system is making audiences even aware of your existence, but not anything more than that. So, it might be that more realistic goals from your advertising are simply getting impressions and some clicks but not expecting conversions. Maybe you just want to increase more ad searches for your business. Setting the right goal measures is critical here so that you can make the best decisions for your business in the long run.

Approach

After you've solidified your ad strategy, here are a few things to consider in terms of your approach.

No. 1: Using Google Ads Versus Other Providers Versus a Specific Site Buy.
For most small businesses, we recommend using the Google Ads network, as it can generally get your display ads in front of the audiences you need and you can use YouTube as well, if you do video advertising. That doesn't preclude you, of course, from looking at other ad platforms or purchasing advertising on specific publisher websites, which offer their own site-related inventory. Many publishers, however, today use programmatic advertising, which means they don't sell their own ad inventory directly, but rather go through ad exchange, which as mentioned above, matches supply-side sellers (publishers ad inventory) with demand-side advertisers (who have specific targeting requests). Programmatic is also the primary method to buy Connected TV ads, or OTT-based ads which targeted devices. Indeed, Google has its own separate programmatic platform called DV360, which it can use for Connected TV and other opportunities, outside of its core network.

No. 2: Using Display, Native or YouTube? Once you look at different platforms (we'll detail the ones we like in the Tools section), part of the approach is figuring out what type of ads you want to produce. Generally, your display ads will come in sizes that meet industry IAB standards.[16] If you decide on display, it's likely you want to focus on more top-of-the funnel awareness, as click-throughs aren't generally the best for display. Unless you're skilled at creating your own ads, we do recommend using a professional designer or an agency, as you can waste a lot of resources here if your ad doesn't visually pop. For native, there are many options, including both native text and native video, depending on

---

[16] https://www.iab.com/wp-content/uploads/2019/04/IABNewAdPortfolio_LW_FixedSizeSpec.pdf

the type of publishers. There are "programmatic" platforms that provide opportunities here (where your ads can be distributed to any number of publishers) or you can opt for more direct buys with specific publishers who sell their own ad inventory. For native, thought leadership content (social currency) tends to work best compared to, say, a display ad.

If you decide you want to do video advertising, that's great. A few things to think about here are:

- Scaling your video production to specific sizes (we recommend starting out with a standard 16x9, high-resolution video for most, but adjust for other sizes as well) so that you can have opportunities to run your video ad on YouTube, specific social channels, or even programmatic video opportunities such as CTV.
- Scaling any video that you produced for content purposes can also potentially work for advertising as well.
- Thinking about your video ad content approach (similar to the steps we went over earlier in the Video section)

No. 3: Ad placement (publisher site) should fit the brand. Obviously, the tone, images, ad copy should accurately reflect your brand identity and brand narrative. But it should also fit with the site your ads end up on, otherwise, it can reflect poorly on you as well. If you choose a programmatic option, you may not have complete control over where your ads end up, but one thing you can do is specify the sites you don't want your ads to run on – especially if those sites that are political, religious or controversial in nature. If that's where you choose to run, that's fine. But just be wary these days as most businesses seek to avoid controversial associations with certain publishers.

Tools

For the tools, either you or the ad agency you might hire will likely focus on a few platforms that will allow you to distribute your ads. (For launching video ads and the tools needed (especially on YouTube) see our earlier Video section.)

Display

- **Google Display Ads Network:** Google serves display and contextual ads on a number of websites (outside of Google itself). The ads are often bought in combination with search (AdWords). Publishers integrate the Google Ad technology to serve ads on their site.

- **AppNexus (formerly Xaxis, 24/7 Media):** Similar to the Google Ads Network, AppNexus has major, first-tier publishers along with some second-tier publishers. It also offers programmatic advertising across its sites.

- **AdMob (Google's Mobile Ad Network):** AdMob is one of the world's largest mobile advertising platforms and claims to serves tens of billions of mobile banner and text ads per month across mobile Web sites and handset applications.

Native

- **Outbrain, Gravity, Taboola, ShareThrough (Native ad specialists):** These are all similar advertising/content platforms that help advertisers increase web traffic by presenting users with links to the ad content in native form. The ad modules generally determine which content within the network is interesting and relevant to individual users, based on what is clicked. Rather than go directly to publishers where you can pay $5 to $20 CPMs for display, you can pay $.35 per click and be integrated into the publisher's site with these services.

- **Programmatic for Connected TV/OTT**

  As mentioned, programmatic-specific options for placements with Connected TV or other services are often done separately in specific platforms. One thing – most of the platforms only work with marketing/ad agencies as the targeting and requirements have to be well defined, in addition to having good quality creative for video in particular. Some also have minimum spend requirements. If you're working with a marketing agency today, you might have them inquire about a few different options here:

- » Brandzooka
- » SmartyAds
- » TubeMogul (A Part of Adobe Advertising Cloud)
- » Simpli.fi
- » MediaMath
- » PubMatic
- » Google DV360

Tactics (Display)

On the tactical side of any display or native advertising, here are a few things you can do to generally maximize your ad's performance.

No. 1: Go big or go home. Throughout this section, we've discussed the importance of focusing ad goals for display and/or native on awareness. That is, just providing a touch point where you can serve your brand in front of a particular audience target. So, that, later, your brand is top of mind when it comes to that point of an individual being ready to purchase. Programmatic advertising helps with this as your display ad can run on multiple sites and placements in front of the same target audience. But here's where it gets a little tricky.

Running a single ad on a single site is likely going to have minimal impact. That's because it's easy for most website visitors to skip over ads entirely. Click-thru rates are generally poor to start with so you might find your ad gains little in terms of your goals unless you make a bigger splash. That means if you're going to spend on display advertising (and it's not about retargeting previous visitors) it pays to go bigger because, to get noticed you need to take up multiple placements. We understand that can get expensive, but otherwise you might be wasting significant dollars just by buying a single ad placement. (Regardless, as programmatic takes over more and more, the days of running a single ad in a single spot are likely coming to an end anyway, but just be forewarned that such opportunities still exist, but may not yield what you'd like unless you think about making a bigger splash.)

No. 2: Ad-specific tactics. Before you place the ad, you need to develop the creative and the copy. If it's a native placement, then you'll have to create either the copy (if it's a text-based ad) or a video (if it's a native video ad). As we said previously, make sure you have someone who has design skills create the ad. If that's you, great. Here are a few other things to keep in mind:

- **Use explicit calls-to-action.** It doesn't matter if this is a button or text, just make sure it stand out as to what you want someone who sees your ad to do next. Begin telling a story with ad, then finish on the site.
    - » Read our free report
    - » Enter our contest
    - » Click to play
    - » Learn more
    - » Buy Now
- **Use images wisely.** It's said that a picture is worth a thousand words and that's in advertising as well. Having a visual that "pops" – whether it's a photo, an illustration or animated rich media – can make the difference between a successful ad and an average one. Make sure any visual you use fits brand-wise/color-wise/look-wise with your landing page as well.
- **Use a relevant landing page.** An ad is typically framed in terms of benefits to the user. Make sure not let them down once they click on it too. That means having a landing page that contains visual elements and cues that work with the ad.
- **Use rich media banners.** Banners that employ images, movement, text, sound, and video and are often interactive, will draw the eye more. These banners are known as rich media in advertising circles and typically have better performance than standard conventional banners with photos and text. If you can, we'd advocate for anything that will make your ad stand out on the page.

No. 3: Use behavioral targeting and remarketing. One of the goals of any advertising campaign is to move individuals further down toward a purchase. With many display campaigns, you're basically starting at the top, getting them aware of your products, services, and/or brand. However, there is data available that will allow you to better target those who may be looking for a solution – or your solution – right now. For example, behavioral targeting can be done in the

Google Ads network in particular in which you can focus ads on those who are searching for a particular thing. For example, let's say we're searching for "red basketball shoes for men." And then when we go to visit a publisher's website, we might get ads for men's basketball shoes. Here's an example of Dick's Sporting Goods targeting a specific ad to us on CNN (even though we never visited the Dick's Sporting Goods site).

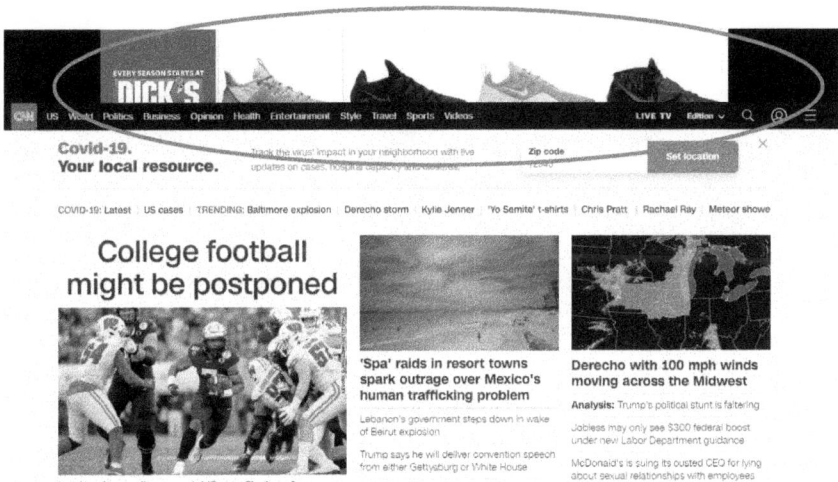

For those who are already familiar with you and have visited your website, we like to recommend remarketing as a tactic in which you can show an ad to specifically those individuals. Because they are already familiar with your products and services and/or brand, performance on these ads tends to be better than those audiences new to you. Remarketing can be set up by uploading a list of emails to a particular

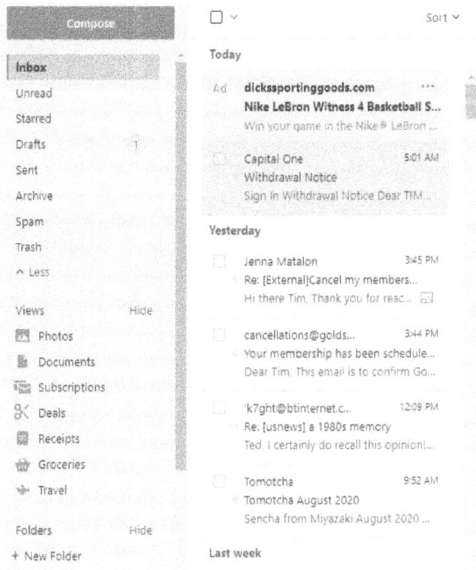

ad platform or by placing a tracking pixel (say from Google, Facebook, or other ad platform network) on your website. For example, we eventually visited the Dick's Sporting Goods website. And then later, went to our Gmail client and saw another ad (right) that retargeted us through a text ad. While not a display ad, this is an example of how to mix together different ads to create multiple touch-points. Also, since we originally searched for basketball shoes, the ads were relevant to what we were looking for.

Other Cases Using Remarketing

- **Repeat Visitors:** Target repeat visitors, say, with a discount promo.
- **Abandoned Carts:** Target a previous visitor who abandoned a cart.
- **Remarketing Using Additional Data:** Use information besides a search query, such as location and device to be super relevant.
- **A/B testing your creatives:** All the major digital ad platforms allow for the ability to test multiple creatives in one spot. A few things to keep in mind as you do a test. For any creative, we'd suggest optimizing for click-through.
  - » Only change one variable at a time. For example, if you're testing a display ad, you might want to test one image against another. Or separately, try a different call to action, but don't change both.
  - » Make sure the test is equivalent. Run the separate creatives to an equal number of members in the targeted audience and see which one is the winner.
  - » After a 24-to-48-hour test, determine which one performed best and use that one. In cases of where it's not so clear (or statistically not a significant difference), you can run the multiple creatives a while longer.

Tactics (Native)

If you decide to run native ads, the tactics can often be similar to display with a few different areas of emphasis.

- Focus on a seamless look with the publisher site. Well-chosen outlets can turn interesting topics into a win for both the advertiser and publisher.

- Like display, deliver a payoff on the landing page. One thing about native ads, in particular, is to make sure your landing page delivers on the message in the ad. If you have a specific topic you're addressing in the native spot, the landing page should provide more detail about that topic.
- Use native for mobile-focused ads. Display ads often don't work well on a mobile device. A better user experience with mobile can often be achieved with a native ad, which works best on a smaller screen.

Implementation

How you actually place the ads will depend on the ad platform you're using. While we can't go through every single platform here, what we can do is take you through the basics of setting up a Google Ads account and how to set up a display campaign in particular. As mentioned earlier, with advertising in particular, we do recommend that most small businesses use a specialist in this area, as the various platforms can require some previous knowledge or experience. That said, we'll walk through the following for those who have an interest in learning more.

- Setting up campaigns
- Setting budgets and conversion types.
- Ad targeting, remarketing and more
- Setting up conversion tracking in Google Analytics and other details

Setting Up a Campaign

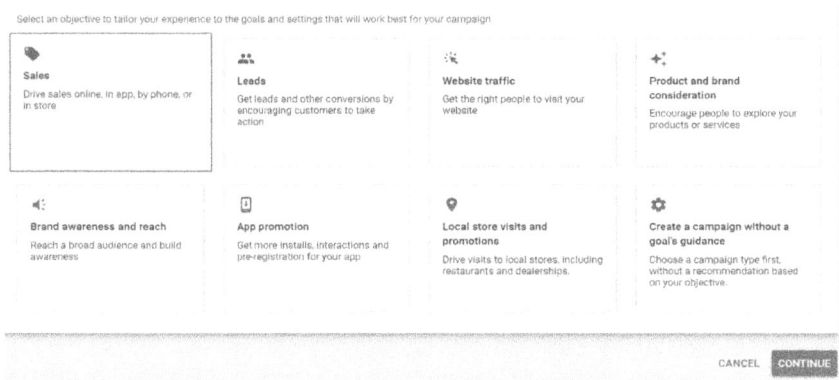

Google ads will ask you for a goal when setting the campaign:

The reason for the question is that Google Ads will recommend ad types (Search, Display, Video, etc.). You can choose one that fits your particular goal/objective or skip it and create a campaign without a goal in mind.

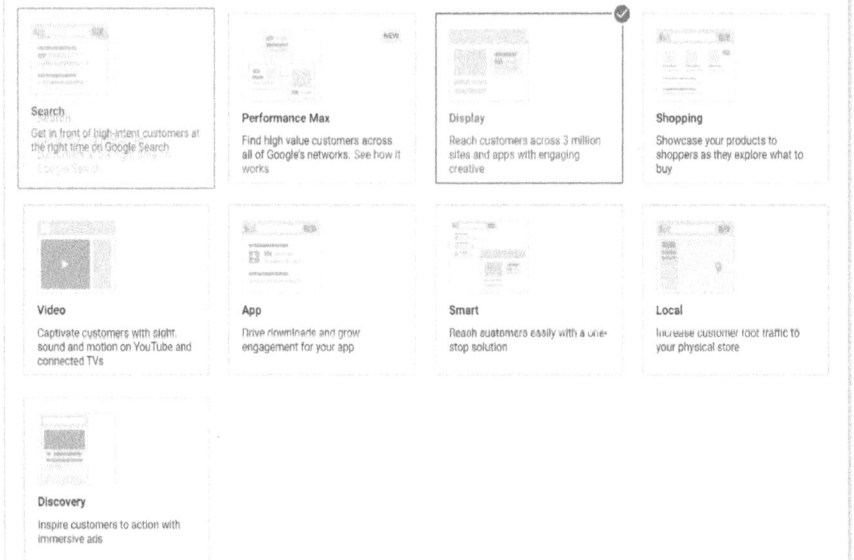

Next, select the Display campaign from available campaign types:

After that, Google provides a couple options:

      a. Smart Display Campaign

      b. Standard Display Campaign

We recommend using the Standard one. Smart display campaigns are an automated way to launch your campaign by letting Google AI engine do the setup and management. Indeed, it even chooses your ad copy and images from your landing page! As we suggest in the inset box, this can often be a recipe for disaster for a number of reasons. For that reason, we say stick with a standard display campaign.

For the next steps after that:

- Give your campaign a name

- Selection location targeting: You can select countries, states, and even enter cities, zip codes and a radius around your target location (if you are doing local ads)

Select any advanced setting options below If needed

⚙ MORE SETTINGS

Ad rotation	Optimize: Prefer best performing ads
Ad schedule	All day
Devices	Show on all devices
Campaign URL options	No options set
Dynamic ads	No data feed
Start and end dates	Start date: January 5, 2022 End date: Not set
Conversions	Don't include view-through conversions in your "Conversions" and "All conversions" columns
Content exclusions	Show ads on all content

Why Google Smart Campaigns Aren't Smart at All

In 2018, Google announced a new feature aimed at small businesses, in particular, called "Smart campaigns" – an out-of-the-box ad solution that relies on AI and machine learning to create Google ads for you. It basically works this way: You answer a few questions about the campaign and, voilà! Google does the rest putting together your ad, including text and images/creatives, as well as targeting audiences.

For small businesses, it's a timesaver and relieves much of the headache around learning how to setup a search or display campaign. After all, you don't need any knowledge of how the Google Ads platform works.

The problem: We've seen small businesses waste a lot of money on Smart campaigns and not get the return they need. That's why we would say such "Smart campaigns" aren't smart at all. Let us explain why.

How Smart Campaigns Work

After you answer the initial questions, Google automatically locates what it thinks are your primary leads based on its AI engine. It then automatically spits out the ad copy and creative that can be displayed across Google's search engine, Gmail, Google Maps, YouTube, and Google's partner websites. If your ads are localized and you've answered the questions properly, your campaigns will show up for those individuals in that geographical area if they include terms that Google determines are related to your business.

So Far So Good, Right? Well...

As it turns out, there are a myriad of problems with those "Smart" campaigns. For starters, you can't optimize the campaigns yourself. Everything is done by the Google ad engine. You may, for example, want conversions but Google might simply deliver traffic to your website. And it often is irrelevant traffic. That's because Google uses only "broad match" for these campaigns – the broadest keyword matching parameter it has – which means your ads will inevitably be showing to those who have no relevance to the audiences you'd ideally want. The campaigns also won't let you know which search words led to your ad being shown or which websites displayed your ads.

In our own experience, we've seen also seen Smart campaigns that use ad copy that would barely pass for English (see right) and ad creatives – "images" pulled from the landing pages – that are cut off or don't make any sense with the copy. No matter how good the AI is – and it's not that good yet – you can't expect a machine to do this part better than a human being can.

Ad ·

Drinking Water Systems | Reverse Osmosis, Pure, Clean

Reverse Osmosis Water Filter-Water Filtration-Water Treatment.Call Now.

Get directions

Call business

Why Data-Driven Digital Marketing Agencies Don't Use Smart Campaigns

The good agencies we know don't use Smart campaigns. And mostly it's because Google has designed this as a way for small businesses to bypass the usual hurdles and specialization required in learning the ins and outs of the platform. In other words, it's a shortcut. And the problem with shortcuts is that they don't allow you to get into the details, something that is critical when it comes to ad performance.

Another thing to point out is that Google, in the end, isn't incentivized to improve your campaign performance or ROI per se – it gets paid with each click. So, while some campaigns might deliver traffic, it can often be audiences that aren't actually in the market for your products or services. And you pay Google regardless of who they send to your site.

To wit, here are the biggest drawbacks of Smart campaigns:
- They're not designed to improve your ROI
- Smart campaigns are all automated so you have zero control over where your ads will appear or where they're placed
- You also have no control over the ad copy or the images
- Smart Campaigns limit your ability to create an exclusion list to weed out any unqualified leads or audiences.
- You get limited detailed analytical reports
- Oftentimes, your ads get shown to the wrong people because of the downsides of broad match. That's because you can't specify keywords or add them manually. You can only specify keyword themes, which are then optimized by Google. Finally, you're limited to toggling them on and off.
- You can't see the specific search terms used to get to your site

- You can't add negative keywords
- You can't add ad extensions

Why 'Expert' Mode Is Better

For small businesses, we understand the lure of a solution that allows you to do something easily, especially when it involves the setup of an ad campaign on your own. But we'd argue what matters most in this case is that your ads perform. And as much as we might encourage anything that seems easy to do, that's not the only thing you should consider. Here are some reasons why a manual setup (or "Expert" mode) is better:

- You choose the keywords that you want ads to show on and when you don't want them to show
- You can write effective headlines and descriptions based on those keywords.
- You can best structure the account between campaigns and ad groups to effectively maximize your CTR and conversion rate.
- You can optimize campaigns for conversion by setting up tracking and events that are most valuable to your business.
- You control any creative and call-to-action copy.
- You can set up bidding strategies that drive conversions or clicks and control the amount you are willing to spend on clicks
- You can improve your landing pages by using data to optimize them for conversion or the action you want users to take.

Conclusion

Considering the downsides of this Smart campaign tool, our view is that you're much better off learning how to manage a regular Google Ads campaign, or getting a third-party advertising agency to work with you. A better managed search ad campaign gives you more control over keywords, targeting, and overall optimization. And with a better managed search ad campaign, your business will be able to rank above competitors, reach new in-market customers, and, most of all, convert those visitors into buyers. To achieve that, you don't need a "Smart" campaign driven by machines, just a smart one driven by human beings.

Setting budgets and bidding strategies

With any Google Ads type, it will ask you to enter a daily or monthly budget. We recommend getting started with at least $500 for the month and then you can make changes to the campaign based on the data you collect from that.

Next, select the type of bidding strategy to focus on. Different bidding strategies are used for different kinds of campaigns and advertising goals. For the purposes of bidding, you'll want to consider five basic types of goals, along with your current campaign settings.

- If you want customers to take a direct action on your site, and you're using conversion tracking from Google Analytics, then it may be best to focus on conversions.
- If you want to generate traffic to your website, focusing on clicks could be ideal for you. In this case, cost-per-click (CPC) bidding may be right for your campaign.
- If you want to increase brand awareness focusing on impressions may be your strategy. You can use cost-per-thousand viewable impressions (vCPM) bidding to put your message in front of customers.
- If you run video ads and want to increase views or interactions with your ads, you can use cost-per-view (CPV) or cost-per-thousand impressions (CPM) bidding.
- If you run video ads and your goal is to increase product or brand consideration you can use cost per view (CPV).

Ad Targeting, Remarketing and More

Here are the options available for targeting:

⚙ ADD TARGETING	
Audience Segments	Suggest who should see your ads ⑦
Demographics	Suggest people based on age, gender, parental status, or household income ⑦
Keywords	Suggest terms related to your products or services to target relevant websites ⑦
Topics	Suggest webpages, apps, and videos about a certain topic ⑦
Placements	Suggest websites, videos, or apps where you'd like to show your ads ⑦

Audience Segments: Audiences are groups of people with specific interests, intents, and demographics, as estimated by Google. They're the people you define that Google will show your ads to. You can also enhance your targeting and bidding by employing specific first-party or third-party data you've collected from your audience sources.

Demographics: With demographic targeting, you can reach people who are likely to be in demographic groups that you choose, including age, gender, parental status, or household income.

Keywords: Keyword targeting lets you choose words or phrases related to your products or services. The keywords you choose help show your ads on relevant websites, apps, and videos. One way to use keywords is to employ them in terms of behavioral targeting of your audience, which we mentioned earlier in the tactics. In other words, show your ad to those who have searched for a particular terms related to your business.

Topics: Topic targeting is a simple way to place your ads on many webpages, apps, and videos that discuss a certain subject. Topics are based on broad industries or interests, such as agriculture or music. For example, by targeting the "Autos & Vehicles" topic, your ad may appear on websites, apps, or YouTube videos with content about cars or other automotive themes.

Placements: Add placements if you want to target specific locations on the Google Display Network or YouTube. On the Display Network, a placement can be an entire website, a specific page of a site, or a mobile app. On YouTube, a placement can be a channel or a video.[17]

7 Things to Consider Before You Buy Ads for a Small Business

We often get a lot of questions that revolve around if and where small businesses should buy digital advertising. Unfortunately, there's no hard-and-fast rule or indicators that say you should, or you shouldn't buy it. And there's no marketing playbook that will tell you exactly where to buy your ads.

Like everything else, much depends on your unique situation – your business type, the stage at which your company is developing, your budget, your risk tolerance, your goals and goal horizon (short-term, medium-term, or long-term), and many other considerations and factors. That said, to try to help you figure this out, we'll dive into each of these considerations in depth and cover some other things you have to know before buying ads.

Consideration No. 1: What Type of Business Are You?

We often say the type of marketing you do depends heavily on the type of business you run. And that's true for the ads you buy as well. If you're a retail business that sells both online and/or, say, in a brick-and-mortar store, you might have one approach. If you're a B2B business, you might have another. Without getting into advertising goals yet, in general, a broad range of ads can work for those types of businesses which might have a shorter buyer journey (say, impulse-type retail purchases), including: social media, Google search ads, display and native ads, and video ads.

---

[17] For Video campaigns only: When you add Display Network placements, your ad may still run in all eligible locations on YouTube. And when you add YouTube placements, your ad may still run in all eligible locations across the Display Network.

If you are a B2B business focused on lead generation and your goals are on a shorter-term horizon, display advertising may not be the greatest choice. In that case, you might consider weighting certain platforms more heavily such as Google search ads, while using display and social for retargeting. Why the difference? Because the longer the buyer journey, the harder it is to convince people with a display ad to convert upfront or talk to a salesperson. The more appropriate ad might be in areas where people are already looking for a solution, such as search. That's not true in 100 percent of the cases and much depends on your strategy, which we'll discuss below, but the data bears that out and is one reason why smaller B2B companies tend not to do a ton of brand and display ads. (The bigger B2B businesses do.)

Consideration No. 2: At What Stage of Development Is Your Company

We've talked to a number of companies over the years. And if one thing is consistent, it's this: When many small companies start out, the bulk of their business comes from those already in their network. In other words, those individuals who already known to you, or their contacts and friends. To save money early on, it makes sense to exhaust your network of contacts first, as a.) You can take advantage of the word-of-mouth aspect of a referral and; b.) It saves on marketing expenses as leads generated from friends or friends of friends often cost very little.

But at that stage when you've hit up all the people you know and need to grow beyond your "network," many begin to think about advertising. That's not to say digital ads can't be used when you're just starting out – and indeed for many retail businesses they need to think about advertising right away – but we would encourage small businesses actually to try to do as much word-of-mouth marketing as they can first to keep costs low. It's at this second stage we describe above where you might want to think about extending your reach through ads. Hopefully, that is also the time when you have business already coming in and can afford both the media cost and any agency services.

Consideration No. 3: What Is Your Risk Tolerance?

Ads carry inherent risk, especially those that are focused on branding and awareness, which takes time to develop. Ad performance can rise or fall on any number of factors including the placement type, the platform (when and where the ad is showing), the targeting, the ad copy and/or any images, the call to action, your goals, and any ad optimizations you might employ. That's a lot of risk for a single creative or placement, especially if there are costs involved. If you are completely risk averse as a business owner, you might think twice about investing in advertising because there are no guarantees that you'll fulfill your goals. But, like the old saying goes, you also can't make money unless you spend money. That's true with any risk taking and it's true when you think about advertising. (One reason to go with an experienced agency like Marketing Nice Guys or another established agency that they will have a track record of helping you craft ads that perform better and get a decent ROI.) Indeed, if you can change your mindset to think about marketing more as an investment in your future, it might help you better see the value for the long run, as any form of advertising will help raise awareness of what you do.

Consideration No. 4: What Are Your Goals and Goal Horizon?

Every small business we know wants more revenue. And the sooner, the better. But those shouldn't be your only goals when it comes to advertising. One thing many small businesses perhaps don't realize about some forms of advertising is that certain placements are better than others at driving direct revenue (money that can be attributed to the placement). For example, if we were to suggest a company buy display advertising on a site in the Google ad network, the goal for that ad may not necessarily correspond to direct revenue. That's because, no matter how good the ad and targeting are, click-through rates on display advertising just aren't that great (as we detailed earlier). So, why would you advertise? To build your brand awareness and keep you top-of-mind in front of the right audiences. To many small businesses, that may seem unconvincing. But if you look at a company such as Coca-Cola, which has banner advertising everywhere and limited means for direct conversion, they haven't done so badly. Its entire business, after all, is built on top-of-mind awareness.

The problem of course is that not every company has a business model such as Coke. On the flip side, many small businesses want to use any advertising they do to generate revenue now. As mentioned above, that's where the time horizon matters. How quickly do you need to see a return on your advertising investment? Brand building takes time and if you have the money and the right strategy, display and other forms of advertising can do a great job of getting your name and products and services out there. However, if that's not the case, then you might want to think about other forms – paid search, for example, which often is much better and provides a more immediate return on your business. Here's a quick way to think about your goals and potential channels:

> **Goal 1: Leads and Phone Calls (Bottom of marketing funnel)**
> **Ad Channels:** Google Search Ads, Facebook Ads (Especially lead ads)
> **Goal 2: Awareness and Brand Building (Top of marketing funnel)**
> **Ad Channels:** Facebook, Instagram, Google Display, YouTube, Linkedin (For B2B)
> **Goal 3: Engagement and Re-Engagement (Middle of funnel)**
> **Ad Channels:** Retargeting on Google Display, YouTube, Facebook and Linkedin

Consideration No. 5: What's Your Budget?

Perhaps the most direct conversations we have with small business clients revolve around media cost and spend. After all, if you have hired an agency (or are paying an in-house staffer) to help you, there's an upfront media cost, then there's also the cost of the resource you're using to place the ad for you. Much depends on the goals you have, but let's take search advertising as an example. Say you want to drive some immediate-term ROI. For that, we'd generally recommend a spending baseline threshold of $1,000 per month on media. (Note: The agency fee to manage will often equal or exceed that — depending on who you hire – and a full-time staffer would cost quite a bit more than an agency.) That's not to say you can't spend less than that in Google search ads and still be effective. You can and we've helped small businesses with smaller budgets. But there are reasons for that kind of media spend threshold, including:

- You can't really drive great conversions if you don't reach more people. If you think about it, it's like any funnel (X number of people will see your ad; X-Y people will engage with your ad and click to your website; X-Y-Z people will actually convert. So, if you don't reach that many people (X), you won't get a ton of conversions.
- Depending on the keywords you buy and the competition, you may not have enough budget, which can limit ad impressions (the number of times your ad is shown to users).
- Your ad rank may suffer due to budget (in other words, in the display of results, you might get beat out due to competition.

Unless you spend a bit of money, you may not be able to optimize your ads and test the way that best practice dictates.

For other, non-search related ad opportunities, you could get away with spending less per month. For example, we know small businesses that dabble in advertising spending only $200 per month on, say, Facebook. These companies simply boost their own social posts or create their own ads to use in display campaigns, but the same issues that we describe in search above can also apply. Plus, we've seen many small business owners become disillusioned between the mismatch in expectations for what they want the ad to do versus what the placement actually delivers. Over time, if you aren't setting the right goals for the right placements, you can easily waste money and time, especially if you are inexperienced in the various platforms (see more below).

Consideration No. 6: 'Where to Spend' (Based on the Goals You Have, Type of Company, Time Horizon, Budget)

There are no hard and fast rules for where to spend your money or even which platform is best for what type of business you have. It's a mix of many of the considerations we've discussed above, including the goals you have, the type of company, your time horizon, and your budget. There are so many options for you as a small business:

1. **Social media.** Typical ad opportunities can be found on platforms such as:
   - Facebook
   - Instagram
   - Pinterest
   - LinkedIn
   - Twitter
   - TikTok
   - Snapchat (though this remains much more the realm of larger advertisers)

Each platform has different ad types and options, depending on your goals. And it's worth investigating what you can do based on the factors we mention above (goals, type of company you are, etc.) A few things to keep in mind about social advertising:

- It can be a great lower-funnel conversion mechanism if the purchase is retail or is impulse-based, or part of a retargeting campaign. Otherwise, social advertising generally is better for top-of-the-funnel awareness.
- Platforms vary wildly in terms of ad engagement and lower-funnel effectiveness. For example, Pinterest is perhaps the best of all the platforms in terms of e-commerce conversion and performance – just note this audience is heavily female – while LinkedIn and Facebook probably dominate B2B for lead generation.

2. **Paid search**. The obvious place to start is Google. But don't forget about Bing, too. The great thing about search ads is that they can be used in all parts of the buyer journey, though many small companies focus, for obvious reasons, on conversions. It's especially useful for e-commerce retail, B2B, or other lead-generation type businesses. For small businesses that focus on local, don't forget about advertising in local search results as well. One caveat – we would strongly recommend small businesses hire a specialist or an agency to help them with paid search (see the "Final Consideration" below).

3. **Native advertising**. For whatever reason, small companies often don't take advantage of native ads (which can come in the form of articles, videos, or other content) as much as bigger companies do. Perhaps that's due to the cost of placements on particular websites, and the need to create compelling content. What's great about native is that, if you are a company that can produce relevant content, you will probably enjoy high rates of engagement with your ads and enjoy click-through rates that average about 1 to 5 percent.

4. **Video advertising**. The 800-lb gorilla of video advertising is YouTube (owned by Google), though individual publishers throughout the Google Ad network also provide video ad opportunities. Video ads are also popular on social media channels. Obviously to take advantage of video advertising you need to produce compelling video clips and that can be a deterrent for some small businesses.

5. **Paid display, programmatic, and mobile app ads.** As mentioned, more than 85 percent of all the digital display ads you see are programmatic ads, delivered as part of an ad exchange which matches advertisers with target audiences on different sites. Google has its own programmatic network and there are other major players as well. For the reasons we've stated above, such opportunities for display and mobile tend to be taken by mid-size to larger companies with larger budgets. For small businesses, one thing we might recommend is using, say, the Google display network to retarget those who already came to your website or perhaps remarketing to those who have searched for an area you provide services in. Beyond that, the upfront budgets and the branding awareness aspect might be a steeper hill than many small businesses can afford to climb.

A Final Consideration: Don't Do It Yourself Unless You Really Know What You're Doing

We don't say this to be self-serving. And we are 100 percent in support of small businesses learning the digital marketing field as they go. But for the average small company, we would recommend they hire an agency like ours (or get someone with a background in paid media advertising in particular who can help.) With digital advertising – and it doesn't matter if you're considering a display campaign, a native ad, social media, video, or search – we've seen a lot of businesses that waste money and not get results because they just dive into it, without understanding some core marketing principles, or even simply knowing more about the platforms they are spending money on.

There's a reason paid media specialists and managers develop an expertise in this area alone – it can be "complicated" to make sure you're targeting the right audiences, focusing on the right stage of the buyer journey, and getting a decent return on ROI. In an ideal world, you should create a plan and an approach for what you're trying to accomplish (it's not always a simple purchase for example), have access to professional design and ad copywriters, and A/B test to make sure you're optimizing performance. That's just the beginning. Unless you know more about certain techniques – such as ad retargeting, optimizing for a particular action by the end user (clicks, landing page views, or conversions), or, tracking KPIs and goals – you'll still likely fall behind others who are better ad managing ads and know exactly what they're doing.

If you know how to do all that, great. But note, we haven't even discussed the nuances of paid search, though we did so in the previous chapter (Chapter 9), including:

- How the Google Search Ads auction works
- Best practices in account creation and campaign setup
- How to develop effective ad groups
- Understanding match types and when to use different ones
- Creating good ad copy and extensions
- Having a thorough understanding about responsive ads
- Understanding bidding strategies and optimization strategies
- Identifying the right keywords

And so on...

Obviously, this area alone is complex. Throw in other platforms – such as more sophisticated programmatic ad exchanges and there's even more to absorb to know how to do it well.

Sure, there are some things you can do on your own. Facebook and other social media services have made it relatively easy to boost a post, for example. But unless you know who your target audience is, create the right message to them at the moment they're looking for it, and have a better sense of what your goal is, you might still find your ROI to be elusive as well. The point here isn't to discourage you, it's just to be realistic about what you want to accomplish in the time you have. And if you feel like your time is better spent elsewhere, agency consulting is the way to go.

Optimization

As with any digital marketing channel, you'll want to look at ad performance. In the case of display and native ads, you'll want to make sure to set up Google Analytics and conversion tracking (something we'll cover in the final chapter) and also ask the following questions:

- **Did your ads hit the reach and frequency you defined? How are you doing on the KPIs?** You should be able to see this from the tracking you've set up in Google Analytics and elsewhere.
- **How good was your CTR compared to a benchmark for the industry?**
- **Do you need to optimize your landing page? Are audiences 'bouncing' after they arrive?**

If your ads aren't performing, one thing that any small business can do is to use MOAT (moat.com) – where you can look up the creatives of any advertiser and see their display ad execution. It's a great site that might provide some additional design inspiration.

CHAPTER 11:

E-Commerce

The great thing for many small businesses is that there are a ton of platform options if you want to sell products (or services) online through e-commerce. Examples of e-commerce platforms designed for small business include: Shopify, Squarespace, or even Woo Commerce (for those with WordPress sites). The bad part, unfortunately, is that out of the box, each of the platforms have some limitations and may not include e-commerce best practices across the board – or can't be reconfigured unless you as a small business upgrade to a more expensive version. Each is also unique in terms of what you get out of the box too. Hence, in the following (rather than go through our PATIO framework, which would apply in the cases where you might redesign an e-commerce site or consider better options for your business), we'll simply cover the best practices for e-commerce in six core areas. That way, you can see where your current e-commerce experience fits or consider what factors are important when you're selecting a new system. Note: In the website section, we've already gone through the core best practices of website design and those apply here too, along with these six e-commerce specific considerations:

- Home Page and Navigation Best Practices
- Search: E-Commerce Specific Search Experiences
- Product Page Formatting
- Cart and Checkout Flow for Optimum Efficiency
- Abandoned Cart Strategies
- Post-Purchase/Loyalty and Follow-Up Messaging

Home Page and Navigation Best Practices

The goal of any e-commerce home page and navigation is to make sure that your visitors get to the products/services they want quickly and easily. For some businesses with only a few products to sell, the home page might simply contain all your products there. In other cases, where you have many products to sell, you've probably broken those down further into categories. For the purposes of our discussion here, we'll cover the latter in terms of our approach. One thing to consider when you do have a number of products in different categories is how to use the home page. Here are a few different options:

- **The category approach** – In this type of home page, most of the links go to category or other promotional pages from where all of the products in your specific category reside. The reason to do it this way is that your visitors may not have a specific product in mind when they come to your website but may want to simply see the different categories of products you sell.

- **The product integration approach** – This approach focuses on mixing in different products along with promoting your category pages. The reason for this approach is that companies sometimes highlight bestselling products to make it easier for customers to find. Amazon, in particular, uses this approach for personalizing certain products people looked at or highlight specific sale items.

With either approach you take, one goal of the home page is to convey the breadth of your product offering, something that less than a third of e-commerce sites actually do, according to one study. To do this, you don't have to promote every product but simply make sure that your site visitors are aware you have products in a particular category.

A few other aspects of a good home page strategy:

- **Personalization**. Like any digital marketing channel, the more you personalize the marketing to your audiences, the generally more effective it will be. There are a few ways you can approach personalization, especially on a home page.

- » **By geography**. If your business has multiple stores to also purchase goods or services in person, your site can reflect (and should) reflect which one is closest to them.
- » By customer profile. Does the customer see choices based on who they are? Or what you know from their login profile?
- » By customer behavior. Does the customer see products they've navigated to previously? Or maybe what they've bought before that they can buy again? For this latter portion, you'll probably need a developer to help you but they can connect buying behavior stored in your CRM with the marketing promotions that can be displayed on your home page.

- Promotions and popups. Some sites use will use a popup or lightbox on the home page to showcase a particular promotion or savings if you enter your information. Or they might promote a newsletter that you can sign up for. This is a particularly smart approach for companies to capture visitors' email information so they can use regular email campaigns to stay in front of them. A few particular considerations for this:
  - » Don't overuse the popups. We've seen sites that employ popups on every page of the e-commerce experience, which we would argue don't work as well. This is especially true for product landing pages. The reason these don't work there, in our opinion, is that they start interrupting the purchase process for individuals who have more of an idea of exactly what they're looking for.
  - » Try an exit popup rather than an entry popup. In other words, many sites serve popups right when a customer comes in, but many users simply close this one by habit. It may be more ideal to use what's known as an exit popup, which comes up just as an individual is leaving the site. This will allow you to hold their attention for a promotion they might come back to later.

Other E-Commerce Home Page Best Practices

Earlier, in the website section, we discussed a few aspects of creating a good user experience. In particular, we mentioned keeping the color palette limited and maintaining an "airy" quality about your site. For e-commerce, those two aspects are particularly important. Why?

Let's cover color first. The more colors you define within your style sheet, the more they tend to draw the eye. When you add more color in the form of product images or product category images onto your home page, the more everything will compete for a visitor's attention, adding to a visual chaos. The more limited the color palette for text and other design elements, the more you'll keep the attention on the right things (products, categories etc.) that you want to promote.

As far as visual design goes, many e-commerce websites we've seen will also try to cram as much as possible into the top part of the page, as they have so many products and categories they may want to promote. But as discussed in the website section, all this does is create an overwhelming experience that will leave visitors confused as to what to do next. Better again, to build in more "air" when designing sections of the home page, where visitors can truly scan what they're looking for and find it easily. If you have a well-designed website, visitors won't mind scrolling or swiping to get to a longer page.

Navigation

When it comes to navigation of an e-commerce website, the same rules for a website still apply. (See our earlier discussion of these in the Website section.) That said, when it comes to e-commerce, don't overwhelm customers with your primary navigation, even if you have a number of product categories. Consider a site such as Amazon, which today probably has nearly every product category under the sun. It limits the navigation to about 9 main elements (roughly the max for most sites). It then uses a megamenu (the curtain that opens on hover over the main category item, showing the subcategory areas) as well as a hamburger menu for all its other main category pages. The bottom line: Keep the main navigation simple and not overwhelming so you can encourage visitors to look around and dive deeper.

Search: E-Commerce Specific Search Experiences

Many of the elements of a site search that we covered in the website section apply here. Given most small businesses will opt for a particular platform such as Shopify, Squarespace, or other e-commerce focused experience, you're pretty much stuck with the search they have that comes out of the box. That said, if you are shopping for a provider, it's good to check for these specific elements of any search appliance. Make sure it:

- **Supports product/model number queries:** In some cases, customers search for a model number, product number or ISBN (in the case of books). Make sure that any e-commerce platform you choose can handle those types of searches and return a result.

- **Implements autocomplete:** When you start typing, it understands what you're looking for and can make suggestions to save you time. In addition, even after your typing in a search, make sure results can also handle phonetic misspellings (example: a customer gets no results for "Kitchen Aid Artysan" when looking for the "Kitchen Aid Artisan" mixer or "blow dryer" if "hair dryer" is searched on the site). Understanding those common mix-ups about what to call something is key to helping your customers find what they're looking for.

- **Uses Faceted Search:** Many websites don't use faceted search, the drilling down into further subcategories of a product such as price, model, whether it's for men or women etc.), despite evidence that it improves the customer experience.

- **Supports Search Queries for Color or Size Variations:** Many products come in varying sizes and colors. And customers are often very specific about what they're looking for so making sure that platforms include such variations in search will also help your users find what they're looking for quickly.

- **Is Visible:** One other simple aspect of an internal website search – that it's both visible on the site and large in terms of placement. Some e-commerce platforms place search in a small corner of the page or just use the magnifying glass to indicate where it is. That doesn't help most customers find it quickly.

One Last Thought: Consider Voice Search

The easier you can make any process for customers the more they'll probably like it and come back. Most e-commerce platforms today don't employ voice search out of the box. But if you have capabilities to customize the ability to talk into your computer or mobile device to allow your customers to search for what they want, that will likely only improve the experience. Indeed, some more advanced e-commerce sites are already exploring it. At Marketing Nice Guys, if you are interested in this option, contact us and we can get you in touch with development teams that can help put this together for you.

Product Page Formatting

Similar to the sections above, most e-commerce platforms are relatively set in terms of how to display the product pages themselves. That said, small business-es that use these providers do have control over a few areas that impact market-ing effectiveness. Here are a few tips on product pages specifically below:

- **Make Product Pages SEO Friendly:** Google is a big driver of e-commerce traffic. Some product pages on major retail sites still aren't SEO optimized, especially when it comes to the core basics such as URLs, image tags, descriptions, and headlines. Make sure to pay attention to detail here, especially those elements we covered in the SEO section.

- **Keep the Visual Weight on the Major Elements That Encourage Purchase:** Visual weight is basically a design concept that refers to items that draw the eye on a particular page. So, the greater visual weight, the more prominent it is. Sites are able to do this in 3 ways:
  - » Surrounding a focus item with whitespace;
  - » Enlarging the size of an item in comparison to other items;
  - » Color or other ways to make something stand out.

For a product page in particular, visual weight should most focus on a few core areas – the product image, the headline, the Add to Cart button and any color selectors. Here's a great example of site we love (Fitbit) that does a nice job with its product page (right). The big thing to avoid? Again, lots of text color and trying to cram tons of content into a single viewing area. Something that will likely only lead to visual confusion on the part of your site visitors.

- **Sharing Buttons for Social Media:** Does the company make it easy to share their products? Adding social share buttons will allow your fans to share they bought this product and/or better spread the word for you. Such services are often built in to e-commerce platforms so make sure to take advantage of them.

- **Suggesting Alternative and Supplementary Products:** If users come to a product page and that product doesn't quite fit their expectations, having other alternatives for them can help stem abandonment. If users purchase the product on the page, having supplementary accessories (products typically bought together) can help them save time and boost their order value per visit.

- **Very Clear 'Add to Cart' Button:** One thing we at Marketing Nice Guys recommend is that you use color here to make the button stand out. While you can use one of your core brand colors, it might make sense to use a different complimentary color or a slightly separate one that fits with your color palette but is generally distinct otherwise. This will make the button stand out on the page and, if you consistently use that particular color, it will help visually indicate that it's a button that will move you to the next step. Remember, color is a strong visual cue too, so anything that can help a website visitor do something without thinking about it, will improve your checkout rates.

- **Reviews:** The best e-commerce sites have reviews of their products; some even have Q&As as well. Such additions are not only helpful for customers but boosts the site's trustworthiness. Many e-commerce platforms offer their own internal product review add-ons or a Q&A feature and/or can work with different plugins from outside providers so make sure to take advantage of those.

Cart and Checkout Flow for Optimum Efficiency

Again, many e-commerce platforms are somewhat fixed in terms of the steps that they take once a product is put in the checkout all the way to a purchase screen. They also can be somewhat rigid in terms of layout flexibility, which can be a pain point for many businesses that want to optimize the process. In general, the fewer steps you can make customers take between putting an item in the cart and having them finally purchase, the better. That said, as a business, there are little things you can do along the way to make sure to maximize conversions. Here are a few areas to consider:

- **One-Page Checkout vs. Multi-Step:** Depending on the platform you choose (or have chosen), you might not have an option for one or the other. To be honest, there's no evidence completion rates are necessarily better for one-page checkouts (where all the information needed is found on a single page) versus a multi-step process. Most e-commerce sites we know do the process as multi-step. The key is to make sure any process is quick and linear with a few best practices:

- **Avoid roundtrips.** This is especially true for multi-step checkouts, where you might sign in or create an account but the individual doesn't actually advance to the next step after they do so. Rather, he or she might stay on the current step with the profile information provided.

- **Make it easy to apply coupons** (especially those that might carry over from an email.
    - » Make sure the code or coupon is easy to remember
    - » Allow individuals to copy and paste it

- Reinforce to customers that the site is secure. You can do this a few different ways:
    - » Add an icon such as a lock on your cart and checkout pages and even your call-to- action buttons.
    - » On the cart page itself, reinforce security by using language such as "Checkout Securely"

- **Allow a customer to save the credit card information for easy access next time.** Note: This is assuming you are using a PCI Compliant payment provider that stores a secure user token.

- **Make it easy to create an account and save your billing address, and various shipping addresses** (Amazon does a great job with this, for example).

- **Keep registration fields short.** Too many sites (about 61 percent according to studies we've seen ask for too much extraneous information). Per Baymard.com (the authority on most e-commerce processes), two areas you should definitely remove 1. The "Address 2" field of most standard forms, as well as any extraneous fields such as "Company." Most sites leave fields such as "Phone Number" but use an information box to explain why they need it. ("In case we need to contact you about your order.")

- **Call-to-action language.** It may seem like a minor thing, but the language you use on your call-to-action buttons matters. To give you an example, we've seen some sites use a final call-to-action button such as "Pay Now" or "Buy Now." While that seems harmless, if you actually take a look at major online retailers, they use a different approach and language such as "Place Order," which has less of a "you-owe-me" or "you're-about-to-hand-over-your-money-to-me" type of intonation and more of a feeling that you are also getting serviced in the process. You might suggest it doesn't matter, but subconsciously such language can make the difference between someone eventually buying and someone not taking that final next step.

- **Use a "sticky" call to action button.** On some of the major platforms, we've seen call to action buttons to "Place Your Order" that don't even appear "above the fold" in desktop or until you scroll down in mobile. That's a bad experience as it's not evident from the landing screen where you can actually

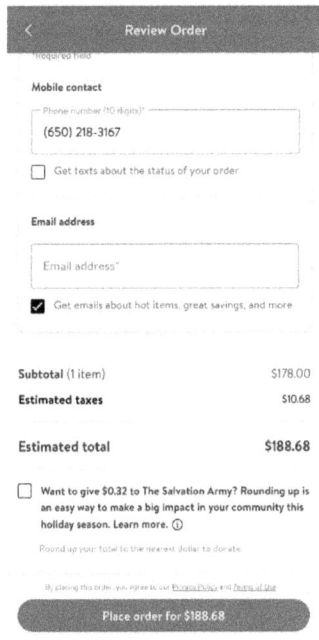

buy what you want. When you're looking at e-commerce platforms, make sure to consider where that button is. If you are able to make some development changes, one thing you can do is to make sure the final "Place Order" button is sticky, meaning it stays on the screen the entire time regardless of whether you scroll down in desktop or mobile. (See the example of what Walmart does here on the right. The button is always in view.) Placement here can mean the difference between someone taking that final last step or not doing anything at all.

Abandoned Cart Strategies

An estimated 70 to 80 percent of all customers abandon their online shopping carts. How do you get some of them to convert? Especially if they reach the point of having signed in, or provided their email address? What many companies do to reach those customers is set up an abandoned cart email, which you can do either through a connection to your email/marketing automation system – or through the e-commerce platform itself. You'll need a developer but they can help you pull a list of individuals who have submitted their email or signed in (remember the majority of people who abandon carts on most sites never actually sign in or submit their email). From there, your developers can automate a personalized email that will typically include a picture of the item and a link to the cart/checkout page to continue their purchase.

Messaging. Like any good email, it's really up to you to draft the copy and subject line that will go out in the automated email. You'll want to make sure to pay attention to this in particular as language can be the difference between someone opening the email and interacting with it, and someone who misses it completely. You'll also want to make sure that any link takes the potential buyer back to a stage in the process as far along to checkout as possible. Some good examples of subject lines for abandoned carts:

- You Left Something Behind (in Your Cart)
- We've Reserved Your Cart for You
- Your [insert item dynamically] Is Waiting for You
- Did You Forget About Me?
- Take XX Percent Off Your Cart (Before It's Gone!)

Frequency. One thing we always recommend to small businesses is to send multiple emails if an individual hasn't bought an item. After all, it can take more than one message to get someone to come back to his or her abandoned cart. To give you an illustration of this, we've worked with companies that have sent up to 6 messages in the first 5 days or so. Why do they do this? Because abandoned cart messages get opened and they get results. In some cases, we've seen such emails boost close rates by 30 percent or more. What's a good frequency? We often say something like this, if you're just getting started.

- One email after one hour of someone not checking out
- If not converted yet, another at 24 hours
- Similarly, one at 72 hours
- Finally, one at one week

Your developer can make sure that the system runs a check in between each email to remove those who have already purchased from you. It's not for every business, but one thing you can think about on the later messages is add an additional discount to entice those to complete the purchase. Given that these are individuals who took the time to put something in a cart, it might be worth it for you to secure a sale with the additional incentive.

Post-Purchase/Loyalty and Follow-Up Messaging

When it comes to e-commerce in particular, one of the most important aspects of marketing for your small business is actually post-purchase. Why is that? If you think about it, those that purchase from you almost automatically become your best customers, the ones who can potentially buy from you again or convince others to buy from you as well. So, it's important to pay attention to details here that will help you make them loyal/lifelong buyers or advocates. A few best practices we can recommend here. Right after purchase, try the following methods to create more engagement:

- Create a "thank you" screen with opportunities for advocacy such as a share-my-purchase-in social message ("I just bought ____" that includes a link back to the product or service.)
- Send a confirmation email post-purchase (within the first 5 minutes ideally).

- Create an automated thank-you-for-purchasing email that will follow up with related products or services, perhaps a few hours or 24 hours after the purchase.
- Send a confirmation email (if applicable) when a physical product has shipped and supply tracking information.
- Improve loyalty for purchases by offering customers who just purchased further offers or ask customers to take a survey (for their time, make it worthwhile).
- A week or so after the product has shipped, ask for reviews and provide a link where they can easily submit both ratings for the product and any testimonial about it.

E-commerce can be a challenge to get right because the various platforms can be somewhat inflexible out of the box. But if you do a lot of business right now through your store, it may pay to upgrade your platform or invest in development updates as small changes can actually make a big difference in conversion rates.

CHAPTER 12:

Mobile Apps, AI and Other Options

Finally, we would be remiss if we didn't cover a lot of the current technologies now being used by many businesses for marketing, including mobile applications, artificial intelligence (AI), or even extended reality (XR) – what is essentially the combined new name for augmented reality (AR) and virtual reality (VR). The challenge with many of these technologies, of course, is two-fold: 1. Cost and; 2. Finding the development or technological expertise to execute any project. That said, let's discuss the ins and outs of the different options in the context of a small business.

Mobile Apps

Do some "small" businesses use mobile apps for marketing? Of course. Many new businesses are built entirely on mobile applications, and the lure of producing an income-generating app remains quite strong. In 2021, for the first half year alone according to TechCrunch, consumers spent $65 billion in the Apple and Google Play stores[18], a huge jump from the same period in 2020. Roughly half of that now is in-app purchases.

But to do an app in the first place, most of those new businesses likely had one of two things – the talent in-house to design and develop the app; or the capital to do so, which from a valuation standpoint might put them beyond what most small businesses would ever dream of. They would've needed one of those

---

[18] https://techcrunch.com/2021/06/28/consumer-spending-on-apps-hit-record-64-9b-in-first-half-of-2021-but-install-growth-slowed-to-1-7/

two things because app design and development are not cheap. In 2020, the median price to create an app by mobile agencies was **$171,450**, according to a recent survey by mobile app agency Clutch. While typical cost range stated by app development companies is **$100,000 – $500,000**. Smaller apps with more standard out-of-the-box features can cost less –between **$10,000** and **$50,000**, so there might be an opportunity, depending on how much you want to commit to serving customers in mobile.

Keep in mind, that's just the upfront cost. Most apps also have yearly maintenance costs and need to make fixes to previous versions – that runs about 20 percent of the original development cost each year. So, if you have spent **$200,000** to develop a new app, expect to spend about **$40,000** per year to maintain it and improve it. Then, consider that Apple and Google will also take 15 to 30 percent of whatever is sold through the App Store or the Play Store. [19]The question is: **Is it worth it for you to spend that much money and not get the full amount of resulting revenue?**

PATIO for Mobile Apps

If you do decide you still want a mobile app, we'll take you through everything you need to consider as a small business. Like the other areas, we'll walk through our PATIO framework to keep it consistent and easy.

Planning & Strategy

When figuring out the plan, here are a few questions to consider.

1. **What's the goal of the app?**
   Do you want to generate revenue? Is it engagement of users/members/subscribers? Is it easy access to related information or tools (utility)? Maybe you want to entertain your customers? Upsell them? Or generate loyalty? Understanding this is key to the development of an idea experience.

2. **How do will this serve the customer beyond a mobile website?**
   One thing to keep in mind is that while people might download hundreds

---

[19] Both Apple and Google announced they would cut developer fees in 2021 to 15 percent from their original 30 percent.

240 :: Chapter 12

of apps on their phone, they might only use a few of them regularly. Research done in the U.K. and the U.S., for example, recently found that consumers use an average of 30 apps per month but spend 80 percent of their time on just five. Will you be one of the 30, much less one of the five? Or will a mobile responsive website work just fine for your needs?

It is true these days that many retailers, for example, will build their own app that mirrors much of the mobile website. But those sites tend to have larger audiences (hence, they are larger businesses) with repeat customers who might buy from them often. Hence, the utility of having a mobile app that has everything stored in it (payment methods, shipping and billing addresses, etc.) in those cases makes sense, even if it is quite similar to the mobile web experience. Plus, many of the retailers who do this have add-ons for augmented reality experiences for example where customers can see literally see how clothes and color options look on them. Such experiences cost a lot of money to build as well.

When should businesses build apps (native app) versus creating, say, a responsively designed web site? The general answer is that an app adds value if one can take advantage of a smartphone or tablet's native functions and provide incremental value or convenience. (An example here would be using the camera, calendar, mapping, music, geo-location, auto-login, alerts that come "natively" as part of the phone itself.)

3. **What budget am I willing to spend? And what's my expected ROI?**
    We've covered the costs already. And it's helpful to build in a financial model for a few years if you want to do this well. We'd estimate the budget costs for design and development, additional marketing costs to promote the app, App Store or Play Store fees, and maintenance. Compare that with the expected revenue, usage and downloads and you can make the best-informed decision.

4. **Who is the target audience?**
    It might be that you create an app for only a portion of your audience. Let's say, for example, you run a retail site for weddings that's used by both end-consumers (those planning a wedding themselves) and wedding planners. Well, odds say, a couple may only get married once and may only use the site that one time. It may not make sense to create

an app specifically for them. However, for repeat buyers such as wedding planners, they may come back often for multiple clients. So, creating an app just for that portion of the audience might work.

5. **What are other considerations to app development?**

From the perspective of development, there's another hidden "cost" that you might have to consider –the need to maintain and support different code bases for different versions versus cloud-based update that everyone gets. In that respect, mobile apps can become more of an IT nightmare. Apps with a lot of integration/customization not only cost a lot to develop but you also have to maintain support for all the different versions and updates as well.

Approach to Mobile Apps

Once you've finalized the strategy, including defining the goals, how an app serves the customers, the budgets, and other considerations, the next step is figuring out the approach. Here are the key areas in this section:

- What category of app do I want to build?
- Personalizing the user experience.
- How can I take advantage of the native functions?
- Earning money

What Category of App Do I Want to Build? And What's the Content Approach?

It's up to you in terms of how you see defining the type of app you want. We, of course, would base it on the audiences you serve and what their specific needs are. The most downloaded apps in the App Store (for both iOS and Android) are typically categories such as the following:

- Games
- Social
- Photo & Video
- Entertainment
- Lifestyle

- Productivity
- Shopping
- Music & Audio
- Communication
- Health & Fitness
- Education
- Dating

The other question here is also, what content approach do you want with the app? Per the STEPPS framework we covered in the Content chapter (Chapter 4), are you providing social currency? Triggers? Emotion? Social proof (public)? Practical tips? Storytelling?

Figuring out this approach will go a long way toward being able to put together the business requirements of any app you decide to develop.

Personalizing the User Experience

Similar to any website, personalization is now a big aspect of any mobile experience. How can you personalize that experience based on what we discussed earlier in the Website section:

- User profile information
- Geography
- User choice or input
- User behavior
- Archiving or storing a mobile user's works or creations

One thing to think about for your app is what information developers need to be able to transfer back and forth. And make sure to think about a two-way integration from the app to your customer relationship management (CRM) software and vice versa. For example, you might have stored data on customers in a particular area that you'll want to bring out on the app. Or, customer might choose or make a selection in the app that you need to store for future use in your CRM. Remember, the more data you need to transfer, the more expensive the upfront integrations and maintenance will be.

How Can I Take Advantage of the Native Functions?

Native functions are those operations that come with your mobile device or from other apps on your mobile device that your app might connect to, such as the camera (with access to photos and videos), the calendar, music, maps, geo-location, auto-login, and alerts. Figuring out a way to include these within the app will provide value to someone who downloads yours.

Earning Money

While not the end goal of every app on the market (some are mainly just about engagement), it's worth considering how creating an app will help you make money. A few categories of apps here include:

- **Offering apps completely free.** The goal here is simply to use the app as way to keep the brand in front of customers.
- **Offering apps for free with ads.** Some apps such as games or social media apps like Facebook are supported in this fashion.
- **Upfront purchase of the app.** Some apps make it easy to do a one-time purchase upfront.
- **In-app purchases.** Games, for example, can be downloaded for free but then they charge a certain amount to complete the game.
- **Mobile payments for in-store purchase.** Some apps are basically mobile payment apps, which allow customers to pay in-store for credit they've bought using an app. With this, you can also consider creating a loyalty program with rewards for frequent purchases. Starbucks' app is a great example of both of these concepts.

There's no one way to do it but make sure to think the user experience and how your audience might be willing to pay (one way or another).

Tools & Tactics

Unless your primary business is going to be as a mobile app, you're likely not going to start off with the kinds of developers you'll need to produce one, and as result, will probably have to choose between an agency or an out-of-the-box option. Given that's where most small businesses are, let's cover the basics of the tactics, since the tools you might need to develop the app are primarily for those who would build the app internally. In this section, we'll cover the following:

- Choosing an Agency or Out-of-the-Box Solution
- iOS: Things to Know
- Keeping Costs Down
- Distribution and Alerts

Choosing an Agency or Out-of-the-Box Solution

There are companies that specialize in out-of-the-box solutions. For example: non-profit event apps, shopping apps, or utility apps for small business that have similar identified needs that can be built of ahead of time and white-labeled with minimal customizations. This might be an option for you if your business qualifies under those circumstances. In general, out-of-the-box solutions will be a lot cheaper because there's limited customization. The apps are essentially pre-built ahead of time and you can create a white-label solution for your business likely under $25,000.

If you have a broader app idea that requires more involved data integration, and more specific needs, you'll probably want to choose an agency to do that. Here are a few tips if you go down that road:

- Look for knowledge and experience with the iOS submission process. (This is particularly important as most apps are still submitted through Apple's iOS process for developers first.)
- Look at past work they've done
- Compare hourly rates (many smaller providers work just fine)
- Come prepared with business requirements

iOS: Things to Know

- **Generally, Apple is the gatekeeper in terms of apps.** If it's accepted by the Apple App Store, which is usually the first submission, it typically will get accepted by the Google Play store.
- **Consider the cost of App Store commissions and don't try to create workarounds to payment or the app may get rejected.** For the first year, Apple takes 30 percent in most cases, though it makes an exception for small businesses who qualify (those who make under $1m in revenue) and may only take 15 percent on all app purchases. Certainly, you'll want to consider the purchase process and avoid trying

to sneak in hidden ways for your app customers to buy subscriptions within the app that go around Apple's App Store process, as your app will likely get rejected. This can cause delays and more developer costs in order to remedy those and submit again.

- **Submission Process:** Depending on how large the app is, it can take a few weeks after submission. Have the agency or company that's building that app submit on your behalf.
- **Bugs/Issues:** Apps often get rejected that have bugs and that can slow the process down significantly. So, make sure both you and your agency perform some quality assurance/usability testing before submission.
- **App Store Optimization:** (ASO). As you submit the app, make sure you and your agency pay attention to a few things so your app can get discovered within the App Store or Play Store:
  - » **Name:** First, the name of the app is critical, especially if you're somewhat of a known brand. One tip in that case: Use a descriptive title that includes the brand name.
  - » **Description:** Provide a keyword-rich description so individuals searching for apps in a particular space can find you.
  - » **Keywords:** Pay attention to the keyword field. You get 100 characters. Make sure to include high-value words, with no spaces in between, separated by commas.

Keeping Costs Down

- **Do your audience research upfront and on your own if you can.** Agencies will often charge for audience research, so the more you can conduct that in-house, particularly geared toward your mobile app, that is always helpful.
- **Have your developers create APIs.** One of the most labor-intensive pieces is synching data with the app. If you have your own backend developers, we would recommend you talking to them about what you want to do and establishing any needed APIs for data exchange upfront. Also, make sure to alert them to be responsive to agency requests for data.

- **Defining your requirements upfront.** Be as specific as possible for what you want to do and what you want to include as functionality. Brainstorming sessions with an agency will cost money and time.
- **Stay involved during development.** Take a good look at the prototypes an agency builds and make sure you are getting what you want. If you don't, you might find that you need to shift direction significantly, which can add to your costs.
- **Distribution and Alerts.** You're in the user's pocket or within arms-reach 100 percent of the time. Take advantage of it. Make sure when you're developing the app to enable alerts for deals, sales, event-related information that could increase engagement. For those with commerce or other purchase apps, alerts have been shown to increase purchases by up to 180 percent.[20]

Implementation

After you've submitted the app (and hopefully it's been approved and available), your job as a small business then transitions to promote the fact that you have it. How do you do that? Here are a few tricks:

- **Promote it in front of your mobile web visitors.** One thing many companies do is push the download of an app in front of their mobile web visitors. Your developers can help you do this by checking to see if visitors are coming from a mobile browser and, if so, prompting them with a button to download the right app based on whether they have iOS or Android operating systems.
- **Promote the app in social.** It's worth it to promote your app in social as far as organic posts go. But it also might be worth doing an ad where you can target app downloads to specific audiences in particular. Most of the social platforms such as Twitter, Instagram, Facebook and LinkedIn offer an ad format that is specifically designed for such activity.
- **Provide app-exclusive offers.** One way to get engagement is to launch offers and discounts that are exclusively available within your app. Or,

---

[20] Data from netmara.com

you can provide an incentive to download it such as 10 percent off your next purchase.

- **Ask for ratings & reviews and respond to ratings & reviews.** We've seen businesses that get an app approved but then they forget about it within the App Store and Play Stores. That's bad for several reasons. First, a lot of downloads are based on the number and quality of ratings and reviews. The higher that both are, the better. That's why you need to ask for reviews anytime you can from customers who download the app. Second, over time, if users aren't happy with the app and give a negative review, those reviews just sit there encouraging others not to download the app. Third, app store reviews can actually be a great source of feedback to improve the quality for the next version. That's why we recommended regular monitoring of your App Store comments and responding if you see negative reviews as well.

Optimization

With mobile apps, there will be a continuous need to update them and improve the experience with each version. A few tips here include:

- Take a look at App Store reviews and the number of downloads to see how your product is faring and get feedback that can help you with the next version.
- Good companies, as mentioned, spend about 20 percent of the initial cost each year on continuous fixes and improvements to app functionality.
- Think about additional distribution in social and on your website to encourage people to get the app.
- Stay focused on app usage metrics. What functions are customers using? Which are most popular? If it's content, ask yourself why something is popular too. If you can, develop more of those features that are popular with audiences for the next version.

Artificial Intelligence (AI)

Contrary to what you might believe, artificial intelligence or AI is already heavily employed in many of the tools small businesses use today. Email and marketing automation platforms, Google and social media ads, and content management systems, for example, all use (or have the capability to use) some form of AI these days.

While the concept itself may seem out of reach for many small businesses, the tools used to develop AI are actually becoming a lot more accessible. Microsoft, for example, recently opened up its Azure platform for developers, helping them take advantage of its machine-learning capability. A good example of AI becoming more widely available are the chatbots, which appear on many small business websites that help steer a visitor toward, say, a salesperson or a particular content recommendation.

While we understand some might shy away from such new technologies, it's critical for small businesses to at least begin to explore some of the benefits as the competition is also investing more heavily in such tools. AI is already being used quite a bit in:

- **Email.** AI embedded in many of the marketing automation platforms will let you know the best time of day to send. It can also evaluate subject lines and automatically segment audiences.
- **Predictive analytics.** This is one area where machines can analyze data and find individuals who might have a greater propensity to buy. AI is already used to analyze behavior that can predict conversion for better qualified leads, for example.
- **Cross-selling or personalizing offers on websites.** AI is already being used by other small businesses to personalize offers on website (based on previous behavior).
- **Sentiment analysis.** A machine has the capability to analyze social media posts in particular to better understand sentiment about a company. Many of the current social listening tools already offer some form of this to even small businesses.

A Note about AR/VR (XR)

We haven't really touched on augmented reality (AR) or virtual reality (VR) to any great extent – (the combined two areas today known as extended reality or XR.) The reasons for that are primarily cost and usage.

Let's take augmented reality for example. Many shopping apps from major retailers employ AR, where an app user can try on clothes or see how a piece of furniture might fit into their apartment (see the image from the IKEA Place app, which shows you how a light might look on your table). In Snapchat too, major companies also play around with AR lenses and filters, allowing you to carpet your desk with grass (such as a recent Scott's Turf Builder ad did). As a small business, you can participate in such technologies as well. The biggest gating factor will likely be the expense. For example, mobile development agency Itrex recently estimated that it would cost anywhere from a few thousand dollars to up to $300,000 for just an app focused on augmented reality[21], not one that even combines other functions.

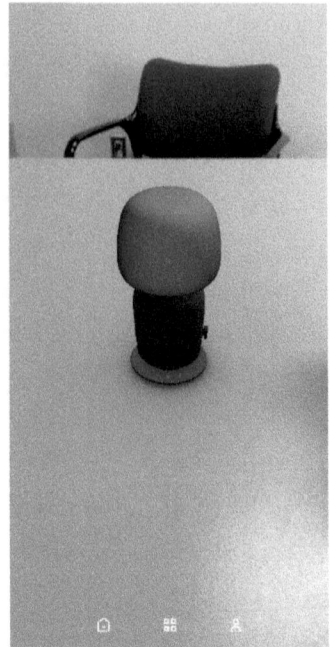

With virtual reality, companies such as BMW and Lowe's take advantage of virtual reality headsets in their showrooms, so their customers can experience, say, driving a car or using one of the tools they sell. That said, for the average small business, it may be that VR isn't yet in the cards from a marketing perspective, because the general public adoption rate remains low and the costs are high – that's regardless of whether you create your own VR experience or if you wanted to advertise on one.

AR or VR?

If you're dead set on using such technologies it may be that AR is a bigger opportunity because of the widespread adoption on mobile devices right now. If you need help, contact us at Marketing Nice Guys and we can help you work with one of our partners on a mobile experience with integrations for different types of extended reality. Or at least provide you a straight-forward conversation on the costs and realities.

---

[21] https://itrexgroup.com/blog/augmented-reality-cost-factors-examples/#

CHAPTER 13

Data, Analytics, KPIs & More

In a nutshell, digital analytics enables brands and website owners to understand how their sites and apps are being found and used. And indeed, in the last 20 years, the availability of data has been a game changer in the field of marketing. The fact that you can see performance data in real-time with digital means you can ideally optimize your marketing performance as you go. Indeed, data analytics has become a burgeoning field in its own right as it encompasses not just the collection, measurement, and analysis of data, but also its visualization and interpretation. With such insights, business owners can improve their strategies, operations and ROI. However, many fail to do so and partly because they don't know how to set up tracking systems or use the platforms available to them. That failure to use analytics can lead to businesses falling behind competitively or not fully optimizing their marketing or business performance.

In this section, we'll cover a few areas:

- Setting overall goals/critical success factors.
- How to set KPIs and some KPI examples to measure
- Marketing attribution and why it matters
- Setting up Google Analytics and basic conversion tracking.

Setting Overall Goals/Critical Success Factors (CSFs)

Also called strategic or operational goals, these are the broader goals of what you want your marketing to achieve. Examples here might include:

- Revenue hitting $2 million for the calendar year
- An increase of 20 percent in revenue year-over-year
- 250 sales-qualified leads in a calendar year

The reason these are important to establish upfront is that they allow you as a small business to set other goals along the way (known as key performance indicators or KPIs) to help you evaluate whether you're on track toward hitting the overall goals/CSFs. For example, let's say you set a goal of your marketing generating $2 million in the coming year for your e-commerce site. Based on your current run rate, you estimate you need 4 million website visits (one KPI), 400,000 users adding a product to the cart (a second KPI), and then 100,000 of those completing a purchase (a fourth KPI) with an average order value of $20 (a fifth KPI). By setting the goal and the related benchmarks you'll be able to figure out how well you're doing as you go. These overall goals can be established for everything you do in marketing or they can be for a single marketing campaign.

How to Set KPIs and Some KPI Examples to Measure in Different Marketing Channels

Key performance indicators (KPIs), as mentioned above, are a set of quantifiable measures that a company uses to gauge or compare performance on the path toward meeting its strategic or operational goals. KPIs vary between companies and industries. For digital, different initiatives require different measures.

Before doing "analysis," it's important to set up KPIs – milestones that indicate how well something performs. One tip: Set up your KPIs based on "reality" – for example, it's probably unrealistic to set 4 million visits to your website if you only did 1 million the past year.

To help you, we've provided some examples of KPIs used in different marketing channels that you can begin measuring:

Website KPIs

Overall

- Page views
- Unique visits
- Bounce rate
- Pages per visit
- Time on site
- Social engagement/shares/comments/reviews
- Browser/device used

Blogs/Content Sites

- Subscriber rate
- Lead/sales generated
- Avg. advertising income per page
- Avg. advertising income per visitor
- Total ad revenue

Lead-generation Sites

- Overall lead generation
- Lead form abandonment rate
- Leads per day/month
- Content downloads/requests per month
- Lead conversion rate

E-Commerce Conversion

- Site Conversion: (% of Orders out of All Visits)
- Product Conversion: (% of Orders out of Product Page Visits)
- Cart Abandonment Rate: (% of Orders out of All Cart Visits)

Revenue

- Avg. revenue per visit
- Avg. revenue per order or average order value (AOV)
- Overall revenue

SEO KPIs

- **Return on investment:** If you've made SEO improvements (technology, time/effort), what's the return in terms of leads, conversions, purchases or other metrics?
- **Ranking improvement:** Improved position for a keyword term or terms
- Overall rank improvement for all monitored keywords (top 100 keywords, for example)
- Top keywords/landing page destinations
- Bounce rate on landing pages
- Pages per visit
- Total traffic (from Google)

Content Marketing KPIs

Reach

- Unique visitors
- Geography (where your content is being read)
- Mobile/device type: what devices are your customers using?

Engagement

- Bounce rate
- Time spent on site
- Page views
- Comments
- Social sharing

Revenue/Lead Generation

- Number of leads
- Conversion rate
- Revenue per visit
- Total revenue

Social Media KPIs

Reach
- Number of fans and followers
- Demographics and location

Engagement
- Number of active followers
- Number of likes and shares
- Comments
- Mentions
- Click-throughs
- Conversions

Video KPIs

Brand Exposure
- Views on video
- Completion rate
- Page traffic
- Bounce rate
- Shares/Social metrics
- Repeat visitor rate

Conversions
- CTRs to product or lead pages
- Revenue lift
- Total revenue

Email KPIs
- Open rate
- Click-through rate
- Conversion rate
- Unsubscribe rate

- Traffic Spike: See if there was a surge in traffic (page/web site/target link) the day of and the day after you sent the email

Goals

- How many leads received? Lead quality?
- Total orders
- Total sales
- ROI?

Paid Search KPIs

- Click-thru rate
- Cost-per-acquisition
- Impression share
- Return on investment (ROI)
- Bounce rate
- Pages per visit
- Keyword traffic (The amount of traffic being generated by each respective keyword in your PPC campaign)

Overall

- Overall traffic
- Revenue Generated
- Impression share

Display & Native Advertising KPIs

- Brand recall: (Typically commissioning a brand study comparing the increase in awareness of the brand among people who have seen the ad vs. people who haven't).
- Click-thru rate
- Direct web site traffic (from clicks)
- Total conversions (lead, purchase etc.)
- Cost per acquisition (if the point was lead generation/conversion or another measure)
- ROI/Revenue contribution

Mobile KPIs
- Total app downloads
- Total reviews
- Upfront purchases (if applicable)
- Total 3-star and above reviews in app store

Usage metrics
- Overall monthly users to total downloads
- Time spent on app
- Total in-app purchases

Marketing Attribution and Why It Matters

Think of marketing attribution as backwards approach. In marketing, it's critical to be able to attribute successful completion of a goal to a particular effort or channel. But it's often not just one channel that contributes. So, while setting goals and KPIs to measure in each channel are important and look at progress toward a goal, it's key to get a sense of what is really driving that eventual conversion/success. Attribution works backward from the conversion goal to look at contributing channels. There are two types:

1. **Last-click attribution:** You send an email to a prospect. The prospect opens the email, clicks, and makes a purchase directly because of that email. That marketing effort was the final touch that made the customer purchase.

2. **Time-decay.** You send an email to a prospect. The prospect opens the email and clicks but doesn't purchase. A week later the same prospect searches for a product in Google, finds your product, and then converts. In time-decay attribution, the email can be given a certain credit for helping that drive that conversion. Organic search (SEO) is given last-click credit and a larger portion of time-decay credit. Time-decay gives you a fuller picture.

Why does it matter to look at this? We often see the following scenario that happens with advertising. We will run an ad for a client that drives traffic to the website or awareness of a product or service. That traffic might not necessarily convert immediately. However, later those same customers come back and do a search for our brand and might find our organic listing. They then buy directly on the website during that session. From a last-click standpoint, you might credit that to SEO, but those individuals wouldn't have searched on our brand at all if we didn't actually advertise to them.

A few more things to keep in mind:

1. When weighting the value of a "touch" in time-decay, the further back you go from purchase, generally the less weight something is given. But that first touch is also important in many ways, even if it was a year or more ago. So, much depends on the buying cycle.

2. Last-click is still important because it tells you what triggered that final move toward purchase.

3. Some examples of marketing attribution tools include:
   - Google Attribution 360
   - Altitude by Impact
   - Visual IQ (Nielsen)

Setting Up Google Analytics and Basic Conversion Tracking

Each platform you might use likely has its own tracking available to measure the KPIs we outline above. For example, you'll likely only be able to get email open rates directly from your marketing automation platform or your Facebook ad performance directly from that platform. It's one reason why many companies use services such as Tableau, Google Data Studio, or Microsoft Power BI to import data from the various platforms and then visualize it all in one place.

For your website, though, we would recommend most small businesses use Google Analytics (as it's free to install and is super-convenient for tracking Google Ads performance as well.)

What is it?

Google Analytics (GA) is a web analytics service that provides statistics and basic analytical tools that allow you to track your website visitors – both where they've come from and what they do on your website. It's available free, as mentioned, to anyone with a Google account.

It can help organizations:

- Determine top sources of user traffic
- Gauge the success of their marketing activities and campaigns
- Track goal completions/conversions (such as purchases, adding products to carts or lead generation)
- Discover patterns and trends in user engagement, especially popular pages, or topics
- Obtain other visitor information such as demographics or device data

How GA Works

Google Analytics acquires data from each website visitor through the use of JavaScript page tags, which are inserted into the code of each website page and sends the data to Google's data collection servers. Google Analytics then generates customizable reports to track and visualize data such as:

- Number of visitors
- Bounce rates
- Average session durations
- Page views
- Goal completions, and more

Important metrics

A metric is a standard of measurement that can be quantified. Google Analytics enables users to track up to 200 different metrics to measure how their websites are performing. From Google itself here are the metrics it tracks:

- Users. A user is a unique or new visitor to the website.
- Bounce rate. The percentage of visitors who viewed only a single page. These visitors only triggered a single request to the Google Analytics server.
- Sessions. The group of visitor interactions that happen in a 30-minute window of activity.
- Average session duration. How long on average each visitor stays on the site.
- Percentage of new sessions. The percentage of website visits that are first-time visits.

- Pages per session. The average number of page views per each session.
- Goal completions. The number of times visitors complete a specified, desirable action. This is also known as a conversion.
- Page views. Total number of pages viewed.

Google Analytics 4

Google Analytics 4, or GA4 is the most recent iteration of this service and was released in October 2020. We recommend most small businesses upgrade to this version as it offers more powerful tracking tools and new user interface. According to Google, GA4 "shifts from reliance on third-party cookies toward the use of machine learning for better data accuracy."

Installing Google Analytics GA4

Here are the basic steps:

- Go to analytics.google.com and create an account.
- Then create a property (the site you want to track) for Google Analytics.
- Go to Admin » Setup assistance

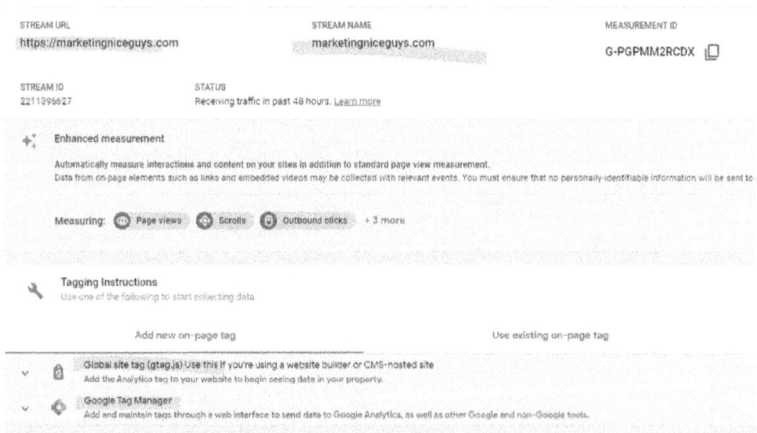

- Create a web data stream. Provide your stream a name and the website URL.
- Next, follow the steps under tagging instructions to setup the tag

There are two ways to do this.

1. Add the Analytics tag to your website to begin seeing data in your property Copy the global site tag into the <head> section of your HTML. Or, if you use a website builder (e.g. GoDaddy, Shopify, etc)

2. Using Google Tag Manager: Which is a free tool provided by Google to manage all third-party tags (Google, Facebook, Linkedin etc) for your website.

Either way, we do recommend working with your website developer or a specialist to conduct this task if you're not sure. For an alternative, many Word-Press websites (for example) have plugins that you can use that will walk you through the process on the website side. We would recommend "Google Analytics for WordPress by MonsterInsights" as a good tool that's a pretty easy set up and installation in which you don't have to go into the <head> section of the code.

Goal Creation with Google Analytics

Goals measure how well your site or app fulfills your target objectives. A goal represents a completed activity, typically a conversion of some kind, that contributes to the success of your business. Examples of goals include making a purchase (for an e-commerce site), or submitting a contact information form (for a marketing or lead generation site).

Defining goals and those conversions are a core part of any digital analytics measurement plan. Having properly configured goals will allow Google Analytics to provide you with critical information, such as the number of conversions and the conversion rate for your site or app.

Popular goal types from Google:

1. **Destination Goal:** Use destination goals to treat a pageview or screenview as a conversion. Enter the screen name or page URL in the Destination field. Specify the match type as Equals to, Begins with, or Regular expression.

2. **Duration Goal:** Measures user engagement by treating a minimum session duration as a conversion. The Hours, Minutes and Seconds fields specify the minimum session time that qualifies as a goal conversion. Any session longer than this amount of time will generate a "conversion."

How to Set Up a Conversion or Destination Goal

1. Go the Admin » Goal section
2. Create a new goal and give it a name. Select goal type as Destination
3. Enter the than you page you wish to track as conversion. As an

example, after someone hits the button for a purchase or a lead, you might send them to a thank-you page on your website. And the only way to reach this page is if you actually "covert" or buy. So, you can enter a destination (thank-you page) as the end goal.

4. Save the goal

Wherever you can, do the same process to track each site conversion uniquely depending on where those events reside on your pages.

CHAPTER 14:

Putting It All Together

Let's face it: Marketing is hard.

It's hard for small businesses and it's even hard for those of us who specialize in the field. That's because there's so much to do, and often not enough resources to get it all done. And as you can see from reading through the book, the strategy and big picture matters but so do all the little details – everything from the copy you use on your pages and ads, to the color of the call-to-action buttons, to the alt tag on the photos. It can all add up to make the difference between a successful marketing initiative and one not as successful. There's so much that we know it can seem overwhelming to even approach.

But there's hope. After all, our reason for writing this book wasn't to bury anyone with dread. We wanted to, of course, be realistic and discuss best marketing practices, but we also feel like much of this is really do-able by businesses themselves. In our view, many small businesses just need a framework where they consider the things that have to be done in any given channel. We've tried to provide that with our PATIO framework, which helps easily distill all the marketing activities a business needs to consider. Armed with this knowledge, you as a business can then prioritize the things you can (or want to) do yourself, versus ones you might hire out for. And even in hiring others, we feel that, after reading the book, you'd be at least better informed to ask the right questions (and get better service as a result.)

One of the points that we hope doesn't get lost is that, while we've provided the best practices within each channel, the bigger issue is that such activities should never be done in a vacuum. They should be integrated so that the efforts in one channel support what you're doing in another. For example, your content marketing should complement your social media, which should complement your email marketing, which should complement your e-commerce. All those efforts together should help push the buyers who are aware of you further down the journey toward purchase. Similarly, your messaging should be coordinated so that you present a consistent narrative to your audiences across all channels. We know this takes a bit of discipline and rigor. But in the end, all the attention you pay to such things will pay off in the long run, as you'll have a stronger brand, and, we hope, marketing that ultimately drives better results. We want to wish you the best of luck in all your marketing endeavors. Don't hesitate to contact us at contact@marketingniceguys if you have any questions or need additional support.

Tim & Boney
September 2022

ACKNOWLEDGEMENTS

The writing of any book, whether it's fiction or non-fiction, is always based to a greater or lesser extent on one's life experiences. In this case, we must acknowledge the insights and guidance that have been provided to us over the years from many people in the field of marketing, whose expertise we have (and still do) rely on. Among those we'd like to call out specifically include

- Toby Trevarthen and Rob McLoughlin of the Narrative Playbook
- Myron Rosmarin (for his guidance over the years in SEO and his participation in our digital marketing class every year where we always learn something new)
- Mini Zhuohan Li of Reingold for her expertise on programmatic advertising and ad targeting
- Bob Wiltfong, for his insights on video marketing and presentation
- Wendy Zajack, head of the marketing and communications program at Georgetown's School of Continuing Studies, who lets us teach a fun class every year
- The many other colleagues, clients, and experts (too many to mention) who've shown us little tips and tricks over the years that we've compiled herein.

Thanks also to our team at Marketing Nice Guys, including Kenan Pollack for reading and editing drafts of this work. (If there are any typos, we'll blame him.) We also couldn't do what we do without the expertise of the Julien Publishing design team and their awesome book design and layout.

Finally, it also wouldn't be a book acknowledgement unless we thanked our families. Boney would like to especially thank his wife Jaynika and son, Reyann, who he hopes will one day grow up to be a better marketer than him. Tim would like to thank his wife Julie for her patience through these long Covid years, and his two sons, Alex and Eric, neither of whom have any desire to go into a field related to marketing.

ABOUT THE AUTHORS

Tim Ito

Tim is a co-founder and principal at Marketing Nice Guys. Our agency has a mission to help businesses and individuals excel in digital marketing. Having more than 25 years of experience developing content, optimizing websites, and running marketing for various organizations, he has particular insight into the challenges faced by companies and their marketing departments. Previous to Marketing Nice Guys, he served as a vice president at the Association for Talent Development (ATD), overseeing the content and digital marketing division. His career has also included stints at ASCD, America Online, Netscape, and AltaVista in content, marketing and product strategy lead roles. Tim started his career as a journalist, as a former senior editor and producer at washingtonpost.com and as a reporter and writer for U.S. News & World Report magazine. He is the co-author of The B.S. Dictionary: Uncovering the Origins and True Meanings of Business Speak (April 2020), with Bob Wiltfong. Since 2015, he has also served as an adjunct professor of a popular digital marketing course at Georgetown University.

Boney Pandya

Boney Pandya is a co-founder and principal at Marketing Nice Guys. Our mission is to help businesses and individuals excel in digital marketing. Boney has more than a decade of digital marketing experience in the B2B, B2C, and association industries, running paid media, email automation and other aspects of marketing operations. He is also currently the founder of Bon Digital, a digital marketing consultancy. Prior to founding Marketing Nice Guys, Boney worked as the director of digital marketing at CSGCreative, as the associate director of digital marketing at the American Association for the Advancement of Science (AAAS) and as the senior manager of digital marketing at the Association for Talent Development (ATD). At both associations, Boney helped increase membership acquisition, improve retention, and boost event registration through digital marketing channels. Boney is Google search certified and display advertising certified, as well as Hubspot certified. Boney obtained his MBA from Drexel University.

www.ingramcontent.com/pod-product-compliance
Lightning Source LLC
Chambersburg PA
CBHW040848210326
41597CB00029B/4769